SYMPTOMS OF CANADA
AN ESSAY ON THE CANADIAN IDENTITY

In this provocative essay on the Canadian identity, Kieran Keohane gives us his outsider's take on Canada's most debated issue. Keohane argues that conflicting objectives have caused the impasse in our search for collective identity. These objectives are marked by official multiculturalism, a proliferation of interest groups, and resurgent xenophobia. Integrating social and political theory with witty examples, he explores how a strong Canadian identity might be constructed.

Keohane steers us away from the pitfalls of universalism or postmodern fragmentation into particularisms. The Canadian identity, he observes, lies in our unique commitment to remaining open to difference. Canadians maintain this commitment with a certain *jouissance*: for us, difference is both painful and pleasurable, conflicting and conciliatory. 'Symptoms' of our relationship to difference appear in everyday phenomena – in our recreation, patterns of interaction, ordinary language, poetry, politics, sexuality, and sense of humour. Keohane draws on two currents of discourse: the discourse on identity derived from Hegelian dialectics and Lacanian psychoanalysis, and the discourse on politics as hegemonic articulation, after Laclau and Mouffe.

Symptoms of Canada breaks the stalemate in our search for the Canadian identity. A refreshing read for Canadians who are tired of the polemics surrounding this issue, it offers valuable insight to all countries where the question of identity is a national concern.

KIERAN KEOHANE lectures in the Department of Sociology, University College Cork, Ireland. He lived in Canada from 1988 to 1994 while completing his PhD at York University.

D0813285

KIERAN KEOHANE

Symptoms of Canada
An Essay on the
Canadian Identity

UNIVERSITY OF TORONTO PRESS
Toronto Buffalo London

Printed in Canada

ISBN 0-8020-0688-4 (cloth)
ISBN 0-8020-7642-4 (paper)

Printed on acid-free paper

Canadian Cataloguing in Publication Data

Keohane, Kieran
Symptoms of Canada : an essay on the Canadian identity

Includes bibliographical references and index.
ISBN 0-8020-0688-4 (bound)   ISBN 0-8020-7642-4 (pbk.)

1. Multiculturalism – Canada.   2. National characteristics,
Canadian.   I. Title.

FC97.K46 1997   971.064'8   C97-931221-3
F1021.2.K46 1997

University of Toronto Press acknowledges the financial assistance to its
publishing program of the Canada Council for the Arts and the Ontario Arts
Council.

Contents

Acknowledgments

I wish to thank Ioan Davies, Karen Anderson, and Himani Bannerji of York University for their guidance and encouragement throughout this project. Thanks also to Virgil Duff, Barb Porter, Judy Williams, and the anonymous reviewers for University of Toronto Press. I hope that many of my friends and colleagues will happily recognize their influence in these pages. Matt Trachman, Kate Sandilands, Patricia Cormack, and Jim Cosgrave were excellent critical commentators and exciting interlocutors. Alan Blum and his students are also important influences. Above all, I wish to thank Carmen Kuhling, my partner and intellectual soulmate, who gave me Canada and who has made my being here so thoroughly enjoyable.

Grateful acknowledgment is made to the following for permission to reproduce material for which they hold copyright: the *Globe and Mail*, Molson Breweries, Susan Musgrave, National Gallery of Canada, Nestlé Canada Inc., James Reaney, Royal Ontario Museum, Tilley Endurables, and Ben Wicks.

Dedicated to the memory of my father, Donal Keohane, to whom I owe my interest in nation, culture, and difference.

PART ONE: THE IMPOSSIBILITY OF THE NATION
AND THE PARTICULARITY OF ITS IMPOSSIBILITY

1

For a Poetry of Canada

Poetry leads to the same place as all forms of erotism – to the blending and fusion of separate objects. It leads us to eternity; it leads us to death, and through death to continuity. Poetry is eternity; the sun matched with the sea.

Bataille 1986, 25

The problem of Canada is fundamental and universal. It is an expression of Hegel's question: how to cancel the opposition while preserving the difference.[1] It is the problem of the spirit of the collective: the desire for the elusive synthetic moment of social solidarity where we glimpse the "'I' that is "We" and the "We" that is "I"' (Hegel 1977, 110). This problem is always posed for us with a sociological particularity; in this case it is a problem for postmodern Canadians, and it confronts us in the form of a crisis of multiculturalism.

Official multiculturalism's project to reconcile unity and diversity has been criticized as ideological, paternalistic, and counterproductive. Critics such as Reginald Bibby, Augie Fleras, and Peter Li argue that it masks and perpetuates structural inequalities, that it reifies and marginalizes so-called 'ethnics' as categories while giving token acknowledgment to the contribution of 'minorities' to the 'mainstream,' and that, by emphasizing differences that divide, it undermines the development of collective identification and social solidarity that it intends to cultivate.[2] The problems of multiculturalism relate to the wider context of the political culture of postmodernity: the proliferation of antagonisms based upon the assertion of the particularity of identities, and the fragmentation of the political imaginary into what Frederic Jameson calls 'private languages' – nationalism, ethnocentrism(s), feminism, environmentalism, and anti-racism.[3]

As a discursive framework that recognizes difference and antagonism, multiculturalism tries to reconcile unity and diversity by formulating Canada as a community of communities. It tries to solve Hegel's problem of cancelling the opposition while preserving the difference, but it cannot do this, because multiculturalism is currently articulated and legitimated within the terms of a self-limiting pluralistic language. The values of 'diversity' and 'equality' upon which the organic solidarity of official multiculturalism is predicated, which it reinscribes in policy and reproduces empirically, presume that the ethnocultural identities constituting the mosaic are discrete elements with preconstituted and apparent interests that can and should be maintained and adjusted/equalized by state intervention. Thus: 'If we protect the individual tiles of our cultural mosaic, the parts will come together to form a beautiful integrated art piece' (Bibby 1990, 3). Because of this, the evolution of multiculturalism can only proceed spatially, identifying and adding new categories to an ever-widening mosaic, while failing to facilitate a synthetic 'poetry of the nation.' The discourse of multiculturalism as currently constituted does not, and cannot, address the frontier effects occurring across the boundaries of the 'tiles.' Richard Rorty argues that these are the 'poetic moments' in culture where antagonistic polarities are synthesized and affinity and equivalencies between them are brought to light (1989, 20, 68). The discourse of multiculturalism needs to be developed and articulated in a language that allows for, and formulates, the openness of the categories, the incompleteness of their relations, allowing the poetry to be written by the people, not the bureaucracy – the state providing the room in which to write.

Canadians need a poiesis that would illuminate the '"I" that is "We" and the "We" that is "I,"' the fleeting synthetic moment of collective solidarity. If not, then we must live with the problems of micropolitics: 'a linguistic fragmentation of social life itself to the point where the norm is eclipsed: reduced to a neutral and reified media speech ... one more idiolect among ... the stupendous proliferation of codes today into professional and disciplinary jargons (but also into the badges of affirmation of ethnic, gender, race, religious, and class-factional adhesion) ... a field of sylistic and discursive heterogeneity without a norm' (Jameson 1991, 17). The problem of micropolitics is that while on the one hand it seems to promise the erosion of oppressive hegemonic orders by innumerable antagonisms, on the other, in so far as there is no articulatory practice which unites them, which collects the idiolects, they are antagonistic towards one another also, and to that extent are unable to formulate an alternative collective hegemonic democratic project.

The possibility of such a poiesis of the collective spirit in the context of cultural fragmentation in late capitalism, Jameson says, is made difficult, 'not only [by] the absence of any great collective project, but also the unavailability of the older language itself' (Jameson 1991, 17). That is, the problem of articulating the '"I" that is "We" and the "We" that is "I"' arises at a particular conjuncture in philosophy and social thought – one that is characterized by a rejection of any talk of origins or essences that ground the collective, an incredulity toward metanarratives that try to collect our experiences, and a scepticism towards any kind of utopian teleology to show us where we might go.[4] But while these postmodern negations of modernist ontology, epistemology, and teleology initially seem debilitating, the promise of postmodern social thought lies in the breakdown in the distinction between interpretation and politics, in the recognition that 'whatever more universal values exist in a certain community will not be the expression of any pre-existing essence, but rather the result of a pragmatic and unstable construction which starts from a multiplicity of points on the social fabric' (Laclau 1991, 57). In other words, when we recognize with Derrida that there is nothing outside the text, no external point of objectivity from which a transcendent logic might be discerned or a telos formulated, we recognize that social theory inevitably enters politics by providing persuasive interpretations of the social that desire to be hegemonic. Accordingly, I offer no apologies for the commitments that are apparent in what follows.

Current theory, such as Donna Haraway's articulation of a 'politics of affinity amongst cyborgs' (1991, 150; also 1992, 295–337), Said's formulation of the 'nomadic imaginary,'[5] and Laclau and Mouffe's project of hegemonically constructing 'democratic equivalencies' amongst diverse identities[6] all recognizes the limitations of micropolitics, and seeks to formulate language(s) expressing a principled way of relating to difference that goes beyond 'pluralism,' 'diversity,' and 'equality.' The principles derived from these values are minimally 'anti-racist' and 'affirmative,' implying boundary maintenance rather than boundary fluidity, when what is required is not simply to articulate principles of non-hostility, but rather to define the terms with which we can hegemonically articulate principles of being 'friendly towards' difference. The challenge is to come up with a language that may be employed persuasively in the public sphere to move beyond the impasses of political correctness in which multiculturalism founders.

We are, thankfully, breaking free from the narrow and totalitarian continuities imposed in the past, the racist, patriarchal continuity endorsed by Mackenzie King, for example, when he said that 'we must always remember that Canada is a white man's country.'[7] But we cannot live with the discontinuity of proliferating antagonistic groups constituted on the particularity of identity either. I am with Bataille, who says that 'we desire to bring into a world founded on discontinuity as much continuity as such a world can sustain' (1986, 19). I hope to contribute to this project of uncovering the register in which we can begin to reformulate the continuity of the collective.

How to Begin?

But where do I begin? An Irishman living in Toronto for five years, what can I say about Canada? My perspective on Canada is mediated/limited by the particularity of the discursive construction of the subject positions that I occupy, the historical contingencies of my insertion into the Canadian conversation: white, male, middle-class, anglophone, Torontonian. I attune with relative ease to what many other immigrants encounter as a hegemonic, exclusive, and oppressive conversation. Everything that follows will inevitably reflect the biases of my ethnocentrism; how Canada appears to *me*.

The conditions of postmodernity have taught us that there is no neutral, Archimedian, external point of view – the transcendental perspective of history, the objective view of the social sciences, or the scrutinizing eye of literary and art criticism – from which we can discern what 'Canada' is. No cultural domain, no canon or corpus can be privileged as repository of the authentic. This has freed people interested in the study of Canada from servitude to a hegemonic (predominantly white, male, Anglo) discourse of Canadian identity, and currently the discourse is characterized by explorations of 'Other Canadas,' deliberately de-centred discourses that explore the experience of being in Canada from positions that have been systematically excluded from the hegemonic regime.

However, postmodernism, or more precisely, post-Marxism, has also taught us that neither can the critical perspective of any particular radical standpoint or standpoints derived from complexes of marginalizations and exclusions from the prevailing hegemony – feminist, Native, regional, economic, racial, or pertaining to sexual orientation, creed, ancestry, etc. – be trusted to give us the true, less ideological, perspective. In so far as the critical account(s) of Canada proffered from any one or a combination of these standpoints grant an epistemic authority to an essentialized subject (Native, woman, Quebecois, for example), and historical primacy to a particular political/emancipatory project (self-government, feminism, sovereignty), the perspectives of Canada offered from radical standpoints are as partial, distorted, and ethnocentric as the hegemonic edifice which it seeks to destabilize and replace (Keohane 1993).

Unfortunately, much though we may wish it otherwise, such ethnocentrism, partiality, and distortion of perspective are inevitable. We cannot unproblematically speak about the Other(s) or assume the position(s) of the Other(s) and speak 'for' the Other(s) or in their interests. Foucault says that the best we can do is to speak 'like' the Other, as another Other, a specific intellectual (1980, 68), articulating as reflexively and truthfully as one can the world 'from my perspective,' as it were, and then risking one's *doxa* (opinion) in the antagonistic conversation; as Hegel would say, by 'subjecting oneself to the infinity of the difference' (1977, 105–6). This requires that one not hide behind the 'objective' authority of the expert or the dubious insider's knowledge of the ethnographer, and equally that one not seek the moral high ground of accumulated victimizations and exclusions, to make oneself the most Othered of the Others. Rather, the hermeneutic approach is primarily reflexive; by endeavouring to locate one's own lacks and limitations, the parameters of one's own ethnocentrisms, and taking these into account when formulating the general picture.

The discourse on Canadian identity is currently characterized by two problematic hegemonic projects. The first is a *reactionary, exclusive* discourse, represented by the Reform party, organizations like the Heritage Front, and Quebec separatist movements. These seek to achieve closure of the question of identity by identifying and excluding excess – all that is not 'mainstream' (Reform), that is not white, Protestant, etc. (Heritage Front), that is not Québécois (Bloc). This is not, of course, to say that these projects are identical with one another. They each have their own unique content and particularity, and their own historical and political specific gravity. They do, however, share a general form: these projects seek to solve the problem of the diversity and multiplicity of Canadian identities by categorically identifying and demarcating a singular centre and systematically excluding elements that do not fit the category. The second hegemonic project is a *proactive, inclusive* discourse, best represented by official multiculturalism and the practices of affirmation that have come to be known as 'political correctness.' These discursive practices also seek closure of the question of identity, by identifying, categorizing, and systematically *including* the multiplicity and diversity of experiences that constitute Canada.

These two general hegemonic projects are competing for primacy to shape the discourse on Canadian identity. It is not my purpose to try to determine which is the more hegemonic. That is a matter for Canadian historians of the future to debate. Neither is it my purpose to offer moral judgment about which of these hegemonic projects is 'bad' and which is 'good.' The judge's attitude is inappropriate, Georg Simmel says, as our task at this point is 'neither to accuse nor to pardon, but to understand' (1971, 339). What we should understand is the fallacy common to both projects: that it is as much a fantasy to think that it is possible to hear the voices form everywhere as it is to discern the singular, authentic or objective voice.[8]

The world appears to us differently according to our particular insertion into it, the unique histories and social relations that make up the traditions and contexts within which the meaning of 'Canada' is constituted. The meaning of 'Canada' is always refracted and mediated through particular experiences – regional, racial, gender-specific, and so on, an infinite horizon of sites of particularity. How then can we speak – or can we speak at all – of that which is common to us?

It is the irony of the human condition that our desire to speak of the general and generalizable, to apprehend and express a shared meaningful totality, is always denied by the contingencies of discourse; that we are constrained to apprehend and articulate from a particular, and thus limited, position. Moreover, these positions are constituted within a discursive terrain that is antagonistic – cross-cut by hegemonic practices of exclusions, repressions, silencings, resistances, subversions, and intrusions. My particular, limited version of Canada inevitably flies in the face of someone else's particular, limited version of Canada.

The unity of what is common to us, let's call it 'Canada,' is an allusive/elusive ideal that is always denied by its being contested and mediated through different particular experiences. While 'Canada' may seem to get lost in the antagonistic mêlée, it never disappears. In fact, it is perpetually reconstituted by the antagonistic discourse, as the assertion of any particularity (Maritimer, gay, Korean) always already implicitly presupposes a unified ideal 'Canada' (which simultaneously excludes and thus constitutes, and incorporates and thus decomposes, the particular identity) with reference to which the differentiation can be made.

I argue then that it is an unavoidable condition of the discourse about identity in Canada that we implicitly invoke an allusive/elusive unified ideal 'Canada' that is common to us, for as soon as we articulate 'how things appear to me' (whether that be an affirmative appraisal of prevailing hegemonies from a position of privilege, or a scathing critique from a standpoint of marginalization or exclusion), conflicting versions of 'Canada' are articulated, which necessarily and unavoidably posit an ideal Canada which our view of the prevailing reality either manifests approximately or fails to measure up to. The best that I can do is carefully to explore Canada 'as it appears to me.' I must work through and explore the discursive formation that I am entrammelled in, hoping to locate, in the particular, elements of a generalizable ideal that is common to the experience of being in Canada.

Awakening the Spirit of Canada: Affinity and Friendship amongst Cyborgs

A spectre is haunting Europe – the spectre of Communism ... It is high time that Communists ... meet this nursery tale of the spectre of Communism with a manifesto of the party itself.   Marx and Engels 1964, 78

Let us take this reminder from Marx and Engels that emancipatory action begins by invoking the powerful spirit of the collective, the spirit of solidarity. The spirit, as Hegel says, is the desire for that which is always ahead of consciousness: desire for the '"I" that is "We" and the "We" that is "I"' (1977, 110). The spirit of solidarity that Marx and Engels are trying to make manifest in the world is Communism. Their manifesto is spellbinding: it is a stirring, powerful, and evocative narrative, intended to awaken a spirit of solidarity that is sleeping in the proletariat, and to harness that spirit, a spirit so potent that it would rupture history and transform the social universe. Marx and Engels are sorcerers calling on the class spirit to come forth and challenge the rule of the bourgeoisie, the spirit of capitalism.[9] What spirits animate and intoxicate Canadians in the 1990s? What spirits are we under the influence of, as it were? What spectres, now haunting the shadows, can be called to manifest themselves, and what spells can we use to invoke their power?

When Mary Wollstonecraft's *A Vindication of the Rights of Woman* was published in 1792 she was denounced as 'a hyena in petticoats': a werewolf, a monstrous woman.[10] Monsters, like Mary Wollstonecraft, are troublemakers, boundary transgressors who can show us the way into the world of spirits, who can de-monster-ate to us the spirits that rule us and that haunt our being ruled. Monsters simultaneously warn us of dangers and promise us possibilities to be realized by awakening the spirit. 'Monster' is derived from the Latin *monstrum*, a divine omen or portent, which is related to the Latin verb *monere*, to warn, to tell of a danger, also akin to *monstrare* (Latin), 'to show,' and *montrer* (French), 'to put on display.'[11] Monsters are beings that warn us, or show us something; things that cause us trouble, that we have profoundly ambivalent feelings towards. Namely, they show us the boundaries, the frontiers of social order, the spirits of solidarities that we are in thrall to. And they tell us of the terrible wonders that lie beyond those frontiers; they warn us that we are on the edge of the abyss.

Monsters show us that there are other spirits, alternative constitutions of the '"I" that is "We" and the "We" that is "I"'; other solidarities that might ground social order. Mary Wollstonecraft's daring extension of the discourse of the rights of man to include woman opened a window to the abyss outside the patriarchal order of her time. The abyss outside the constraining solidarity of patriarchy is not empty. Rather it is full; full of the infinitude of possibilities to which the established hegemonic order stands in relation, alternative possibilities for collective life that the dominant order must exclude, deny, and repress in order to constitute itself, alternatives that persist despite their suppression, and their assertion of themselves appears to the established order as threats of disorder and chaos, sources of meaninglessness and fear. But there is much more to the abyss than a void of nothingness or an infinitude of chaos, something to be feared. Mary Wollstonecraft's monstrous suggestion was also a source of excitement and inspiration. It called up a new, larger, more generous spirit of solidarity. The abyss which she showed appeared as an attractive, alluring frontier; a window to an other world of possibilities where bold and adventurous people could surpass themselves, change the world, become emancipated.

A quarter-century later, Wollstonecraft's daughter, Mary Shelley, gave us the archetype of the monster haunting modernity: Dr Frankenstein's unnameable creation.[12] Frankenstein's monster is the metaphorical figure of the wonderful but also tragic and horrific consequences of the dialectic of Enlightenment; the expansion of human powers of reason, science, and production, creating new conditions, possibilities, and forms of life, but also unleashing uncontrollable destructive forces and unsuppressible desires that could eventually turn on their creators and destroy them. The predatory culture of capitalism is one aspect of this monster, but the monster of capital has an antithesis, another monster, its nemesis, lying dormant, brooding inside the very belly of capital; the proletariat, 'new-fangled men ... as much an invention of modern times as machinery itself,' as Marx recognized,[13] a monstrous creature brought to life by the bourgeoisie who then denied it liberty and chained it in dungeons, and it is the spirit of this monster, its powerful unconscious desire to be (for itself), that Marx and Engels want to call up.

Our powerful postmodern monsters are cyborgs.[14] On the one hand we have the menacing figure of the 'Terminator,' a metaphor for a rapacious transnational New World Order. The lifeworld colonized by technoculture, the extreme alienation of a world of machine-made-machines; the 'Globe-o-cop,' enforcing order in a world rendered transparent by the panop-tical machine of 'Skynet'; a grid of command-control-communication-intelligence imposed on the planet, exponential bureaucratic and scientific practices of classification and hierarchical organization, individuating, iden-tifying, categorizing, and corralling people in ever more complex rational systems of power/knowledge. The Terminator is also a metaphor for the white man/god: Paul Bernardo, the sexual predator who thought he was the king; Marc Lepine, who travelled back in time to kill the feminist engineers who threatened the security of his future. The Terminator seeks to extermi-nate what it perceives to be inferior biological life-forms: eugenicists who hold professorships at our universities, the Heritage Front's legion of knee-jerking automatons, guided by a logic of termination that drives the action of 'ethnic cleansers' of every stripe: the Zionist, the Islamic fundamentalist, and the black race purist as much as the white supremacist.

But the Terminator also has a nemesis, its dialectical antithesis, a cyborg doppelgänger, a monster created by the same historical forces that fabri-cated and unleashed the Terminator, and this cyborg is the spectral figure haunting postmodernity whose power we must try to invoke. 'Cyborgs,' according to Haraway, 'are creatures of social reality as well as creatures of fiction, who populate worlds ambiguously natural and crafted. In the late twentieth century, our time, a mythic time, we are all chimeras, theorized and fabricated hybrids; in short, we are cyborgs. The cyborg is our ontol-ogy; it gives us our politics' (1991, 149–50).

Cyborgs, Haraway says, acknowledge and take pleasure in the confusion of boundaries, and take responsibility for their construction. Cyborgs have no truck with seductions to organic wholeness; cyborgs don't have a species being, they don't belong to a singular class or a unitary race or gender. The real conditions of their lives and their relations with one another are in flux, always in a state of becoming, indeterminable, and so cyborgs are resolutely committed to partiality, irony, intimacy, and perversity. Cyborgs are oppo-sitional, utopian, and completely without innocence. Cyborgs are wary of holism but needy for connection; cyborgs are not afraid of permanently partial identities and contradictory standpoints; cyborg unities are mon-strous, incomplete, and illegitimate; unities of affinity – related not by blood but by choice, avidity' (Haraway 1991, 150–1).

The cyborg is a metaphor for a vivisectionized postmodern subjectivity; fragmented, split, incomplete, hybrid, occupying a multiplicity of often contradictory subject positions. 'We have all been injured, profoundly. We require regeneration, not rebirth,' Haraway says. The cyborg has a spirit, a desire for an '"I" that is "We" and [a] "We" that is "I"' that holds out the promise of regeneration; a potent collective solidarity grounded not in a common language or a common origin in a singular real condition such as class, race, gender, nation, or human nature, but in an 'infidel heteroglossia' of changing conditions and relations with others, achieved by the skilful restructuring of the boundaries of daily life, by building and destroying and rebuilding machines, identities, categories, relationships, spaces, stories.[15]

The possibility of a new radical politics envisaged by Haraway as 'an affinity amongst cyborgs' is echoed today by many writers. The challenge is to reformulate 'left' politics in the aftermath of postmodernism/poststructuralism's critique of the metanarrative, the destabilization of the subject and the corresponding standpoint epistemologies of fragmented political identities. Cyborg politics is, in my opinion, best developed by Laclau and Mouffe, who formulate the dissolution of boundaries separating antagonistic identities in terms of a hegemonic new left 'common sense' of a 'radical and plural democracy' (1985, 182). Laclau and Mouffe argue for the possibility of a radical political imaginary where struggles are linked in a chain of equivalences by articulatory and hegemonic practices. For Laclau and Mouffe, political struggles are consolidated and attain richness and depth according to the extent to which they are articulated with other struggles. It is not enough that struggles be fought simultaneously, nor do they simply require linking up. The struggles must be articulated in such a way that they change one another's identity. Laclau and Mouffe argue:

The strengthening of specific democratic struggles requires, therefore, the expansion of chains of equivalence which extend to other struggles. The equivential articulation between anti-racism, anti-sexism and anti-capitalism, for example, requires a hegemonic construction which, in certain circumstances, may be the condition for the consolidation of each of these struggles ... a 'democratic equivalence' [requires] the construction of a new 'common sense,' which changes the identity of the different groups, in such a way that the demands of each group are articulated equivalentially with those of the others – in Marx's words: 'that the free development of each should be the condition for the free development of all.'   1985, 182–3

This is the conjuncture of possibilities that I will be exploring. I want to locate the moments of openness in identities and the ways in which they might be attuned to one another. I am interested in the particular idiom of boundary transgression and reintegration of antagonistic identities in contemporary Canada. I will formulate the synthetic frontier effects at the boundaries in terms of friendship. I will argue that the idea of friendship provides a principled way of relating to difference/Otherness that is sensi-tive to the particularities and peculiarities of contemporary Canada.

A friendship among cyborgs could collect a spirit of solidarity amongst the diverse, scattered, hybrid and partial beings who constitute Canada: beings, I will show, that have a peculiar relationship to nature, beings without pure origins, whose identities begin in the confusions, conjoinings, and co-minglings of First Nations, Founding Nations, travelling cultures. Canadian cyborg friendship might be a solidarity based on a nomadic imaginary; a spirit that finds its enjoyment grounded in boundary confu-sions, that takes pleasure in the polymorphous perversity of the illegitimate progeny of immigrants, that finds enjoyment in the interpenetration of hybrid, technicoloured beings with many cultures, voices, identities, and sexualities, that develops moral fibre by taking responsibility for the daily, hourly negotiation of the ethics of inevitable and necessary boundary trans-gressions; this might be the kind of monster to challenge the rule of the Terminator in Canada. I will consider the particularity of a Canadian cy-borg spirit of solidarity and how we might invoke it.

Interpretive Symptomatology

From each point on the surface of existence ... one may drop a sounding into the depths.   Simmel 1964, 413

I will look for the spirit of cyborg friendship in symptoms of Canada, by which I mean everyday superficial and familiar phenomena that are signs of trouble, symptoms of Canada in so far as they show the impossibility of Canada, its radical ontological non-existence. But showing that impossibil-ity is the easy part, the cheap shot at nationalism and positive versions of national identity. Anderson (1991) and Hobsbawm (1983), among others, have already done this work (though not, of course, with reference to Canada). I differentiate my own perspective from Anderson's and Hobsbawm's by posing the thorny question that persists despite that disap-pearance of the real: namely (as Heidegger puts it) 'a nation "is," but where is its being situated?' (Steiner 1978, 42). That is, when we recognize the impossibility of the nation, that the nation exists only as symptoms of its lack, we must still deal with the particularity of its impossibility. All nations are imagined communities, all traditions are invented, but it would be absurd to be content with this generalization. If we are to talk about 'Canada' as opposed to any other – equally imaginary – community, we must attend closely to the idiom of the symptom: we must search for the difference, for what is particularly 'Canadian,' in the symptoms of the non-existence of Canada.

Heidegger's phenomenology stresses that human subjects are formed by the historical cultural practices in which they develop.[16] These practices form a background (a lifeworld) that can never be made completely explicit, and so cannot be explained in terms of the beliefs of a meaning-giving subject. That is, the subject's version of the lifeworld does not exhaust the lifeworld. There is meaning embodied in these background practices; they embody a way of coping with things, practices, and institutions. This meaning Heidegger calls 'interpretation.' Heidegger's method, which is to give an interpretation of the interpretation embodied in everyday practices, is hermeneutics. In *Being and Time*, Heidegger elaborates what he calls 'an interpretation of *Dasein* in its everydayness,' by which he means that there is a 'primordial understanding' evident in our everyday activities, practices, and discourse, which is overlooked by the practitioners, but which they would recognize if it were pointed out to them.[17] Heidegger holds that the understanding in our everyday practices is partial and distorted. Later in *Being and Time* he argues that the partial interpretation, the partial or mis-understanding, is a motivated masking of the truth. Heidegger says:

Dasein's kind of Being demands that any ontological interpretation which sets itself the goal of exhibiting the phenomena in its primordiality should capture the Being of this entity in spite of this entity's own tendency to cover things up. Existential analysis therefore constantly has the character of doing violence whether to the claims of the everyday interpretation, or to its complacency and its tranquilized obviousness.   (Heidegger 1962, 359)

What the violence of analysis reveals, according to Heidegger, is the deep truth hidden by everyday practices, 'the unsettling groundlessness of a way of being that is interpretation all the way down' (Dreyfus and Rabinow 1982, xxii).

Lacan calls this masked deep truth, this original trauma, the 'Lack' (of the real) and thus the 'real' truth of existence.[18] In Laclau and Mouffe's usage, this deep truth is called the 'constitutive antagonism' of the social, which competing hegemonic political projects try in vain to suture (1985, 122–7). The 'everyday interpretations,' what sociologists would later call the 'ethno-methods,'[19] are what we use to mask this trauma and produce a shared meaningful lifeworld.

For Heidegger and Lacan, the original lack persists in the very heart of the lifeworld, and we can always find in each and every social phenomenon the moment where the motivated masking fails and the lack is glimpsed. This original lack has a thoroughly paradoxical character. In so far is it is a lack of solid grounding and meaning it is utterly horrible and fearful, yet it is simultaneously a lack of restraint and limit, and thus the source and guarantor of enjoyment and emancipation. Thus we desire simultaneously to protect ourselves from the terror of the emptiness of this lack and at the same time to have access to the free space of the lack.

Following the Lacanian usage, in my work 'symptoms' are the background of everyday practices (the lifeworld structures) that embody interpretations that sustain meaning and protect us from the lack, and which simultaneously expose us to the lack enough to animate us. My hermeneutic (Heideggerian) or analytic (Lacanian) move is to do an interpretation of the symptoms of Canada. I want in my interpretation to find in the symptom what Lacan calls the '*object petit a*,'[20] the little piece of the real that persists in the phenomenon, the point where the mask slips, as it were, constituting a window to the abyss. I am looking for the moments where the symptom declares the real (the radical openness and contingency of the prevailing discursive order) and its moment of motivated masking, where it shields us from the real.

The corresponding orientation to the symptom, the collective sensibility, is what I'm calling 'ironic conceit.'[21] That is, a conceit of closure, of groundedness, grants protection, but irony grants us freedom of access to the lack. It is by ironic conceit that we can mask, and thus live with, Heidegger's deep truth of unsettling groundlessness. Ironic conceit keeps the window to the abyss open, granting us respite from the hegemony of the ruling spirits and keeping alive the promise of transformation.

We are familiar with the usage of 'symptom' in the discourses of medicine and psychoanalysis. The symptom refers to superficial phenomenal manifestations of some hidden, underlying trauma, which we can only approach and begin to discern by interpreting these symptoms. The symptom is a partial, distorted expression of the trauma; the underlying trouble is never apparent in any one particular symptom, so we proceed by reading many symptoms, interpreting how they relate to one another, and then hypothesize that, taken together, they indicate, or point towards, a hidden 'something' that never in fact presents itself to us in its own sheer particularity. And of course it is only by carefully working through the symptoms that we can get near to the trauma and deal with it. Thus the object of interpretation is the unified ideal that unites the symptoms.

My job will be to try to set up what Alan Blum calls a 'reflective equilibrium' between the symptoms.[22] In other words, I am proceeding with the assumption that the phenomena which I'm looking at bear some relation to one another, and their relation to one another points to some unity beyond them, an ideal unity that we structure and fill out by fantasy. But it is an ideal that we are trying to bring into view, and necessarily that unified ideal that is implied by the symptoms will always remain ahead of us. The symptoms all add up to the ideal, yet the unified ideal is more than the sum of the symptoms.

This elusiveness of the ideal implied beyond the symptoms, the fact that the ideal will always be outside our reach, an otherness beyond representation, causes us to rethink the status of the symptom. For if what is beyond symptom is what we desire to signify, but cannot signify, then the symptom is what is. The symptom is all that there is, and beyond the symptom is the void of the real which we protect ourselves from by the fantasized utopian ideal, an ideal that resists signification and thus compels our desire.

Lacan says:

The symptom is a signifier, more precisely a metaphor (unthinkable outside a rhetoric of the unconscious) which produces the individual as a unique combination of the three exigencies: the imaginary, the symbolic and the real. The symptom is the peculiar notation of the human dimension.[23]

The 'unique' and 'peculiar' notation of the human dimension. The symptom is literally who/what we are, the symptom is ourselves. The aim of analysis, Lacan says, is to lead the subject through the fantasy to face the real, and to return again to the symptom, so that one may recognize in the symptom the only support of one's being in the face of the real. Thereby one is compelled to love thy symptom as thy self. Lacan's ethical commandment to love thy symptom derives from the recognition in the real of the lack of any ultimate source of meaning, the unresolvable character of the foundational antagonism, that there is no ultimate cure that will fix the underlying trauma. Thus one must face up to the responsibility of managing the symptom, of knowing oneself and taking responsibility for one's agency.[24] In Laclau and Mouffe's political terms, 'going through the fantasy' (Žižek 1989, 124–8) means discarding totalizing meaning-giving metanarratives, Marxist teleology, the conceit of epistemologically and politically privileged historical agents (whether conceived as workers, women, or third world revolutionaries) and recognizing instead the radical contingency of the prevailing discursive order.[25] The prevailing discursive order thus appears as symptom formation, and a new left political project must work out a responsible relation with it.

My goal is to try to find some of what is unique and peculiar about being in Canada by going through some Canadian fantasies. I know that I will not find that elusive ideal thing that is Canada, but by going in search of it to the point where we glimpse its radical ontological absence, we will bring to light our symptoms, those things unique and peculiar to us. By this I mean that the object of my inquiry is to help us to get to know our symptom so that we may take responsibility for it and shape it hegemonically. The very elusiveness and impossibility of the object of our inquiry is not an obstacle, but on the contrary is the incentive that makes my work, and (I hope) your reading of my work, enjoyable.

Canada exists as symptoms of the real thing which doesn't exist, but which has real effects. I'm approaching Canada by 'looking awry'[26] at it – that is, by looking at it from various (often odd) angles, provided by the everyday staging of Canada by ordinary Canadians being Canadian, doing Canada. Looking straightforwardly, from the conventional standpoints of sociology, political science, and history, we get a (usually blurry) overview, but we invariably miss the divine details of the spirit of Canada. I could proceed by looking at any (infinite) number of symptoms, or perhaps just one symptom complex. Baudrillard says that 'all you need to know about American society can be gleaned from an anthropology of its driving behavior. Drive ten thousand miles across America and you will know more about the country than all the institutes of sociology and political science put together' (1988a, 54–5). I've chosen to examine a few symptoms, ones that strike me as somehow telling. I am a newcomer, enjoying living here, attuning to Being in Canada, a bit of a schizo-cyborg, making connections, making friends, so the symptoms that I zoom in on will be esoteric and somewhat arbitrary. There is, however, a strong guiding principle that connects the diversity of phenomena explored here.

My attempt to bring the unique and peculiar notation of Canada into view is founded on the Hegelian premise, shared by Heidegger and Lacan, that being comes to know itself from 'the *return* from *otherness*' (Hegel 1977, 105). That is, Canada is realized by its reflection from otherness: that Canada is constituted by a process of reflexive realization whereby it comes to know itself and recognize itself, and becomes knowable and recognizable, in its returning from encounters with otherness. My exploration of otherness in Canada takes diverse forms simultaneously. Sometimes otherness figures intersubjectively, as a particular; sometimes as a general form, a beyond of representation; sometimes as philosophical, sometimes as social alterity. In all of this I am exploring specific Canadian relationships to otherness. However, the forms of this otherness are not necessarily equivalent, or sutured in a monolithic field. Others have relations to otherness as well, and otherness from the perspective of others may be quite other than hegemonic constructions of alterity.

To sum up then: there are three steps to the method of interpretive symptomatology by which I will try to speak about Canada and the possibility of evoking a cyborg Canadian spirit:

(1) A series of takes on Canada, interpretive forays into the symptom formation, to the points from which the real – the absence of Canada – is glimpsed; these moments when Canada dies are also the moments when Bataille says we experience our continuity as Canadians.[27]

(2) Hegemonic extrapolation of the interpretations of diverse symptoms in pursuit of the unity implied by the symptoms. That is, the symptom desires that its meaning be interpreted, that its relationality with other symptoms be clarified. Signs want to be read, and this is what we pursue, but ironically, knowing the limitedness of our reading, that our reading can be at best a persuasive hegemonic interpretation, entering a field of competing antagonistic interpretations, the field of politics, of persuasive argument.

(3) Symptoms imply a unity; that is, the particularity of the symptoms says something about what they are symptomatic of, in particular – an ideal unity of a cyborg friendship that would constitute an emancipatory spirit of Canada. Our interpretation is guided by the aspiration to grasp and fully express that unified thing which is particularly Canadian, as implied by the symptoms of Canada. So, knowing that we cannot answer the question, we ask, nevertheless: What essentially belongs to Canada? When we take away what it isn't (that which defines it), what excess, leftover, is there that is what it is?[28] This leftover is what Lacan calls a hard kernel of enjoyment.[29] Not the lack (for the lack is what is shared by what is Canada and what is not Canada), but the particularity of the symptoms of the lack, a particularity of enjoyment which only becomes perceptible when we treat symptoms as *sinthome*, that is, a signifying formation penetrated with enjoyment; the sensory dimension of Canadian *Dasein*; the taste and smells, the look and feel of things Canadian, what Bataille would call the erotism of Being in Canada.

2

National Identity and the Theft of National Enjoyment

The problem of Canadian national unity is one of identification; that is, of leading a diverse collectivity to a mutual recognition of a shared relationship to something called 'the nation.' We cannot say what this nation-thing 'Canada' is exactly, but we say that it manifests itself or that it finds expression in 'our way of life.'[30] This is true of identities in general. If you ask me what it is that makes me Irish, or I ask you what it is that makes you Canadian, we find that 'it's hard to say, exactly,' so we resort to listing to each other unique aspects of 'our way of life': our food, our music, our customs, our festivals, our forms of recreation, and so on. What we relate to one another are the ways in which our enjoyment is organized; the unique things that we enjoy, that others do not have.

The 'way of life' of an ethnic group, a community, or a nation takes the form of an articulated constellation of bits of enjoyment: a discursive construction articulated around a central void; a thing that resists definition. While it is impossible to say what this thing is essentially, it is definitely there, because we can readily point to cultural practices where it is apparent as 'the real thing,' or 'a western thing,' some thing that is 'just so Toronto.' At Caribana recently, 'Island pride' was expressed in similar terms. Trinidadians sported T-shirts with the slogan 'It's a Trin. thing. You just wouldn't understand.' Membership is about having a shared relationship to this thing; a thing that exists only as enjoyment incarnated. The discourse of Canadian nationalism is concerned with Canadian national enjoyment. It is an antagonistic discourse because it is charged with allegations of theft, a theft of enjoyment. This charge of theft is voiced most explicitly at the moment by the Reform party. A party spokesman at a recent convention in Toronto began his address by saying, 'Canada is being stolen from us. It's being stolen by Quebeckers, by Ottawa bureaucrats, and by ethnics who won't join the mainstream.'[31]

This theme of theft of identity/enjoyment is not solely a concern of the Reform party. It is central to the discourse of nationalism in general. According to the national anthem, we are always 'stand(ing) on guard' against possible threats to our way of life. Someone or something is constantly threatening to 'steal' our enjoyment. The Free Trade Agreement is discussed in terms of whether and in what ways it threatens our Canadian enjoyment: will the U.S. drain our economy, take our jobs, suffocate our culture? People who oppose immigration most often do so because they fear that it will alter the ethnic composition of the country, and thus 'endanger our way of life.'

And yet when we ask, 'What is the Canadian way of life?' it proves impossible to give anything like a definitive answer. The best we can do is to give examples of cultural practices that are 'typically Canadian,' such as for example are portrayed in the lifeworld of the characters Bob and Doug McKenzie on SCTV (eh!) or in the advertisements for Molson's Canadian beer – the advertisements that begin: 'In Canada, on Saturday night [on weekends, in winter] young people indulge in a unique ritual: it's called "strutting your stuff" ["opening the cottage," "going out with the boys"].' The advertisements then depict 'typical Canadians' doing 'uniquely Canadian things': dancing at a cool Queen Street club, unloading a canoe, chopping firewood, buying ice, cottage-ing; skiing, skating, tobogganing, hanging out at the campsite, and so on. The advertisements conclude: 'Molson's Canadian: what beer [read 'what being Canadian'] is all about.'

What is interesting about these advertisements is that they inadvertently show the hollowness, the original 'lack' (of meaning), that underpins the identity 'Canadian.' It is nothing 'essential': it is a contingent precarious identity; something socially constructed; a hegemonic construction; constructed in this instance by Molson's advertising department. Identity is a constellation of elements articulated together as moments of a discourse. Discursively produced identities are contingent, and ultimately precarious, because the elements that compose them may be subject to different competing (antagonistic) articulations. The elements of the discourse are ultimately arbitrary. One doesn't necessarily have to be Canadian to engage in the activities depicted in the ads, does one? Americans, Swedes, Japanese, or just about anyone might enjoy the same things. And we can also imagine Canadians who don't enjoy these things, but who are still Canadians. One could imagine other articulations of 'what Canada is all about' – a portrayal of the enjoyment of Afrofest or Caribana – or the enjoyment of various Others not represented in the dominant articulations – a representation of life (existence/enjoyment?) on a Native reserve, or of a drunken husband beating up his wife. Isn't that equally 'what beer [read 'what being Canadian'] is all about'?

There are several important axes of relationality across which the current Canadian identity crisis is constituted. The most prominent of these are the identity relations Canada/U.S., Quebec/the rest of Canada, Canada/Native peoples, and Canada/ethnic groups or immigrants. While these axes of problematic relationality appear and are articulated politically as distinct problem complexes, they share a basic dynamic.

The salient differences in the project of identity construction and maintenance are those of 'enjoyment,' that is, the fragmented and various practices, languages, symbols, and rituals, to which we lay claim as the 'unique' aspects of 'our way of life'; something which 'we' have and 'they' do not; which 'we' enjoy and 'they' cannot understand or appreciate. But possession of national enjoyment is tenuous. 'They' always pose a threat to it: their difference threatens to steal our enjoyment. Americanization threatens to steal our Canadian enjoyment of crime-free cities and harmonious ethnic relations. Their 'culture industry' threatens to rob us of our culture. Their unfettered market forces would steal the enjoyment of our medicare system, our seniors' retirement plans, and so on.

The rest of Canada threatens to steal Quebec's enjoyment in the same way: it does not (cannot, some would say) appreciate Quebec's 'distinctiveness.' The rest of Canada frustrates the Québécois project to be 'maîtres chez nous.' English creeps into the Quebec vernacular, stealing Frenchness. A signs inspectorate and language police are needed to keep the thief at bay. Meanwhile, elements in the rest of Canada feel that Quebec is stealing its enjoyment: bilinguals and francophones allegedly get preferential treatment in employment. Quebec, say Maritimers, gets more political clout and proportionately more than its fair share of federal transfer payments than the neglected Maritimes. Vampirish Quebec feeds on the rich black oil-blood of Alberta. Hydro-Quebec's mega-projects in James Bay allegedly steal Natives' traditional lands. The enjoyment of our shopping, even of our breakfast bowl of bran flakes, is somehow infringed upon by bilingual packaging!

The most general formulation of the problem of antagonistic relationality and identity is Hegel's discussion of the dialectical relationship between the master and the bondsman in the struggle for self-consciousness.[32] The master depends upon the bondsman for his own freedom, for the constitution of his own identity as master. But in his practice of turning the bondsman into an object, he is objectifying himself simultaneously, because self-consciousness is the return (reflection) from otherness: the master and the bondsman are equally unfree. While the bondsman is complicit in his subjugation, he participates in the action of the master – that is, he makes an object of himself – and his becoming a being-for-himself depends upon his engaging in a struggle 'to the death' against the master, by which the bondsman frees both himself and the master from their relation to one another as objects.

For Hegel the achievement of being-for-self can only be released in dialectical struggle. The independent shape has no being-in-itself. It must 'subject its existence to the infinity of the difference.' The supersession of individual existence through the fluidity or general dissolution of differences *produces* individual existence. When being itself (simple existence) places the Other within itself, it supersedes the simplicity of its essence. In order for this supersession to take place there must be an Other. Being itself 'must proceed to supersede the Other independent being in order thereby to become certain of *itself* as the essential being ... in so doing it proceeds to supersede its *own* self, for this Other is itself' (Hegel 1977, 107, 108, 111).

Slavoj Žižek derives a complementary formulation of this dynamic from the psychoanalysis of Lacan.[33] Namely, the problem of relationality with the Other is that the Other is always already part of the One. This is so because without the Other there is no One: the One is the original lack. The Other are hated and feared because its presence threatens to reveal this original lack. Hatred and fear of the Other are, therefore, hatred and fear of the self. Hatred and fear of Quebec's distinctiveness reflect a fear and hatred of the rest of Canada's lack of distinctiveness.

What is hated and feared about the Other is the Other's 'enjoyment'; that is, how the Other's existence is animated. Why is this enjoyment of the Other's feared/hated? The Other's enjoyment shows the contingency, precariousness, or absurd improbability of the One's enjoyment of its own identity. The redneck hates 'Paki food' because it reveals the absurdity of southern fried chicken in Petawawa. In other words, the Other's existence/enjoyment constantly reminds us of the lack, the semantic void at the heart of the social that underpins our own existence/enjoyment. It does this by presenting and confronting the One identity with the infinitude of alternative forms of enjoyment, showing that the form of life, the enjoyment, the way in which the existence of the One is animated is simply one of an inexhaustible number and variety of ways of existence. It shows that 'our way of life' is not the only way; that there is no way of saying that it's the best way; that our existence/enjoyment is, or may be, absurd, improbable, and meaningless. The presence of Other is therefore a constant source of existential angst.

The social is constituted as an antagonistic force field of relationality between contingent articulations of identities around a basic paradox: that the integrity of identity is contingent upon the identification of elements that are not-the-identity; that is, a field of Otherness, outside of the identity, which stands in antithetical relation to the identity. These Other elements simultaneously both constitute and negate the identity: that is, while they are necessary for negatively defining the identity (the One is not-the-Other), they are also a threat to its integrity. In the first instance, Quebec *is* 'not-the-rest-of-Canada,' and yet for Québécois 'the-rest-of-Canada' decomposes Quebec. The inverse of this is the truth for the Reform party. How is this so? Because the original identity is a contingent historical construction, a precarious constellation of (what are ultimately arbitrary) elements. In other words, the identity has no essence that gives it transcendent being outside of a particular socially constructed historical context. This original lack (lack of essence, lack of fixed meaning) is the traumatic kernel of social existence. The presence of Otherness is a constant reminder of this lack, and thus is a source of existential angst and anomie.

The enjoyment of a historical identity – that is, the innumerable social practices, languages, signs, codes that animate a particular identity – is constantly under threat of being stolen away by the necessary coexistence of Otherness, because the Other's enjoyment, or, rather, the infinitude of the difference apparent in the Other's enjoyment, an infinitude that appears as the Other's excess enjoyment, exposes the arbitrariness and contingency, the improbability, precariousness, and fragility of the enjoyment of the One. Because of this the Other is feared and hated, and attempts are made to annihilate it. But this fear and hatred is a projection, or a displacement, because what is actually feared and hated is the lack, the absence of the real underpinning the existence of the One. And campaigns to annihilate the Other, because they would simultaneously result in the annihilation of the One, are practices of self-hatred.

At the same time, this very infinitude of difference apparent in the enjoyment of the Other, the excess of enjoyment that is the source of angst and fear for the One, also constitutes the terrain or the space into which the enjoyment of the One can be extended and grow. We hate the Other for its excessive enjoyment, and we desire the Other for its excess enjoyment. Canadians express dislike of Americans in terms of their being 'excessive.' Americans are allegedly crass and vulgar. They over-consume shamelessly and are untidy in their enjoyment. They are obese, loud, wasteful, arrogant, and 'out of control.' Quebeckers are disliked because of their excess 'Frenchness.' Their language is exclusive. They are promiscuous, sexy, seductive. Their culture is too rich. ('Rest-of')-Canadians point to Quebeckers' penchant for dining out in boulevard cafés; all the sugar and confectionery that they eat; how they drink; how they sell wine and beer in corner stores; how their bars stay open to three a.m.! Their public spaces, their cities are excessive: all those night-clubs in Hull, just across the river from orderly Ottawa. Canadians contrast cold, anal-retentive Toronto with lively Montreal, which has that ever so slightly decadent (and alluring) excess, cosmopolitan Parisian pretension.

In the discourse of racism, immigrants too are disliked in terms of their excessive enjoyment: their strange exotic customs, their large families, their laziness, their promiscuity. We accuse them of loafing around, drinking beer and smoking drugs, stealing our women, and corrupting our youth. Paradoxically, in the racist discourse, immigrants are equally hated for their 'unnatural' capacity for hard work, or their apparant willingness to 'work for nothing,' or for 'only employing each other,' and thus stealing Canadian jobs. Thus the 'sucessful' immigrant and the 'lazy' immigrant are rendered equivalent in the racist discourse, as both are marked by some obscene excess enjoyment. For example, Asian immigrants have recently been constructed in terms of an excess of crime – more precisely, of an excess of criminal enjoyment. Chinatown, we are told by the tabloid press, is run by secret societies. Organized crime organizes a perverse Oriental enjoyment – drugs, gun-running, protection rackets for restaurants and clubs, prostitution rackets, speak-easies, and gaming houses. Asian gangsters are portrayed in terms of their excess enjoyment – they all drive Porsches, keep women (possibly even white women!) as slaves, rule over empires, and so on.[34]

But it is this very excess, pertaining to the Other's enjoyment, that constitutes the object field of desire. The same qualities that we hate in the Other are those qualities that we envy, that we desire. Canadians desire Americans' supposedly higher standards of living, lower taxes, greater control over their elected representatives. The Reform party, for example, is a vehicle that structures Canadian desire in terms of a fantasy of Americans' excess enjoyment. The Reform party pursues this fantasy by constructing an electoral platform on the argument that if Canadians could have American's excess enjoyment – their taxation system, their system of government – it would fill our lack. We would have a new national enjoyment; Preston Manning's 'New Canada.'

But of course American enjoyment is no more secure than ours. Americans fret that their enjoyment is being stolen by Japanese competition, by drugs, by blacks and Hispanics, and they must periodically engage in spectacular lynchings of thieves such as Manuel Noriega and Saddam Hussein to allay these fears. The fulfilment of the Reformer's desire, the overlapping of two lacks, cannot constitute the real: there will still be a lack. Manning's 'New Canada' will be under threat of being stolen away by other Others, and so Reformers also fight 'feminists and homosexuals' who are allegedly stealing the enjoyment of our nuclear families, 'bogus refugees' who steal our houses, services, and welfare, and 'ethnics who don't join the mainstream.'³⁵ The desire for national enjoyment cannot be satisfied; it is always under threat by some Other. The magic knot of nationalism, tightening to squeeze out the thieves of enjoyment, tightens until it disappears. It cannot grasp the void.

Otherness constitutes the field of adventure that sustains the vitality of the enjoyment/existence of the One. Otherness is the object domain of desire, the fantasy space of growth and development. Relations towards the Other are always ambivalent. At one and the same moment the Other is articulated as the thief of Canada and as constituting Canada. Quebec and bilingualism make Canada Canada, vis-à-vis the U.S. Similarly, immigrants bring diversity, adding to our national enjoyment, our 'mosaic,' which we proudly differentiate from the unwholesome stew of the American 'melting pot.' Caribana, Thai food, and the bustle of Chinatown become integral parts of Canadian enjoyment.

One aspect of this growth into the field of otherness is what Hegel calls Being coming to know itself from its reflection from otherness; where, in Lacanian terms, we seek from the Other affirmation of our enjoyment and thus hide the lack from ourselves. Canadians derive enjoyment – have their enjoyment affirmed, certified, and approved as authentic, as it were – by seeing immigrants become more like themselves, but, note, not indistinguishable, not the same as themselves. The difference must persist in order that the reflection is from Other.

A refugee settlement organization in Toronto currently runs an advertisement inviting Canadians to play host to new arrivals. The slogan runs 'Show a new Canadian what us old Canadians are made of' (that is, have someone from a foreign country tell you how nice you are and what a wonderful country you've got). White anglophone Canadians get a kick out of seeing blacks and Asians skating and skiing, and out of asking them whether they have ever seen snow before, whether or not they will ever get used to the cold, and so on. The satisfaction is derived from the contribution of these interactions towards fulfilling the desire to fill the lack (of meaning) through seeing the Other enjoying the enjoyment of Canadian life.

Thus Preston Manning would (have us believe, at least, that he would) welcome immigrants regardless of race or creed. 'Immigration,' says the Reform party, 'has been, and can be again, a positive source of economic growth, cultural diversity, and social renewal' (that is, immigration is welcome when it contributes to our national enjoyment). 'The Reform Party stands for the acceptance and integration of immigrants into the mainstream of Canadian life' (whatever that is!) and 'The Reform Party supports the principle that individuals and groups are free to preserve their cultural heritage, using their own resources.'[36] (That is, immigration and difference are welcome to the extent to which they satisfy our desire to have our enjoyment confirmed.) Quebec separatists' approach to immigration is exactly the same: we welcome immigrants to the extent to which they shore up and protect Quebec's enjoyment (that they are francophone and economically productive). We accept difference only to the extent to which immigrants join the mainstream of Quebec society (learn French, educate their children through French, settle in Quebec, and so on).

But the dialectical encounter with the Other is never on terms dictated only by the master. The encounter with the Other is antagonistic, and placing the Other within the self, subjecting the identity to the infinity of the difference, alters the identity. The dialectical encounter is played out in terms of wars of position, the conduct and outcome of which are undetermined, though the stakes are quite clear: the identities of the antagonists, where 'they' become more like 'us' and 'we' more like 'them.'

As I have indicated above, the witch-hunt for the thief of enjoyment is echoed in Quebec, amongst Natives, amongst racial and ethnic minorities, and in many groups who feel, with varying degrees of justification, that they are not getting their fair share of the action in Canada as it is currently constituted. And, as I have argued, while they accuse each other of the theft of their enjoyment, paradoxically they look to the secret, excess enjoyment which they impute to the Other as the object domain of their desire, the source of the restoration of their enjoyment. Who holds the key to the resolution of the national identity crisis, who can restore our enjoyment? They can, those same Others who are stealing it.

The rest of Canada says that if Quebec's excess enjoyment was shared, if Quebec would accept that the other provinces were as equal as itself, then we would be happy. If only the rest of Canada had as strong a sense of identity as Quebec has, then the country would not be breaking up. On the other side, Quebeckers say that if only we had that excess enjoyment of political power which the (federal government of) the rest of Canada enjoys – a quasi-sovereign distinctiveness, more control over immigration, more control over the federal budget, more clout on the Supreme Court, power of veto on constitutional amendments – the enjoyments denied/stolen from us at Meech Lake – then we would happily be part of Canada.

Both Québécois and rest-of-Canadians say, if we all only had that special relationship with the land that we suspect Natives of enjoying, even though those same Natives deny us our enjoyment of golfing at Oka and by their pitiful drunkenness embarrass us out of enjoying our city streets, then we would all have a sense of place. If we only had the prosperity of the Americans, even though that prosperity is stealing our jobs, guzzling our resources, and would leave us to die on the sidewalk and beg in the streets, there would be no problem. The same ambivalence and paradox are at the heart of the talk about immigrants in the nationalist discourse: if only we had the drive and the discipline of the Japanese, the industriousness and resourcefulness of the Chinese and the Asians, the easy-going-ness and the 'soul' of the Hispanics and blacks – those very people who are making our houses unaffordable, taking our jobs, scrounging our welfare, and making our streets unsafe – then we would not be in this mess.

The threat of discarding the Other, bidding adieu to the rest of Canada, letting go of Quebec, shutting the door on immigrants, is a potent but empty threat. There is no letting go. The centrifugal forces that we fear will tear Canada asunder actually reflect the increased tempo of the spiral dance of the dialectic in which the oppositional Others are mutually bound. They cannot release each other, because (a) they depend upon one another's presence for their integrity, and (b) their boundaries and frontiers have been melted into one another. No sooner are the lines of solitude reestablished than they are melted away again by the heat of the antagonistic friction of the wars of position. What gets sucked into the swirling vortex of the dialectic and melted down are those elements of the symbolic orders of outdated enjoyments: Mounties' hats and uniforms, oaths of loyalty to the Queen, Sûreté du Québec police cars, ignorant stereotypes of Natives, racist and sectarian institutions, 'official-language' barriers and an artificial multiculturalism that produces hyphenated Canadians, reified traditions as artifacts and controlled commercialized spectacles.

What is released and generated is a sumptuous and fruitful pastiche; a symbolic order representing a new enjoyment – the work of Michael Ondaatje, Tomson Highway, Daniel Lanois, Deepa Mehta, Jean-Pierre Lefebvre. The new enjoyment finds space, and grows – on St-Denis, in Kensington Market, on Queen Street. It grows, but does not thrive, in hot-housed and enforced conditions: staged and gawked at by the curious in the confines of ethnic clubs during Caravan, or, when, like Caribana, it is escorted along the Gardiner Expressway by police with practised smiles, kept at a safe distance from the city lest its exuberance prove infectious. But it flourishes in restaurants and coffee shops, bars, clubs, and speakeasies, in neighbourhoods, schoolyards, and baseball parks. Its growth is agonal and terrifying, often violent, sometimes sputtering out in the dimness of a crack house, sometimes lying bloodied on the sidewalk. The space of the new enjoyment must be, and is, fought for – on the steps of the Royal Ontario Museum, at the doors of night clubs, and on the streets of Halifax. It struggles for space in art galleries and on bookshelves, for elbow-room on the streets, for a fair crack at the whip in the workplace, for a place to eat, sleep, laugh, love, and die: for a place to call home, a site of enjoyment/existence.

The national identity crisis is anxiety-laden because of a lag or a slippage between the melting down of the old symbolic order and the production of the new. Canadians become aggressive and divisive over Mounties' hats and mug-shots of Her Majesty, ironically because they claim them to be symbols of unity in a country where such symbols are relatively scarce. Undoubtedly they are, or rather were, symbols of national unity, but unity under a dominant hegemonic order that is rapidly disintegrating. Outdated symbols of exclusive disunifying enjoyment are vanishing, leaving a yawning chasm. Canadians catch a glimpse of the abyss. Who are we, what are we doing here, are we enjoying ourselves? We desperately try to fill the gap, to cover the lack as quickly as possible. It seems to me that the lack cannot be covered solely by legislation, by legal, rational institutions such as the Charter of Rights or medicare. Unfortunately, human rights, hospitals, and pensions just do not turn people on. The stuff of desire that can fill the lack must be amenable to fantastic construction; it must be sublime. It must be sexy, heroic, majestic, and wonderful, but in new ways; able to fuel the fantasies of a very diverse spectrum of people. We need some new sublime objects of identification and we need to do new takes on our old ones. We need to work on, revise, and produce a Canadian tradition.

In light of this, the possibility arises for a federal administration to promote the production of the sublime objects of identification, the symbols that would represent and give order to a new hegemonic project. Such symbols would act as nodal points, *points de capiton*, around which elements could be articulated that would quilt a new social fabric; that would give form to a new organization of enjoyment, a new imaginary of community, or imaginaries of communities, radically different, but not 'marked' in subordination to any centre. In other words, an appropriate project of political leadership at the present juncture might be to foster a new political economy of cultural production and distribution, actively to seek out new symbols and artifacts representing the new enjoyment. This may well be an urgent task of political leadership if one is concerned that Canadians increasingly tend to pursue their desire to fill the lack, to construct their fantasy, in terms of the object domain of the United States – shopping, vacationing, watching TV and vicariously fighting the Gulf War – tending towards identification with the Other as a strategy for dealing with the trauma of the lack.

Such a project is not difficult to conceive. One tactic might be a vigorous pursuit of internationally visible spectacles spotlighting Canada. In an example that Canada might follow, the Spanish government hoped that the Barcelona Olympic Games would knit Catalunya, one of Spain's many equivalents of Quebec, more firmly into the fabric of the nation. Canada might cultivate some heroes. Ben Johnson was one, placed under tremendous pressure to merit the pedestal on which he was forced to stand as a sign of the nation, and when he fell, a victim of the strain of our focused national desire, the frustrated rage of a nation anxious about its impotence was vented upon him.

A federal government might give more resources and sponsorship to artists – commissioning works that seek to represent the new community, inviting forums of artists and public forums from across the spectrum to conceive of representations of our collective enjoyment. There were traces of this in the Spicer Commission.[37] Keith Spicer appeared to know intuitively what was needed – a poetry of the nation. He should have been given free rein to find it or to let people write it. Instead, any poetry was apparently ruthlessly snuffed out by the cold electric eye and the mechanical hand of the bureaucracy. People urgently need such a poetics, a symbolic representation of enjoyment. We grope frantically to represent our enjoyment, sometimes with ludicrous results: the world's biggest goose (Wawa), the world's biggest moose (Moose Jaw), the world's biggest nickel (Sudbury), the world's biggest perogie!! currently under construction outside some prairie town. Edmontonians have a cathedral of consumptive enjoyment, the world's biggest shopping mall, and Torontonians proclaim their enjoyment to the world with the twin absurdities, the world's tallest free-standing erection and the world's largest moving structure.[38]

While some of these sublime objects unequivocally proclaim a nightmarish state of corporate technocratic excess and an aesthetic wasteland, it is inappropriate to scorn them, as they also represent an investment of desire in a search for pride and identity. Giant perogies and soaring concrete penises from the top of which you can see New York are fantasy vehicles that structure desire for many ordinary Canadians. The question that Federal Canadian leaders might ask is whether and how they should intervene in the realm of fantasy. It has been done before with some success – the

Maple Leaf flag replaced the red ensign, 'O Canada' replaced 'God Save the Queen' as the national anthem. Both are artificially fabricated nodal points of the symbolic order representing the new enjoyment. Granted, they are not entirely successful as the sublime objects of inclusive national fantasies, but they succeed to a surprising degree. Is it possible to cultivate more? The train, a modern fantasy vehicle par excellence, and one that literally and metaphorically ran like a central thread through the entire fabric of Canadian society, might have been used as it is in Europe to draw together London, Paris, Brussels, and Frankfurt in the patchwork of the European Community. Instead it was cut up.

Perhaps bureaucratic unwieldiness and want of leadership make it likely that a project of a new political economy of culture emanating from the top down would be counterproductive. Is there an alternative strategy to reconstitute national enjoyment? It strikes me that the alternative is already being pursued. Canadians are already working out the problem of national identity, in the streets, in the workplaces, in bars, and in bedrooms across the country, where racially and ethnically mixed neighbours and lovers struggle for mutual respect, constituting the terms of a new enjoyment on an everyday basis. The stakes for a new political economy of culture are already being fought for in the wars of position for inclusion in the new Canada. Perhaps a hegemonic task is one of articulating the elements to form an imaginary where difference would be radically antagonistic. A hegemonic project of the new Left might be one of *not* forming a new community, but actively de-forming hegemonic projects of imaginary construction; resisting efforts to foist upon the social versions of 'community' invariably based on excluding some Other(s) existing as elements within that very community. The hegemonic task may be one of continuing the practice of preventing the suturing of the social, and subverting the efforts at totalization; preserving the dynamism of radical indeterminability.

3

Symptoms of Canada:
The Enjoyment of Endurance

'Society doesn't exist,' Slavoj Žižek says, 'and the Jew is its symptom' (1989, 125).[39] In other words, 'society' is a precarious constellation of discursive formations, suspended in an infinite space/time continuum, carved out of a field of differences, and all of our most determined efforts to suture or to totalize the social, from rigorous modern science to pervasive commodification and bureaucratic administration, are doomed to failure. Ernesto Laclau concurs: any structural system is always surrounded by an 'excess of meaning' which it is unable to master; consequently 'society' as a unitary and intelligible object that grounds its own partial processes is an impossibility (1990, 90; see also 1985, 27–42). For this reason, say Laclau and Mouffe, we need to study not what society is, but what it never is able to become.[40] The Jew, as the historical scapegoat for these failed projects of suturing and totalization, all the futile efforts to domesticate the field of differences, is the symptom of this non-existence and impossibility of society.

Similarly, one might say that Canada doesn't exist, and that the Sikh Mountie is one of its symptoms. In 1989, when a Sikh recruit to the Royal Canadian Mounted Police sought to wear his turban rather than the usual uniform hat, a public controversy erupted. T-shirts and lapel pins were sold depicting a line-up of multi-ethnic Mounties variously attired, with a single white 'traditional' Mountie in their midst. The caption read, 'Who's a minority now?' A less hysterical, less overtly racist discourse centred on the importance of the Mounties' uniform as a symbol of a national tradition. It was argued that the need for unity ought to transcend the need to recognize ethnic particularity. Others contended that Canada's traditions were in fact practices of pluralism and tolerance. Historians pointed out that the uniform had changed several times over the years, and that the broad felt hat is an arbitrary symbol of Canadianness. The arbitrariness of the signifier then reveals the arbitrariness of the signified: not only does the tradition, the unity, of the Mounties not exist, but neither does the thing which the Mounties stand for, Canada.[41]

The nation/thing is a void around which enjoyment is structured and organized. I have outlined three faces of the hegemonic projects responding to the non-existence of Canada: (a) The reactionary nationalism of the Reform party and Québécois separatists, who are attempting to force the nation into positive existence through a hard, conservative suturing of the social; (b) The Liberal, centrist project, which broadly collects the three main political parties in an effort to practise a looser suturing, a suturing around an 'implant' (a revised Constitution, a Social Charter), but which faces the political, hegemonic task of investing it with sublime qualities so that it fills out the gaps in the symbolic order; (c) A radical subversion of attempts at suturing the social, a project that maybe doesn't even need to be developed hegemonically, as it is in the nature of the social (lifeworld) to overflow whatever nets of signification are being cast to suture the social.

The antagonistic phenomena of the theft of enjoyment in the discourse of Canadian nationalism are symptoms of the lack of Canada. That is, the phenomenal 'reality' of the antagonistic discourse of Canadian nationalism is symptomatic of a foundational impossibility of suturing the social, of positively constituting Canada. But having just argued that Canada does not exist, I now want to argue that it does exist – in a sense. Canada exists in so far as the symptoms of its lack have a particularity. That is to say, Canada doesn't exist, but the symptoms of its lack do. It is the particularity of the symptoms of its lack that constitutes what is Canadian. To rephrase this in terms of a question one might ask: What is it that is Canadian about the non-existence of Canada? To be sure, we cannot give a full answer to this question, we cannot hope either to net the symbolic order of Canada or to distil an essential core, but clearly we still want to talk about 'Canada' as opposed to any other – equally imagined – national community.

If Canada doesn't exist, and a Canadian subject doesn't exist, then what does exist? A Lacanian answer would be that symptoms of Canada are all that exist. According to Lacan, we must conceive of symptom as *sinthome* – that is, a signifying formation penetrated with enjoyment, a bearer of 'jouissence,' enjoyment-in-sense. Žižek says of the Lacanian symptom:

What we must bear in mind here is the radical ontological status of symptom: symptom conceived as sinthome is literally our only substance, the only positive support of our being, the only point that gives consistency to the subject. In other words, symptom is the way we, the subjects, 'avoid madness', the way we choose something (the symptom-formation) instead of nothing (radical psychotic autism, the destruction of the symbolic universe) through the binding of our enjoyment to a certain signifying, symbolic formation which assures us a certain minimum consistency to our being-in-the-world. If the symptom in this radical dimension is unbound, it means literally 'the end of the world' – the only alternative to the symptom is nothing: pure autism, a psychic suicide, surrender to the death drive even to the total destruction of the symbolic universe. That is why the final Lacanian definition of the end of the psychoanalytic process is 'identification with the symptom.' The analysis achieves its end when the patient is able to recognize, in the Real of his symptom, the only support of his being.   Žižek 1989, 75

The symptom masks the void, and simultaneously, by its inevitable failure, it declares, or betrays, the void. Nationalism introduces the fantasy of the nation to fill out the void, but the elusiveness of the nation, and the antagonism arising from the exclusionary practices that attempt to constitute it, betray its fantastic character. The subject must 'go through the fantasy' and face the real; that is, confront the radical nothingness behind the symptom formation, come to terms with the fact that the nation doesn't and cannot exist. Finally, Lacan says, the subject must come to love the symptom because the symptom is all-that-there-is. By loving the symptom Lacan means taking responsibility for the precariousness and contingency of the symptom and guarding against projects that seek to do violence to the social by attempting to force a closure, attempting to achieve a totalized suturing.

Social solidarity, Canadian nationalism in this instance, derives from common identification with particular symptom formations that mask the lack underpinning the social. Thus identification is with the symptoms by/through which enjoyment is organized. Collective identifications are permeated with 'jouis-sense,' sensory enjoyment, and so we must think of our collective identity as achieved and sustained by hegemonic practices that quilt, or bind, our subjective enjoyment with symptom formations. These symptom formations are hegemonic discursive constructions of 'our,' 'shared,' enjoyment of such ephemeral sensory phenomena as 'the taste of our food,' 'the freshness of our air,' 'the rhythm of our music,' 'the joy of our laughter,' 'the sound of our voices,' 'the look of each other,' 'the play and sense of our conversations,' 'the silence of our forest parks,' 'the nuances of our wit,' 'the flavour of our beer,' 'the sharpness of our prairie light,' 'the call of the loon,' 'the chill of our winters,' 'our awesome wilderness,' 'our mannerisms and idiom,' 'our laid-back attitude,' 'our politeness,' 'the warmth of our hospitality,' and so on. Articulatory and hegemonic practices that link the subject to discursively organized complexes of phenomenal sensuousness are essential to identification in general. We must, quite literally, 'feel' that we belong.

Hegemonic projects that seek to organize our sensory enjoyment find clearest expression in such things as coffee-table 'photo journey' books like *A Day in the Life of Canada*, *The Real Canada*, and so on. These try to organize a sense (literally) of the country. They both succeed and fail. They succeed in capturing for us a 'sense' of the country, in so far as there is something in the photographs more than themselves – the *object petit a*, the little piece of the real – the vital enjoyment that the photograph gives us a glimpse of. Yet by the same measure, somehow, they necessarily always fail. There is always something that the photographic projects miss, fail to capture, and that too is the little piece of the real that overflows the organization of the symbolic.

To get a take on the particularity of Canada then, one needs to get at Canadian symptoms as sinthome. One needs to look at and think about the discursive construction of Canadian food, Canadian sex, Canadian play, Canadian recreation. Canada exists only as symptoms that organize collective enjoyment, and enjoyment exists only in its excess, in the re-creation of surplus enjoyment. The sites where Canada is reproduced then are recrooms, kitchens, and bedrooms, pubs, clubs, restaurants, and speakeasies, hockey rinks, baseball diamonds, streets, and schoolyards, and so on, the sites of the everyday lives of the diverse people who are Canada, who reproduce Canada in their enjoyment of Canada.

The problem with Canada is, we are told, that we do not have such national symptoms by which our collective enjoyment is/can be organized. There is a dearth of hegemonic projects that bind enjoyment for the collective. We cannot remember why or how we are Canadian; we cannot 'feel' Canadian. We have regional identifications, ethnic identifications, class identifications, generational identifications, and so on, but nothing that collects our enjoyment. Instead, as I have shown, we accuse one another of stealing the enjoyment, and believe that the politics of the ongoing national identity crisis hinge upon the generation of a symptom: the hegemonic deployment of some means of articulating our collective enjoyment. In what follows I will argue that there is a knot of articulations and associated values central to the symbolic order of Canada. The first of these is the equivalential articulation of enjoyment and endurance. This articulation of enjoyment and endurance has been the basis of the value of tolerance. Second, there is an equivalential articulation of endurance and lack of particularity, which is the basis of the value of unpretentiousness. In combination, at the heart of the symbolic order of Canada is an enjoyment of the endurance of the lack of particularity, associated with values of tolerance and unpretentiousness.

It is not at all difficult to locate equivalent articulations of enjoyment and endurance as a recurring feature in symptoms of Canada. Take, for example, the centrality in the historical imaginary of heroic epics of endurance: the Franklin voyage,[42] the Yukon gold rush, settling the prairies, and so on. Interestingly, the articulation of enjoyment/endurance is frequently made in terms of a failure. This has a continuity from Franklin's quest for the North-West Passage to Terry Fox's 'marathon of hope.' Throughout Canadian popular culture there are discourses that celebrate an enjoyment of endurance and a valuation of tolerance. Take, for example, our shared enjoyment of enduring Canadian winter. What do we mean by the casual greeting 'Cold enough for you, eh?' It asks, Are you enjoying the cold? Can you endure the cold? How much cold can you tolerate? The friendliness of the remark depends on the interlocutors sharing the value of tolerance, of presuming the equivalence enjoyment/endurance. What about endurance recreation – skating, cross-country skiing, canoeing, camping, trekking? The heroic endurance/enjoyment of the voyageurs is recreated in the contemporary practice of endurance driving: the person who delights in telling you how they left Brandon at four a.m., had a coffee in Thunder Bay, drove down to Toronto, on to Montreal, had to be back in Sudbury the following night, 'got an hour's sleep, eh,' before leaving for Calgary.

The articulation of enjoyment and endurance is evident in the practice of Canadian domestic architecture and design. The Canadian rec-room is a marvellous site of the enjoyment of endurance. The rec-room is where the endurance of winter is made enjoyable. Rec-rooms have one or two very large refrigerators chock-full of goodies – lots of beef and steak, some frozen pies. There is a well-stocked bar, a couple of bottles of distinctive ethnic origin for a taste of 'the old country,' a bottle of Mescala with a worm in it that somebody brought back from Cancun. Usually there is a collection of some arbitrary thing or other – baseball caps, crests of golf clubs, miniature ethnic figurines, dinky little glasses – adorning the bar. There is a TV, a VCR, and a stereo in the corner; a recliner and a large couch. Should you wish to build a rec-room, George Dalgleish of Winnipeg gives you many helpful hints in his booklet 'Building a Rec Room':

Your rec room should be constructed so that the family can really 'live' in it. Design it so it can serve a number of purposes. For example, father can entertain business acquaintances, teenagers can do 'their thing,' mother can entertain her bridge club, or the whole family can get together and spend an evening watching T.V. or play games. And parents, would you not rather have your children enjoying themselves at home rather than at the local 'joint'? ... In planning a recroom, decide first on how the *whole* family can get the most out of it. For example, what hobbies do the family have? Maybe father's hobby is photography and he would like a darkroom ... Maybe teenagers like to dance or play pool or ping-pong, so a large enough area could be planned for this. Mother wants a clean and well lighted laundry area where she can do her ironing and sewing in comfort ...[43]

According to Dalgleish, the rec-room really comes into its own during those long cold winter months; he gives us some good sensible advice on installing a fireplace, and stresses the importance of insulation. How is the rec-room valuable? It provides a space in which enjoyment is organized, where we can tolerate the contingency of the social – father's tiresome friends, the trauma and excess of teenage life, mother's domestic drudgery. The rec-room is a tolerant space, where we can enjoy enduring winter, where we party, entertain, and amuse ourselves. It is where the symbolic order of the fictional 'Canadian family' is recreated: a sort of enjoyable/ endurable suburban paunchy patriarchy.

Endurance is wonderfully evident in the enjoyment of Canadian food. The Beaver Club, established in Montreal in 1785, was an exclusive drinking establishment for the trapping and fur-trading aristocracy (Newman 1989). To be admitted as a member one had to have spent at least one full season in the high country. Each member wore a medal with the motto 'Fortitude in Distress.' This is an interesting motto. What does it say about the values that the Beaver Club endorses? A member of the Beaver Club values tolerance, tolerance of the distressing contingencies of life in the wilderness. A Beaver Club member enjoys enduring distress. Fortnightly club meetings consisted of feasts of venison steaks, roasted beaver tails, and pickled buffalo tongues, washed down with gallons of good liquor. Meetings tended to be boister-ous, as members enjoyed recreating feats of endurance on their expeditions. A member might, for example, 'shoot the rapids' by riding a wine keg along the table and onto the floor. The Beaver Club is still active, but it's not the only place in which one can enjoy/endure Canadian food. French Canadian pea soup, cream of fiddlehead soup, smoked fish, Montreal smoked meat, boiled dinner (cabbage, salted cod, and potato), bannock, wild rice, poutine (gravy and cheese curd on French fries), roast moose, marinated beaver tails, boiled bears' feet, followed by shoofly pie, maple syrup, and Nanaimo bars: I do not have the complete menu, but these were some of the delicacies that, as reported in the *Globe and Mail*, guests enjoyed/endured at the gala opening of the new Canadian Embassy in Tokyo in 1991. At a formal embassy banquet, Canada is identified and represented to both Canadians and Japanese through the enjoyment of the endurance food of the voyageurs, loggers, and fur traders.

Canadian cookbooks are full of examples of the equivalential articulation of enjoyment and endurance as quintessenntially Canadian.[44] What is also interesting is the way in which the articulation of enjoyment and endurance collects and unifies difference. Canadian cookbooks have sections on 're-gional food,' 'ethnic food,' 'Quebec food,' and so on, all of them finding unity under such categories as 'frontier food,' 'practical food,' 'cabin food.' In a recent collection, Cooking Collections: Canadian Feasts from Land and Sea, menus representing the various provinces include, from Newfound-land, figgy duff and curried squid chow mein; from Nova Scotia, Solomon Grundy and Bavarian strawberries; from New Brunswick, cream of fiddle-head soup and curried shrimp; from Quebec, Quebec baked beans, maple glazed carrots, and Chinese asparagus; from Ontario, corn bread and ka-bobs; from Manitoba, wild rice and chicken cacciatore; from Alberta, Murray's pepper steak, Sharon's beef stew, and stir-fried ginger beef; from British Columbia, deer or elk soup, roast caribou, Grandma Schultz's moose-meat sausages, and tandoori chicken. But where is the 'Canadian' in Cana-dian food? What collects this diversity? 'Backwoods beef stew,' 'Survival spaghetti sauce,' and a chocolate bar that protects you from hypothermia called 'the Canadian cold-buster.' The 'good' of Canadian food, what makes Canadian food 'good food,' the value of Canadian food, is its heartiness, its enabling Canadians to tolerate the demands and contingencies of the worka-day world.

In the discursive construction of 'Canadian food' there is an equivalential articulation of enjoyment and endurance. What is 'Canadian' in the enjoy-ment of food is the 'survival' in spaghetti sauce. But isn't there something absurd in this articulation of enjoyment and endurance in Canadian food? Pickled buffalo tongues with wild rice and bannock; is that Canadian? Surely not, because, frankly, Canadians don't eat that kind of stuff. Dishing it up at a state banquet in Tokyo is patently absurd. It perfectly exemplifies a symptom of Canada: a hegemonic attempt to produce something Canadian, which, by its failure, shows the impossibility, the non-existence, of Canada. The categorization of Canadian cuisine is impossible; what is Canadian defies being located in food, the food defies being located in Canada. Cana-dian food is roast beef, chow mein, perogies and lasagna, Big Macs and Kraft Dinner. Canadian food is derivative, modern, international, and convenient. Roti and cabbage rolls, and for that matter boiled bears' feet, are all symptoms of Canada: that is, symptoms of the non-existence and impossibility of Canada. The same is true of the previous examples. We have already seen that 'Canadian' recreational activities are not really that unique; anyone might enjoy them, or for that matter steal the enjoyment of them, simply by enjoying something different. *Canadian Living* has similar difficulty in locating and specifying 'the Canadian home.'[45] The magazine depicts 'the Quebec farmhouse,' 'the Victorian manor,' 'the Acadian country kitchen,' 'the True North style,' but what is it that is 'Canadian' about Canadian Living always eludes us. The 'modern townhouse,' or the 'natural look,' bears the stamp of massification. Similarly the basement rec-room is a suburban phenomenon that can be found anywhere in the North American mid-west. George Dalgleish tells Winnipeg homeowners how to 'transform your basement into a Hawaiian outdoor café, an English pub, a Mediterranean villa, or any other theme you choose,' but he cannot tell us what a 'Canadian' rec-room would be like. The particularity then is not given by the material – that is to say, by the 'Canadian content' of the examples. It is only the equivalential articulation of enjoyment and endurance that puts a Canadian form on the content.

The second equivalential articulation in the symbolic order of Canada which I wish to identify is that of enjoyment and lack of particularity. This is most evident in Canadian humour. Take for example a recent advertising campaign by Molson's called 'Great Events in Canadian History': 'Great event in Canadian history' #1: 'After a night of lousy hands Grant Skinner is dealt 3 aces, draws 2 queens, and cleans up.' 'Great event' #2: 'Against all the odds so-and-so's parents allow him to have the cottage for the Labour Day weekend.' #3: 'So-and-so and so-and-so throw a party and become legends overnight.' These ads cleverly play on a Canadian enjoyment of the lack of particularity. They openly acknowledge their symptomatic character: that there is nothing behind them, that there are no 'Great Events of History'; that there is nothing other than that which lends coherence and organization to enjoyment. History is nothing more than the resubjectification of enjoyment, and so Canadians must love their symptom as themselves. The ad works to sell beer for Molson's in so far as Molson's successfully articulates itself and its product as a symptom that intervenes between the consumer and the lack, which Canadians can identify with and love, thereby facilitating the reproduction of consumptive enjoyment.

Bob and Doug McKenzie on SCTV provide another example of this particularity of the enjoyment of the endurance of the lack of particularity. The bare, more or less empty set declares the recognition of the lack of particularity. The 'Great White North' constitutes the real, the nothingness that lack of particularity exposes them to. The toques, jackets, mitts, and boots are the symptom/sinthome which permit their endurance, which allow them to pursue their enjoyment, the consumption of beers and smokes, eh! and the pursuit of excess enjoyment, more beers and smokes. Samuel Beckett could have written Bob and Doug: absurd, minimalist, existentialist. How can it work as comedy? Only if it assumes an ironic relationship to the lack underpinning 'Canadian society.' Only if it assumes that we can enjoy the lack, that we can value the particularity of the lack of particularity.

Recall again the Molson's commercials: 'In Canada, on Saturday nights [on the weekend, in winter ...] young people indulge in a unique ritual, etc.' We know that it's not 'unique,' that the practice is arbitrary. We are ironic about our 'uniqueness.' What these mundane examples reveal is a crucial aspect of the symbolic order of Canada. What is being endured and enjoyed in the recurring themes of endurance in symptoms of Canada is the particularity of the lack of particularity. At the heart of the symbolic order of Canada is an ironic relationship to the lack. Canadians can be goofy about the lack. We know that we lack particularity, and that acknowledgment of the lack is our particularity. We can enjoy the endurance of our lack of particularity. The sustaining value of national identity is enduring the lack, and the moral commitment required of Canadians is to not pretend to particularity. The moral commitment that sustains Canadian solidarity is a commitment to not being pretentious – a commitment to not pretending to be something that we are not, a commitment to not pretending that we are 'positively,' 'essentially' Canadian. While others may pretentiously posture as 'all-American,' 'true Brit,' or whatever, a real Canadian would never pull such an absurdity. Durkheim says that every society has a version of an ideal type member. 'This ideal type which each society demands that its members realize is the keystone of the whole social system and gives it its unity' (1975, 57). The ideal type member of Canadian society is the tolerant unpretentious person, who calmly pursues his or her business without any fanfare, and is respectful of others who do likewise. Wayne Gretzky then is the perfect national hero, enjoying to perfection the activity demanding the most endurance, displaying a distinctive tolerance in a sport marked by tests of tolerance. Distinct, unmistakably world class, but not in the least bit pretentious about it. In *Cooking Collections: Canadian Feasts from Land and Sea* there is a 'celebrities' favourite menus' section. The 'Great One,' in true Canadian form, offers us an unpretentious, hearty, multicultural menu, which can tolerate the contingency of all sorts of people turning up for a Canadian dinner party - 'chili à la Wayne.' Wayne says:

This delicious recipe is perfect for impromptu gatherings. No measuring is required. It depends on how many people and what your tastes are. You need: ground beef. Can(s) of: tomato paste, brown beans, kidney beans, tomatoes. Carrots, broccoli and cauliflower. Tabasco sauce, Worcestershire sauce, salt and pepper. Then: brown the ground beef, add the other ingredients, and stir. Cover and simmer for one hour, and remember, the longer it cooks, the thicker and richer it gets.

Cooking Collections, 136

On a national unity caravan, the then prime minister, Brian Mulroney, tried to play on this value of Canadian unpretentiousness. Speaking to a meeting in Alberta, Mulroney said that what Canada was became pretty clear during the rescue in Alert. The rescue was conducted in a typically Canadian way – without fanfare, without much ado, quietly and with competence. There were French-speaking Canadians and English-speaking Canadians, neither asking the other where they were from or what language they spoke. Up there, in the Arctic in the wind and cold and the terror of encroaching death they were all Canadians.[46] Pretentious posturing is dispelled by close encounters of the real kind, Mulroney implies. And he may be correct. In the face of the real it becomes clear that a morality of compromise and cooperation based on mutual respect is all that there is.

At the heart of the symbolic order of Canada is a knot where endurance and enjoyment, and enjoyment of endurance of lack of particularity, are articulated. This knot of meanings supports values of tolerance and unpretentiousness. What the Mulroney example shows, however, is that precisely because these values depend upon contingent articulations, they are open to a wide range of articulatory and hegemonic projects – liberal projects of (as per Mulroney's effort), or neo-conservative projects that would say that we have endured enough, that our enjoyment is infringed upon by the law of diminishing returns (as per the Reform party). Unfortunately there is no guarantee that the ironic relationship to the lack, the unpretentious endurance on which the value of tolerance depends, is 'safe,' that the value of unpretentiousness will be hegemonically articulated in terms of a liberal tolerance and a respect for difference. There are many different versions of unpretentiousness, some of which mask deeper insecurities.

The articulation of enjoyment of the endurance of the lack of particularity, and the values of tolerance and unpretentiousness, all come together in the quintessentially Canadian fashion statement, 'Tilley Endurables.'[47] And here also we will find the pretence of unpretentiousness and tolerance masking Canadians' deep-rooted anxiety about the theft of enjoyment. Tilley Endurables produce a range of clothing that aims to be 'the best travel and adventure clothing in the world.' Rugged but stylish, eminently practical, Tilley hats, jackets, shirts, and pants can tolerate all the contingencies of an adventurous encounter with difference. The washing instructions say 'give 'em hell,' Tilley Endurables can tolerate it. Tilley Endurables are clothes for a Canadain enjoyment. Tilley Endurables advertise the fact that their products are 'logo free': no pretentious posing of designer labels here! One Tilley store employee told me proudly, 'We're so middle of the road that nobody notices us.' But, oddly, and of course this is exactly the pretension of unpretentiousness, everybody does notice. During the Gulf War, Tilley hats were regular issue for Canadian forces. A member of the Royal Canadian Navy tells us that 'It's definitely a Canadian hat. You can't get it anywhere else.' Being recognized as having a 'definitely Canadian hat' was important in Saudi Arabia, lest the Arabs confuse our boys with the Americans, I suppose. And of course, in a Tilley hat one was appropriately dressed for that adventurous encounter with the Other. War is, after all, the ultimate adventure travel experience.

Tilley Endurables have another distinguishing feature worthy of note. Tilley Endurables are famous for having 'security pockets' and 'secret pockets.' One of their top-of-the-line products is a jacket with sixteen pockets, only nine of which are visible. Some pockets are so secret, in fact, that customers are not informed of their whereabouts until after they have purchased the jacket. Why should one need such a jacket? If one is to enjoy/endure/tolerate the adventurous encounter with the Other, while maintaining one's distinctively Canadian unpretentiousness, one needs a Tilley jacket because the Other might be light-fingered. We can enjoy/endure the encounter with the Other, but we must be careful lest they pick some of our pockets and steal our enjoyment. And where might an unpretentious Canadian encounter the light-fingered Other? Where else but the field of difference that is Yonge Street in the adventure travel of everyday life. Tilley Endurables express the subtleties of a characteristically Canadian ambivalence towards the Other: enjoying, enduring, tolerating the encounter with the Other, but remaining sceptical and reserved, fascinated and careful of the thieves of enjoyment.

Many Canadians are anxious about their identity because they are too close to the real, and this anxiety is currently being picked up on by various xenophobic projects. The task of democratic political leadership may be to take them through the fantasy, and face up to the lack, and then to come to identify with their symptom as themselves – to identify with the lack in the Big Other and to make a commitment to unpretentiousness, a commitment that would demand that the openness be kept open, protected from xenophobic nationalist hegemonic and articulatory practices that would seek to close it.

4

Ironic Conceit: The Living Room
of Canadian Enjoyment

Where is Canadian enjoyment to be found? What space in the social does it occupy? Where does enjoyment find the room in which to live and thrive? I am concerned here with locating Canadian enjoyment more precisely, in order to return and develop some of the themes introduced above. To explore the alleged theft of enjoyment more productively we must locate the site of the robbery. To understand the economy of desire for identification with symptoms of Canada, we need to find the space where the enjoyment of identification is possible. This chapter will try to show the space of enjoyment, a space 'cleared out' of the social by practices of ironic conceit.

We have seen that Canada doesn't exist, that there is an empty space at the heart of the nation, and this lack is the source of irreconcilable social antagonism. Nietzsche formulated this foundational lack underpinning modernity in terms of the death of God, resulting in a condition in which everything is permitted and shaped only by the will to power (see e.g., Nietzsche 1967a and 1967b). Contrary to Nietzsche's position, a Lacanian view holds that the terror of modernity is that everything is prohibited, because the father returns to rule as Name-of-the-Father; the symbolic order as Big Other (see Žižek 1991, 253–73). We recognize in the death of God and in the beheading of the king that all-that-there-is is the product of the collective, contained within a symbolic order. The symbolic order is a pervasive order that contains everything, an order outside of which there is nothing, except what Beckett calls 'the unnameable' (1991, 265), the real, thing, that resists symbolization. From this perspective, social life, one might venture, is shaped not so much by the will to power as by the will to enjoy: the will to live enjoyably with the collective in the face of the void.

This pervasive order to which there is no outside becomes tyrannical in that there is no point to which to appeal for intercession. As Derrida puts it, there is nothing beyond the text, no God to be prayed to, no king to be persuaded, no Archimedean point of objectivity from which to get some perspective on things, and no hereafter to escape to or to be elevated to. Claude Lefort[48] argues that when power has been set free from God and from the arbitrariness of personal rule of the monarch, and belongs to no one except to the people in the abstract, it threatens to become unlimited and omnipotent, and take charge of every aspect of social life. The symbolic order thus becomes the Big Other, the abstract collective that is omnipresent, omniscient, and omnipotent. The rule of Name-of-the-Father in the symbolic order is absolute. But the Name-of-the-Father is ultimately impotent, His rule is precarious. There is nothing beyond the symbolic-order-as-Big-Other, except for the nothingness of the real, a traumatic original lack that radically undermines the Name-of-the-Father: His rule is ultimately groundless, without foundation. The symbolic order then can be read as a symptom complex: symptomatic of the void beyond it. The symbolic order – as Big Other – has a thoroughly ambiguous character: it protects us from the void, and, by declaring its existence as nothingness beyond it, it exposes us to the void.

The Big Other, to borrow usage from its appearance in the discourse of the Metro Toronto police, 'serves and protects.' It serves as the medium in which we live, as all-encompassing and necessary as water is to fish swimming in it, and it protects us from the nothingness outside of it. But just as the police have a tyrannical face as 'police force,' the Big Other, in its absolutely necessary unrelenting pervasiveness, prohibits exploration beyond it; the penalty for doing so is psychotic autism, resulting from the destruction of the symbolic universe, or death (see Žižek 1989, 75). The contemporary social condition is one in which we are faced with living always in the light of the paradoxical presence of the Big Other who serves and protects. We must live in the light of the benign/facilitative, harsh/prohibitive gaze of the abstract collective. The question is, how is enjoyment possible under the gaze of the Big Other? Here I want to explore this accomplishment of enjoyment, an accomplishment which Hebdige (1988) calls 'hiding in the light.'

According to Žižek, ideology does not offer us a point of escape from our reality, but offers us social reality itself as an escape from the traumatic kernel of the real.[49] Ideology is a fantasy construction by which reality appears to be coherent, its elements drawn together, thereby masking the traumatic, constitutive social division that Laclau and Mouffe conceptualize as 'antagonism' (1985, 122–4). The practice of hegemony involves the articulation of ideological fantasy which supports reality, makes reality tolerable: or more, which makes our reality enjoyable. The subject can enjoy the symptom formations that constitute his or her reality only in so far as the logic of the ideological fantasy by which they seem coherent escapes them. We produce and reproduce the symptom formations in our everyday lives; the logic of the ideological fantasy structuring it is not beyond us or outside of us somewhere, so we must examine how we allow the logic of the symptom to escape us even in our reproduction of it. What is the logical structure of the ideological fantasy by virtue of which we can enjoy the symptom?

Enjoyment is possible only if it is protected from exposure to the real by a network of discursive constellations that fix or quilt the symbolic order in such a way that it appears successfully sutured or mastered. That is, enjoyment needs the security provided by an ideological quilt. But at the same time enjoyment is only possible if the symbolic order is not totalized – that is, closed – because enjoyment needs a 'beyond' where desire feeds on what fantasy can introduce there: enjoyment is possible only while there is a promise of adventure in the real. Enjoyment lives in a paradoxical space where the social is sutured: where it is drawn together across the void, and, at the same time, where it is always becoming undone. The symptom formations that constitute the social fabric are woven by an ambivalent economy of desire – for surety and simultaneously for unfixity. The enjoyment of the collective lives in a clearing demarcated by these symptom formations. The space where the enjoyment of the collective lives is cleared out by practices of ironic conceit: that the real is mastered (that the real is not mastered).

When I say that enjoyment depends upon conceit I mean that enjoyment needs to be protected from the real, and that this protection is given to it by a conceited orientation to the symptom. The symptom is overestimated. The symptom is regarded as more than symptom. It is fancifully held to have integrity, to be totalized, to be successfully sutured. This conceit of suture means that the lack is hidden, and enjoyment is possible. The conceit then is a generalized highly favourable notion of oneself, of one's situation, facilitated by a lack of evaluation of the real – symptomatic – character of the symptom.

In its disrespect for the symptom, conceit can be offensive. We enjoy by conceit, our enjoyment depends upon it, but the conceit would be offensive and enjoyment would be spoiled if we were simply conceited. Conceit alone would make our enjoyment stupid. We would be simply fooling ourselves: fooling ourselves that the symbolic order was closed, we would be stupidly subject to the Big Other. But if the conceit is playful, if we are ironic about it – that is to say, if our conceit is a ruse, a game we play with the symbolic order, an ironic game – then it's a different story.[50] The sectarian or racial bigot exemplifies conceit without irony. Mike Myers's character Wayne Campbell of Saturday Night Live's 'Wayne's World' exemplifies the game of ironic conceit: 'Canada is a great Nation ... Not.' 'Wayne's World' is one of the many Canadian dimensions of Saturday Night Live. The characters Wayne and Garth, the suburban rec-room setting, the idiom are all derived from Myers's adolescence in Scarborough. A cartoon on the editorial page of the Globe and Mail, 4 March 1992, depicts Joe Clark and Brian Mulroney as Wayne and his sidekick Garth. Wayne (a.k.a. Joe Clark) says: 'Like ... eh ... there's constitutional problems ... but we're wildly optimistic about the Canadian spirit of compromise and goodwill.' 'Not!' says Garth (a.k.a. Brian Mulroney).

According to Alan Blum and Peter McHugh, in the *Phenomenology* Hegel outlines the irony of the human condition: 'that the Ultimate Truth is denied by its dependency upon discourse and by the need to be grasped and expressed, and that the absolute character of discourse is denied by its being *in medias res* (in the middle of things)' (Blum and McHugh 1984, 144). Thus the social is underpinned by a radical contingency and indeterminacy that requires that we adopt an ironic attitude to 'reality.' The cultivation of an ironic sensibility in the lifeworld is one of the hallmarks of modernity (Meucke 1970). Irony arises from a sophisticated, resigned awareness of the contrast between what is and what ought to be. It is the resource that allows us to live enjoyably with the discrepancy between the appearances of a situation (the conceit that we are sovereign subjects, living in a symbolic order that is coherent and ultimately meaningful) and the actual circumstances (that we and the symbolic order lack, and that existence is surrounded by the void).

Writing of Canadian ironies, Hutcheon says that irony can be seen as 'a general cognitive principle ... of metaphor and metaphoric structure, ... a mode of indirection and deferral of meaning' (1990, 12). Thus irony, as it appears here in the Globe and Mail cartoon (I will treat Socratic irony in a moment), takes the form of a statement whose surface meaning is qualified by the implication of a contrary meaning or attitude. Irony is the mode of speech by which the intended meaning is the opposite of its literal sense. Irony is a form of indirection, or misdirection, producing an incongruity between what is expected and what occurs. Irony: the *implication* of a contrary meaning or attitude. Note the use of 'Not' in the signature irony of 'Wayne's World.' For example: 'Canada is [x] ... Not!' There is an ironic implication in the first clause already; before Wayne or Garth says 'Not' we suspect they are being ironic. The initial assertion is always a little too strong ('wildly optimistic'), the tone of delivery too serious (Wayne's poker face foiled by Garth's hint of a grin). So when Wayne or Garth says 'Not,' there is a double irony: the 'Not' is also ironic. The first (ironic) affirmative clause mocks the lack (the failure of the statement to sustain itself, to achieve closure). And the second (ironic) negation of the assertion in the first clause has, counter-intuitively, a suturing effect; it undoes some of the damage to surety wrought by the ironic implication of the first clause.

In this way Wayne and Garth, and, as my argument below will hold, many ordinary Canadians in their everyday lives, are Socratic ironists, and something more besides. Socrates' ironic practice was the feint: he feigned ignorance in order to expose the weakness of his opponent's argument. Wayne and Garth and ordinary Canadians engage in a similar kind of trickery, a stratagem to show the other's weakness. In this case the other is the Big Other, and the weakness which our irony shows is its lack, the point where suture fails, where things fall apart. But enjoyment also requires that the ironist not be made to drink hemlock by the collective. The lack must only be shown with subtlety. We cannot do an 'out-ing' of the Name-of-the-Father and make a spectacle of His lack. We must only catch a glimpse of it, awry, obliquely; it can be shown only as a hint, a promise. And this is why our ironic practice must take the form of conceit. It is not enough that we expose the lack; our exposition of it must simultaneously hide it.

Hutcheon says that contemporary (Canadian) irony is characterized by destabilization; 'its function is to undo certainties, even its own,' and thus to constantly perpetuate 'aporia.'[51] Ironic conceit makes for a slippery playfulness. It always escapes, slips away from dogmatism. It always keeps a way open for itself, it keeps an option on not meaning what you have taken it to mean. 'The social is sutured ... Not.' 'My identity is essentially [blah blah] ... Not.' 'Canada welcomes immigrants ... Not.' 'The Canadian character is imbued with a spirit of compromise and goodwill ... Not.' It is, and it's not, simultaneously. By its evasiveness and ambiguity, ironic conceit keeps a space open for enjoyment, and for hegemonizing.

Games are played in this space of enjoyment, one of which is the game of politics, played by persuasive discourse in the form of hegemonic articulatory practices. Judith Butler's discussion of Gayatri Spivak's politics of 'strategic essentialism' is an obvious example, especially in Butler's current formulation of the space of politics as the space of misrecognition.[52] But politics is not the only form of play that goes on in the space of enjoyment cleared out by ironic conceit. Some of the practices of enjoyment are ritualistic, reproductive, sedimented, not contentious or antagonistic for the most part, although they may become so again. And some play is oriented to the value of playfulness itself, towards keeping the conversion going, idling, if you like. Not idle, but ticking over, running on. This is what Simmel (1971, 127–31) calls sociability; inter-action for the sake of interaction, that is constitutive of the life of the collective, society, as such.

When conceit is not ironic it becomes a stupid bigotry. Likewise, irony is endangered by the possibility of its degenerating to sarcasm. We want to be ironic about Canada, but not sarcastic. Irony loves the symptom, plays with it, cares for it. Sarcasm mocks the symptom, scorns it, hates the symptom for not being 'real.' Sarcasm hates the symptom for what it is symptomatic of, the lack. Sarcasm hates the symptom for what it's not; it hates that the symptom does not live up to the expectation that it be 'real.' Irony loves the symptom for what it is: itself, in its fragile phenomenality.

Enjoyment is ob-scene. It is sneaking. It lives surreptitiously. It needs the Big Other's protection from the real, but it must escape the Big Other's overbearing tyranny. Enjoyment lives by self-deception: that the Name-of-the-Father is a powerful totalizing force which has mastered the real, and that He, the Big Other, lacks, as we do, and is thus impotent, assuring our freedom. Because of this sneaking quality, enjoyment thrives even in the most seemingly inhospitable of places, even in Canada. It is a sort of commonplace, especially I think with regard to WASP-ish Toronto and 'hardship' frontier towns, to say that Canada is unfriendly to enjoyment, that Canadian culture is marked by a Protestant retentiveness and a frostbitten disdain of excess. Canadians have told me, laughingly, that, like 'military intelligence,' 'Canadian enjoyment' is an oxymoron. The joke illuminates a beautifully Canadian ironic conceit: an enjoyment of the unpretension of the pretence to lack of enjoyment.

In what follows I will explore some facets of Canadian enjoyment. They are enjoyments that live in space cleared out by practices of ironic conceit. In general the ironic conceit that makes the space for them is one of mastery and closure; a closure of the symbolic order and an ob-scene, transgressive enjoyment of the failure of closure and the impossibility of mastery. The ironic conceit of mastery and closure allows transgression a way to back out, as it were. Irony transgresses the conceit; that is, irony allows us to transgress ourselves, our own conceit. Ironic conceit allows us to let the cat out of the bag, so to speak, but for just a moment; we keep an option on the transgression. We are always able to backtrack and say, 'I wasn't really transgressing, see.'

Enjoyment of course may be found in an infinite number of places, wherever ironic conceit can clear out a space for it. I am concerned here, though, with a particular enjoyment; the particularity of Canadian enjoyment. So while my primary concern for this chapter is to show the contingency of enjoyment on irony and conceit (I will deal more explicitly with the particularity of Canadian enjoyment in later chapters on Canadian sex and humour), the examples I have chosen, have, I think, a peculiarly Canadian particularity to them. They are: (a) the enjoyment of being close to nature; an enjoyable playing with nature, where both parties are simultaneously dominated and endangered by one another. (b) The enjoyment of alienation; that is, of having some distance from the symbolic order and an irresponsibility towards/for it: exemplified by Canadians who invoke their ethnic heritage or similar signs of marginality, such as 'I'm from the West,' or 'I'm a Newfie,' to say: 'I'm not really a Canadian, so this doesn't refer to me.' (c) The enjoyment of membership, by virtue of estrangement; that is, Canadians who derive their identity from the presence of the stranger, or who invoke their hybrid ethnicity (by virtue of which a moment ago they enjoyed alienation) to say 'I guess you could say that I'm just a typical Canadian – not hyphenated, or alternatively, just as hyphenated as the next fellow.

I'm going to consider ironic conceit in the paradox of transgression by looking at these faces of enjoyment as they show themselves in various places: going to the cottage or whale watching seem likely practices through which one might explore the Canadian enjoyment of being close to nature, but for the moment I will explore the enjoyment of being close to nature in the less obvious practice of visiting a museum of civilization, which of itself is a peculiarly Canadian enjoyment if only because, for a country whose problem is said to be a surplus of geography and a lack of history, Canada has an excess of museums. I will look for the enjoyment of alienation in souvenirs of Canada, in the enjoyment of souveniring (of reminding ourselves of) Canada and the non-existence of Canada. And I will explore the enjoyment of membership in the practice of discrimination; the enjoyment of recollecting the collective by the mediation of the stranger, and of finding in the stranger the means to escape the tyranny of the collective.

The Museum of Enjoyment

It's early morning in spring at Long Point on Lake Erie. A Canadian family are standing on a dock made of rough planks, surrounded by a soft marsh of golden rushes and dark mud. A gentle breeze blows through the marsh, a breath of fresh pine and pungent swamp. The air is filled with a raucous chorus of birdsong; calling, answering, thrilling, interrupting one another. The family look around, pointing things out: 'Look, look, there's a fox, hiding in the bushes.' 'Hey, there's a beaver.' 'That's not a beaver, it's a groundhog.' An arm's length away a mallard drake preens his feathers. A startled widgeon scrambles into flight. A Canada goose, tired after her long migration, sleeps on a clump of yellow grass, a dry islet in a sea of wet mud.

Like the figures on Keats's Grecian urn, however, the smartly dressed mallard will never woo a mate, and the widgeon cannot escape our rude intrusion. Unfortunately spring is frozen at Long Point, and nightfall is six p.m. (eight p.m. on Tuesdays and Thursdays). We're not 'really' in the middle of a swamp on the shore of Lake Erie. Long Point is part of an exhibition entitled 'Ontario Wetlands' at the Royal Ontario Museum on Queen's Park Crescent in Toronto.[53] The Long Point installation features thirty-nine species of wildlife, stuffed and mounted in characteristic natural settings. The curators have made the installation very realistic – natural light, birdsong on stereo – and have even managed to waft a scented breeze through the marsh. While the whole thing is a clever simulation, it seems to have a life of its own. 'The marshes at Long Point teem with birds,' a notice tells the interested visitor. 'Many are migrating, using the marshes as a rest stop. Others are settling down to begin breeding.' Visitors say things like: 'It smells like the country, doesn't it?' 'It looks like real water, eh.' 'Look, look at the heron!' (excitedly, as though it were going to fly off!) 'They're not really real, are they, dad?' 'Sure they're real. Look at them swimming. That one's scratching.' And then the smart-aleck kid calls his mom to see the very special bird concealed in the brush – a fire sprinkler. The game is up and the family group moves on. 'Bye bye duckies,' says his baby sister.

It seems odd somehow that this encounter with the Canadian wilderness occurs in the 'museum of civilization' in downtown Toronto. After all, what can swamp life tell us about civilization? Perhaps Ben Wicks's cartoon character 'Bill' can explain it.[54] He's downstairs in the entrance hall, introducing the public to museology.

This cartoon character is a sombre, heavy-set, middle-aged man in a dark suit and trilby hat, cranky, middle-class, unmistakably anglo. In the ROM, Bill is employed to introduce and to guide visitors through an exhibit called 'Mankind Discovering.' This exhibition is a précis of museology, a story of how the ROM goes about its business, a story about how 'modern scientific method' is employed by the ROM curators – ethnologists, archaeologists, life scientists, art historians, paleontologists, and earth scientists – in their quest to 'discover mankind.' Bill is the 'subject of knowledge' in a large cartoon that explains to visitors the four stages of modern scientific method; hypothesis, fieldwork, analysis, and synthesis.

In the first frame Bill is seated in a study, behind a desk, in his customary dark suit, dour expression, and furrowed brow, cartoon thought-clouds rising over his head. The object of contemplation in his thought-cloud is a strange creature, a wild looking thing, possibly human(oid), its body pitch black, big white savage/frightened eyes. In frame 2, Bill is in a safari suit, pith helmet, a large net in his hand, binoculars hanging from his shoulder, water bottle and revolver on his belt. The dour, contemplative expression is gone, replaced by a look of eager determination. The strange black creature that caused him puzzlement in his study is cowering in a tree, awaiting capture. Frame 3, 'analysis,' depicts Bill and his captured specimen in a laboratory. Now Bill is wearing a white coat. He is surrounded by test-tubes and bunsen burners. Bill is staring intently down a microscope at the wild black thing with the big eyes, sitting passively on the microscope slide. The closing representation, 'synthesis,' depicts Bill at home, in the bathtub, in the manner of Archimedes. He's thinking again. This time his thought-clouds are filled with bits of a jig-saw puzzle, jumbled at first, then all fitting together around the centre-piece of the black thing. Bill has a great big satisfied smile, no longer troubled, the puzzle all fits together, even the black thing is no longer strange. It fits nicely into the integrated picture in Bill's thought-cloud.

What we have here is an account of the way in which 'modern man' deals with the existential dread evoked by the Other. The stage of 'hypothesis' is the anxious moment of encounter with the element of difference that does not fit the picture, that disrupts the elements of the prevalent hegemonic discursive order. Bill's thoughts are troubled by a black thing which does not 'fit the picture.' While the black thing is troublesome, worrisome, terrible, keeping him awake nights, it also provokes him to hypothesize, it constitutes the field of adventure, as we see in the 'fieldwork' frame. The black thing leads Bill on, it has captured his desire, it constitutes the space into which he can extend himself and develop. Tracking down and capturing the black thing is invigorating and satisfying. The element of difference is cornered, netted, shot perhaps, and brought back to the laboratory for analysis, systematically observed under the gaze of the microscope, everything about it carefully recorded. It becomes the object of power/knowledge. The end of analysis is a comforting synthesis. The anxiety caused by the encounter with the element of difference is overcome when it can be integrated into the prevalent discursive order. The bathtub enjoyment of this white, middle-class, anglo man depends upon his putting the Negroid in his place.

If we go back upstairs now to the 'Ontario Wetlands' exhibition we can see the satisfying synthesis achieved by the modern scientific method in the

Long Point installation. The Canadian wilderness constitutes a field of differences and chaos, many black things, troublesome unknown elements. In the modern Canadian imaginary, the wilderness as dangerous and alluring terrain holds the place of an even wilder space, the void; the space Nietzsche calls the abyss, and Lacan calls the real: the terrifying and alluring infinite unknown outside the order of civilization, the negativity outside Being that phenomenal reality stands in relation to and derives its positivity from. The Long Point installation expresses the desire for the achievement of order, the domestication of this field of differences, the suturing of its elements so that the void beyond it is hidden.

All the elements here are thoroughly known: mapped, measured, systematically observed. The secrets of nature, or, more precisely, the secret enjoyments of nature, are uncovered: how the frogs survive the cold weather, what the fox eats, the migratory routes of the various birds, the great distances they cover by gliding on currents of warm air, the exotic places they visit – Florida, North Africa. A lot of attention is given to their mating practices: their plumage, their songs and dances, their domestic life of nesting and chick rearing. All the elements of the field of differences are captured, studied, shot, gutted and stuffed, and then re-presented to us in a 'lifelike' exhibition. All the elements are put in their place, articulated moments of a discourse that contains the wilderness. The ROM has 'captured it perfectly.' The Canadian wilderness is produced and made known to us by the ROM.

The Long Point installation then is a barbaric place, a monument to the terrible practices of modern science, to a history of sustained violence, rape, and predation. Long Point celebrates the principles of modern scientific method that Sir Francis Bacon recommended: that 'Nature should be hounded in her wanderings, that She should be ravished by the scientist, have Her secrets penetrated, so that She may be commanded by man's action.'[55] 'What men want to learn from nature is how to use it in order wholly to dominate it and other men,' say Adorno and Horkheimer (1982, 4). Long Point is a testimonial to the domination of nature and man, to Enlightenment totalitarianism.

And yet, this cannot be the whole story. Despite the violence of science, the Long Point exhibition is still a site of enjoyment. Visitors stand and listen to the (recorded) loon calls, they enjoy the 'view' of the lake, forest, and distant hills, they savour the rich smell of the mud and the rushes. They say: 'It's just like ... such and such a place, remember?' They say: 'Ooh, look at that one hiding up there'; 'See that little one, drinking.' They treat it as if it were 'natural.' Visitors to Long Point somehow feel close to nature, while knowing full well that it is a simulation. How is this possible? Such enjoy-ment of being close to nature is only possible in a space that exists between mastery of nature and failure of mastery of nature. The enjoyment is pos-sible only where mastery of nature is an ironic conceit. In the absence of mastery an encounter with nature would be terrifying, but if the limits of mastery, the failure of mastery weren't apparent, if nature were 'wholly dominated,' then the visitor to Long Point would encounter an equally terrifying monumental *techne*. It is only because the visitor can see how the ROM has 'captured it perfectly' and yet simultaneously 'missed it com-pletely,' can see that the gesture of mastery is futile and that Long Point is still 'really' out there, teeming with life, that the museum can be experienced as enjoyable.

The Long Point installation is a symptom. On the one hand, the simula-tion tames the wilderness and masks the real, protecting us from existential angst. And at the same time, by the same gesture, it declares the real and confesses that the order of simulacra is under threat of reabsorption by the real. The museum exhibit testifies to the absurdity of national history and geography projects, the precariousness of the nation in the context of the infinity of the field of differences. The simulated wetland, for all the vain tyranny of the ROM, is still a wild space. It confirms the success of hege-monic projects of order, and at the same time it shows the limits of such projects: that they cannot capture the real, suture or totalize the social; that knowledge/power and control of 'the land of Canada' is a precarious and elusive achievement. Long Point allows us the conceit that we have mas-tered Canada, at least in so far as Canada is 'the land of Canada,' but at the same time warns us, and promises us, that it has escaped us, that it is 'out there,' evading us, enticing us ... it is this space, a tense space where we might yet get it, but equally where it might get us, that is the space of enjoyment.

The 'being close to nature' that visitors to Long Point enjoy is only possible while their orientation to the exhibit is one of an ironic conceit of mastery. This ironic conceit that sustains their enjoyment is a very delicate achievement. Enjoyment is disturbed when the conceit is made too obvious; when the smart-aleck kid calls his mother's attention to the 'very special bird,' the fire sprinkler hidden in the bushes. When the mastery is declared and exposed, enjoyment is in jeopardy, it's 'just not the same any more.' The conceit is that we have mastered nature (but we know that we haven't really). That is, our conceit is ironic, and this allows us to approach Long Point enjoyably. We're fooling ourselves so that our encounter with techne is tolerable, and our encounter with nature is tolerable.

In the tension between the assurance of mastery and the promise of adventure in failure of mastery, enjoyment is possible. The enjoyment is disrupted if the conceit is exposed: if techne makes a vulgar appearance, or an impotent, futile gesture, giving away, as it were, the limits of mastery over the field of differences. The fire sprinkler in this case does both. It shows us that the 'lifelike' wetland is a dead thing, the life has been shot or poisoned out of it, cut away, scraped, dried, stuffed with straw, and stitched together again. But also, just as the fire sprinkler unmasks techne, we can see how it shows the monstrous face of nature. The fire sprinkler shows the futility of the Frankensteinesque enterprise; because the installation can never be 'lifelike,' the museum's pathetic effort is subject to sudden reabsorption by the elemental natural force of fire.

Enjoying the visit to the ROM depends upon this ironic conceit of suture: that on the one hand 'we've got it all under control,' that the symbolic order is closed, totalized. But on the other hand, that it is not totalitarian, that there is some 'room to manoeuvre,' that the social still affords us some living space. This conceit of mastery and ob-scene enjoyment of failure of mastery is not just for the visitors. The curator's and researcher's enjoyment depends on the same ironic conceit. We can see this if we return to the 'Mankind Discovering' installation. Part of this exhibit is a desk, presented to view as if the visitor had just walked into a museum researcher's office. We are shown the researcher's work, but we are also offered a glimpse of the researcher's enjoyment. A drawer is open; we can see a stapler, a roll of scotch tape, two rulers, maps, photographs of buildings in a 'Third Worldy' looking place, a box of aspirin, envelopes, index cards, some Tic Tacs (candy), pens, an eraser, and a rubber stamp. Lying on the desk in a haphazard order are some books (*Survey Field Book; Sotheby's Catalogue of Classical Egyptian and Near Eastern Antiquities; Archaeological Technique*), a small pile of pottery fragments, a magnifying glass, paper clips and rubber bands in an old vessel, something preserved in a jar, a desk calendar with the day divided by half-hour intervals, a fossil, a telephone, a paper offering an account of the 'DNA replication mystery,' a coffee mug, some Post-it memos, some more photographs, etc., etc. What are we to make of an exhibit like this?

One could of course be cynical, and say that this is a perfectly typical Canadian museum exhibit: the kind of thing that one might expect of a country with a lack of history, which nevertheless has a museum or a heritage centre everywhere one turns one's head. The *Official Directory of Canadian Museums and Related Institutions* by the Canadian Museums Association lists some 4060 museums. By comparison, the *Guide de Musées de France* by the Centre National de Lettres and the *Tutti i Musei d'Italia* list 2750 and 2500 institutions respectively. Canadian museology and historiography, finding nothing 'out there,' make an exhibition of themselves.

One might also take it as an indication (and this is a less cynical, but perhaps a premature reading) that Canada is an utterly postmodern society, where modernity has become a museum exhibit. Certainly the desk is a modern relic. It allows us to peer into the world of one of Max Weber's 'specialists without spirit.' The desk tells a story of 'mechanized petrification, embellished by a kind of frenzied self-importance.'[56] This is the desk of a suturing technician, a cog in the giant modern machine built for tracking down those wild elements, mapping, measuring, and knowing them, articulating them into the prevailing discourses, achieving that desired closure of the symbolic. The researcher's desk is littered with the paraphernalia of a compulsive modern economy of desire for order.

The research scientist is a puritanical bureaucrat, mechanically applying the scientific method. The desk is a smorgasbord of signs of the desire to master the field of differences by the application of modern technique: the panoptical, surveillant regime of power/knowledge represented by the maps, rulers, magnifying glass. The orientation to the Other is ambivalent. On the one hand, we can see the desire to master it, classify it, to constrain it (the index cards, staples, and paper clips on the desk referencing the chains, machine guns, and prisons used to put order on the Other when encountered more directly). On the other hand, we can see the fascination with the Other and the aestheticization of the Other, signified by the 'touristy' photographs, the small earthen vessel, and so on. And of course, permeating all of this, the mark of capitalism: commodification, the ethic of accountancy, rationalized acquisitiveness, betrayed by the Sotheby's catalogue.

But the exhibit indexes more than modern regimes of power and mastery. We can also treat this desk and its contents as indexing the limits of modern regimes, and admitting to a conceit of mastery that facilitates the researcher's ob-scene enjoyment. At an elementary level, the troubles of the researcher, the worries, doubts, and anxieties of the workaday world, are betrayed by the aspirin, coffee mug, and mints. A desk cover, covered with doodles (a rabbit, a shopping list, abstract shapes), hints at a subversion of the bureaucratic work by the outside world of everyday life and by the unconscious.

The best clues to a conceit of mastery, though, are three pictures pinned onto the front of the desk. The first one shows two scientists in a laboratory amid lots of technological gadgetry. One is chained to the wall, as in a dungeon. The other says: 'Me, mad? Yes, but I do have tenure.' Next to it is a 'Broom Hilda' strip. Broom Hilda says: 'You know what the museum is, don't you?' 'Yes,' her sidekick replies, 'it's where you go to take a nap standing up.' Alongside this is a still from the movie *Raiders of the Lost Ark*. It shows Dr Indiana Jones, the buccaneer archaeologist, giving a lecture at the university, while his female students flirt with him.

The interesting problem posed by the pictures on the desk is that – amid the violence of science, faced with the Weberian/Foucaultian scenario of specialists without soul, subject functionaries in a total web of power – we find reflexivity and irony. There is a recognition of the lack here by the 'cogs' themselves – the caricature of insane science, the playful 'not taking ourselves too seriously' relation to the tedious, boring aspect of the work, the preserving of the fantasy adventure: 'Classification, cataloguing! Who the hell wants to do that?! We're with Indy, scoring babes and cheating the Nazis ... Not!'

Amid all the trappings of power/knowledge there is a playful, ironic self-mockery of the apparatus. There is a recognition of the limits of the apparatus of mastery. Here again we find the space of enjoyment in the conceit of mastery – the moment where the researchers' orientation towards their own work is ironic, making possible an ob-scene enjoyment in the space between the two lacks. Enjoyment is contingent upon the ironic conceit of suture: the surety (the failure of surety of) the Big Other (the assurance of science, the recognition of the limiting lack in science); the certainty (the uncertainty) of the positivity of the identity of the researcher; the confidence in (the humility of) the human lack.

Souveniring Enjoyment

We can catch another glimpse of the space of enjoyment by looking at souvenirs. Souvenirs remember enjoyment. But souvenirs are always inadequate to what it is they are supposed to recall. They cannot do justice to enjoyment. They are given apologetically: 'Here's a little something from Canada.' Souvenirs are tokens, inadequate reminders of enjoyment, but effective nonetheless in so far as they remember particular enjoyment, a particularly Canadian enjoyment in this case. Souvenirs 'work' by appropriating little bits of the symbolic order that reference sublime objects of identification. Souvenirs souvenir (remember, bring back) by setting off strings of associations, lighting up quilting points in the social fabric like lights on a pinball machine. Souvenirs light up symptom formations like neon signs, signs that warn us of, and welcome us to, the real.

In the case of the museum we saw that enjoyment was made possible by clearing out a space in the social by practices of ironic conceit. The enjoyment of the Long Point exhibit was made possible by an ironic conceit of mastery of nature – 'We've got nature under control ... Not!' In souvenirs, or 'souveniring,' we see a conceit of distance from the symbolic order, a conceit of separateness, apartness from the symbolic order, making possible an enjoyment of not-being-responsible-for-it, –or-to-it.

Before we begin to look at some souvenirs, we should address a problem of distinction. Though of course one may give a souvenir as a gift, are souvenirs-of-Canada the same as gifts-from-Canada? Is there a distinction? Is the souvenir, for example, something that visitors take away to bring back for themselves the enjoyment of the visit, and the gift-from-Canada something that the Canadian takes outside to give to the non-Canadian, to present Canada, a bit of Canadian enjoyment, to the outsider? But the non-Canadian could not be absolutely strange to Canada, for if he or she were, the souvenir would be meaningless and the Canadian gift giver would be embarrassed and would have to explain the thing. The gift-from-Canada must souvenir 'Canada' for the non-Canadian, in order for it to be distinguishable from the gift-from-some-guy (who just happens to be from Canada). The souvenir-of-Canada and the gift-from-Canada both depend upon access to the particularity of the symbolic order of Canada: they recall Canada to both the Canadian and the non-Canadian. The point is even clearer in the case of the Canadian who buys a souvenir of Canada, or a gift from Canada, for him- or herself, as a souvenir of a visit to some other part of the country.

When Marion, my sister, gave me a sweater that she bought in Germany, as a present from Germany, as a souvenir, for me, of her visit to Germany, it worked as a souvenir not because the sweater had any Germanness in it. (It was made in Mauritius as far as I recall, but clearly it's not a souvenir of Mauritius.) The sweater is rather a souvenir of Germany because when I wear it or see it in my closet I can access the symbolic order of Germany by it, but only via my sister's visit. Nobody else can. To anyone else it's just a sweater. The souvenir from *Germany*, the gift from *Germany*, is a different thing. It's there for all to see, it's easy to read. It announces its particularity without the mediation of personal narrative or sentiment. The souvenir is, in this sense, a vulgar or a cheap thing, a common thing, which the collective can enjoy. Now, if my sister had brought me lederhosen, or a beer tankard with a lid on it ... It is artifacts and objects of this latter kind, which present themselves as promiscuous signifiers of Canada, an easy read for the collective, that I am concerned with here. So, for my purposes, such gifts-from-Canada are subsumed under souvenirs-of-Canada.

There are souvenirs for every market, remembering enjoyments marked by class and taste. I will look at some samples from two sources, from the shelves of Eaton's and The Bay, representing the mass market, and from some of the more specialized and up-market craft shops and galleries, such as one may find in Toronto's Yorkville or in the boutiques of the Château Frontenac. The souvenirs range from plastic Native dolls in suede dresses made in Taiwan, available for $19.99, to whalebone carvings by Inuit artists from Inukjuak and Frobisher Bay, selling for several thousand dollars.

Let's unpack some traits of souvenirs. First, souvenirs are representations of the quilting points of hegemonic discourses that order the social. Souvenirs recall for us, and reassure us of, mastery and domination, and at the same time they promise us adventure in the failure of mastery. We can see in souvenirs the continuation of the conceit of mastery that made enjoyment possible in the museum (which is why, as one might expect, museums invariably have souvenir shops in them). Two motifs predominate the Canadian souvenir market: Natives and Nature. They do not simply stand alongside one another – 'Brewster the Beaver' sharing shelf space with the (nameless) 'Native Doll.' They are intermingled and collapsed into one another, an intersection of nature and culture where boundaries are blurred and identities become indistinct. The Native is not simply 'close-to' nature, the Native is 'part-of' nature. The Native is equivalent to the beaver and the forest, a wild element ordered by the trap, the chainsaw, and the gun, put in its place by the museum, and 'now available in selected retail outlets.'

The souvenir of Canada remembers this blurring of identities and offers a reassurance of their hegemonic ordering. This is most obvious in items like polished and lacquered pieces of hardwood, with clocks and calendars built into them (the chronological order of modernity imposed upon timeless nature). The plastic figurine of the Native boy dressed in the felt Mountie's uniform (the savage policed. More: here is a souvenir of Foucault's model of power, the care of the self: the savage policing himself; the imperatives of the surveillant order internalized by the savage, the self-disciplining order outwardly expressed and celebrated).[57] And – how about this – a pair of Native heads in soapstone, by a Native artist, as bookends! (the severed heads of butchered Natives propping up the canon of Western civilization).

And what about the other side of the conceit, the promise of adventure in the impossibility of mastery? Cards accompanying Native and Inuit craft work promise the purchaser that the carving is a representation of some Native legend or other, that this thing is used in some 'sacred ritual,' that this artifact 'is believed to have magical powers.' One store invites shoppers to 'Come view the largest collection of Iroquois soapstone carvings ever in Toronto.' A card accompanying the pieces reads: 'Symbols in these carvings were part of a religious belief of the Woodland Indians; they represented the spirit world and the dancers who emulated these powerful beings.' Decontextualized, sketchy, obscure, the promise is that the carvings souvenir an unknown domain, an excess that remains inaccessible to consumers even after they have paid hard cash for it. In fact it is this hint which the Native carving gives of an ineffable world of secret enjoyment that makes 'all of them marvellous, but this one especially wonderful! ... There's just something about it ...'

And one should not assume that access to the secret excess enjoyment of primitive spirituality is only for yuppies. Eaton's carries a range of gifts that promise the same enjoyment for the less well heeled or for those of less discerning tastes. One might perhaps choose something from the 'Native Renaissance' jewellery collection, or perhaps a 'Canned Grizzly Bear,' a 'Canned Bald Eagle,' or a 'Canned Moose.' The label on the front of the can warns: 'Danger: Contains Canadian Grizzly Bear.' Inside (unsurprisingly) is a miniature snuggly teddy bear. The real surprise is the label on the back of the can. It explains what 'real live' grizzly bears are like, how ferocious and dangerous they are, and instructions on what to do if you are confronted or attacked by a real grizzly in the wild.

In the Eaton Centre? Please! But then again, if we are to believe the tabloids, you might be 'swarmed' by something equally dangerous and primitive; a pack of black youths, 'wilding.'[58] The Eaton's souvenir department promises the adventure with nature in one form or another. The shopper in the Eaton Centre enjoys the space of ironic conceit: 'We've got nature canned (but it's still out there and dangerous).' 'The mall is such a well-ordered place (but what are those wild-looking kids up to?).'

This is the conceit that makes the mall a fun place, that makes shopping enjoyable. But it is not what makes souvenirs enjoyable. The enjoyment of souvenirs is the enjoyment of separation from the symbolic order. But to see this we must unpack some more souvenirs.

Souvenirs celebrate and reaffirm the surety of order, and at the same time play on the ambiguity and unfixity of the moments in hegemonic discourses, protecting enjoyment and promising to nurture it with unspecified fantastic adventures. But there is more to the economy of desire of the collective than a dialectic of fear and fascination for the Other. Souvenirs make a utopian gesture towards the Other. Souvenirs recognize the Other, and recognition is always utopian because it is a recognition of the Other in the self, of the lack shared by the Other and the self, and consequently of the interdependency of the destiny of the identities upon one another. The one desperately needs the Other. Souvenirs beg the Other to deliver us both from the terror of the lack. This utopian gesture is evident in the most pathetically vulgar of souvenirs, the 'crying Native' dolls, the 'cute' plastic figurine of the pretty Native woman or child with the forlorn expression and blue tears in their sad brown eyes.

Crying Native dolls can be had in several outlets in the Eaton Centre, a mall that anticipates almost every conceivable consumer need. An intelligent toilet in the mall anticipates when to flush. One store anticipates the misogynist frivolity of the master, and comes up with golf tees in the form of nude women. It anticipates his boredom, and supplies executive desk toys. It anticipates his nostalgia and provides old-fashioned razors, suspenders, etc. What do the dolls for sale next door anticipate? Why are the dolls crying?

The master's enjoyment depends upon a continuation of domination, which the consumer of the Native (i.e., the Native doll, i.e., the Native, reduced to object, commodity) can share. There may be a filthy enjoyment in complicity with practices of butchery, certainly, but for this the doll need not cry. It should be sufficient that the doll, as representative of the objectified, dehumanized Native, blindly or blankly return the master's equally inhuman gaze. But the dolls are crying. They are not returning a cold gaze. The crying dolls do not reflect the master's indifference, it's not that he doesn't care ... The crying doll anticipates the master's extension of domination in a futile search for mastery and the doll cries for the master's painful failure. The crying dolls anticipate the master's guilt, the denial of his guilt in his need to see the results of his tyranny as 'cute.' The 'crying Native' souvenir souvenirs the master's recognition of the impoverishment of the relation between the master and the slave, their status as objects to one another. The dolls souvenir his repressed desire for the slave to set him (and thereby them both) free.

This utopian moment, the desire for a collective emancipation, is also expressed by the expensive souvenirs in the Yorkville craft galleries. One, for instance, carries a range of Canadian crafts downstairs which 'take their inspiration from the primitive style.' Upstairs, the 'Eskimo Gallery' features carvings by Inuit artists, not simply 'inspired by the primitive' like the artists represented downstairs, no, this is supposed to be the real, genuine, primitive article. Gallery staff drew my attention to some work by a particular artist, remarkable because the style departed from the naïve norm and displayed a 'modern' influence. The exception brings to light a significant aspect of the resource of the primitive to facilitate enjoyment. Enjoyment requires a naïveté, an innocence. An innocence of what? An innocence of the modern, metropolitan Big Other, a freedom from the tyrannical authority of the Name-of-the-Father to which the modern is subject.

And of course the exception is also enjoyable, and not simply because of its exceptionality. If the domain of the primitive were purely naïve, the modern would hate it and fear it for its excessive difference. If the big Other of the modern had no dominion over the primitive, the innocence of the primitive would radically expose the lack. The exception, showing the modern influence, demonstrates how the Other affirms the enjoyment of the modern as authentic: just when the Other exposes the lack by its naïveté, it disguises it, covers it up again, affirms the totalized character of the modern symbolic order by showing that order's mark upon it and admitting to being influenced. The soapstone carving with the modern influence promises that there is a domain beyond – beyond the reach of the big Other – but in the same breath it reassures us that it too is under control. The modern soapstone carving is a signpost of the playground of enjoyment: free of the direct supervision of the big Other, but checked out, vetted, and designated safe by Him nonetheless.

Staff told me that the clientele of this craft gallery are mostly Canadians buying gifts for friends abroad. These pieces are seen as 'very Canadian,' and of course, I was reminded, very collectible. Yuppie enjoyment is nourished by the promise of primitive spirituality in Native culture embodied in the ineffable quality of primitive aesthetics. Native aesthetics serves as a resource pool for Canadian identity, a pool that Canadians can dip into when they wish to give something 'very Canadian' to someone else. But of course, Native art is no more – or no less – authentic, 'real,' than the plastic doll made in Taiwan. The pool of the primitive that the Canadian draws from contains nothing other than what his/her fantasy has introduced there to begin with. What the Canadian receives from the Other (Native, Inuit) is the reflection, refraction, distorted echo, of his/her own plea for something 'real' with which to fill out the lack. An impossible request, to which the Other, also lacking, sends back an absurdity, a stone walrus.

But where is the utopian moment in this pathetic economy – buying something 'Canadian' from someone who is quintessentially Canadian, but yet somehow outside of Canadian society, radically Other? The Other is not-the-identity, yet constitutes the identity. The Other negates the identity, yet is its only resource. The utopian moment that reflects this recognition emerges in an unlikely form. It emerges in the emphasis on some kind of 'respect' for the Other, expressed in the way the market knows best: terms of trade. 'There was a time when these could be had for a case of beer or a carton of cigarettes. Not any more, thankfully. It's much fairer now. It's all handled by the co-operatives which are run mainly by the Natives themselves,' a gallery owner explained, as part of the sales pitch. Two important points here. The fairer terms are achieved as a result of struggle, a moment of victory in a dialectical antagonism between the master and the Native bondsman. The 'thankfully' expresses recognition by the master of the emancipatory effect of the struggle, for both the Native and the white consumer – recognition of the improvement in the quality of their relation to one another. The improved terms of trade reflect, at another level, the recognition that master and bondsman relate to one another now, under these less crassly exploitative conditions, more as subjects than as objects.

So far our exploration of souvenirs of Canada has made a number of points clear. First, there can be no art/mass culture distinction made between the plastic doll and the Inuit carving. They are rendered equally sublime and equally vulgar when they are articulated within the modern economy of desire, consumer capitalism. Second, souvenirs represent quilting points in hegemonic discourses. (They are like light bulbs flashing on and off over quilting points.) Third, souvenirs make a utopian gesture, they reach out to the Other and try to come to terms with it. But none of this gets at the dimension of enjoyment in souvenirs.

To see the space of enjoyment in souvenirs we must see how souvenir(ing) is a practice of ironic conceit where we recognize the impossibility of collecting the symbolic order, where we simultaneously pay tribute to its integrity and mock its lack. Souvenirs try to crystallize the symbolic order of Canada, they attempt to pull it together around a point (a Native doll in a Mountie's uniform, a soapstone polar bear) and, by the inevitable inadequacy of the souvenir, its failure to capture the symbolic order, thereby let its lack be seen. The lack appears as an excess, a 'much-more-than-this' that the souvenir cannot collect. And this is just what we expect of the souvenir, that it be inadequate, that it be 'just a little something,' that it represent the symbolic order, affirming its integrity by being recognizable to the collective, but that it let us sense a lack.

Souvenirs are always inadequate, and at the same time they are spoiled by being excessive: 'Oh you shouldn't have ... (given me this cheesy thing) ... It's too much.' 'Well, it's nothing really ... (but I spent a day looking for it, and it cost a bundle).' Souvenirs are inadequate because they are trivial, and they are excessive in their triviality. They are inadequate in their failure to capture the symbolic order, they are trivial in the face of the absence, the immateriality of that which they fail to capture. They are excessive in their absurd inadequacy to the vastness of the absence which they show. Souvenirs are marked by excess; in fact, what souvenirs souvenir is precisely excess. Just like enjoyment: endangered, fragile, somehow spoiled by its insufficiency, and yet possible at all only by its being excessive.

The space of enjoyment in the souvenir is the coincidence of its lack/ excess, but how does the souvenir give us this space? The souvenir clears out a space for enjoyment by doing extreme violence to the symbolic order in its very affirmation of it. The sublime object of ideology that quilts the symbolic order is an ordinary object, an everyday thing that is elevated to the status of the sublime thing, the impossible/real object of desire. In the symbolic order of Canada, a leaf and a rodent are such sublime objects of collective identification. Souvenirs do exactly the inverse of elevation to the sublime. They take the sublime objects, the maple leaves, the beavers, the flags, the Mounties, the Natives, which by their sublimity grant particularity to Canada (and save Canadians from the lack of Canada), and make them profane, ordinary things that one can buy in the store.

The ironic conceit of the souvenir is that in its tribute to the Big Other, that is, by its declaration of its (the souvenir's) inadequacy, it affirms the authority of the Big Other. The souvenir souvenirs that our enjoyment is protected from the lack. And simultaneously, by profaning the sublime objects of ideology that quilt the symbolic order, the inadequacy of the souvenir souvenirs the lack in the symbolic order and declares the impotence of the Big Other. When we recognize, in the inadequacy of the souvenir, the impotence of the Big Other, it gives us some space to enjoy a distance from the symbolic order, an irresponsibility towards it. Souveniring is a practice of ironic conceit that pushes back the symbolic order to create a clearing; it clears out a space for enjoyment. Souvenirs show us that the space of enjoyment is contingent on an ironic conceit of separateness, of alienation from the Big Other. In the souvenir we can see something that we know isn't Canada, and yet, this is exactly what Canada is. The souvenir shows us that space where we find a very Canadian kind of play; a keeping an option on being Canadian, an option of standing outside the collective and claiming some kind of immunity from its authority – like the person who says, 'Of course I'm not really a Canadian, you know,' I'm German on my father's side and Ukrainian/Danish on my mother's.'

Enjoying Estrangement

Souvenirs souvenir an enjoyable alienation, a separateness, a freedom from the Big Other. The overwhelmingly familiar remembers strangeness. But the souvenir has that ambiguous quality of being both inadequate and excessive – 'That's not what Canada is about at all,' and yet, 'That's exactly what Canada is.' It 'says it all,' 'sums it up' (think of the punch line that closes the Molson advertisement, '[E]x says it all'). Because of this ability to declare the lack by admitting to not being able to do justice to the symbolic order, and simultaneously cover up the lack by making the excessive claim to being able to 'say it all,' the souvenir both opens up the playground of enjoyment and gives it some boundaries to make it safe.

The stranger can also show us the space of enjoyment. The encounter with the stranger is the inverse of the encounter with the souvenir. While the familiar souvenirs the strange, the radically different reminds us of our collective similarity. This makes possible an enjoyment of membership, an enjoyment of our shared collective relationship to one another under the rule of the Name-of-the-Father. The stranger reminds us of this shared relationship, which he or she lacks. From the stranger we derive the enjoyment of closeness, of being subject to the authority of our collective. And yet, by virtue of our being able to identify with strangers we can partake of their estrangement, and derive an enjoyment in distancing ourselves from our collective.

This is the ironic conceit at the heart of racial discrimination that makes racism enjoyable. And racist discrimination is enjoyable; at least it is for the racist, if its persistence as a practice can be taken to be sufficient evidence. And now of course one may raise the obvious objection to this line of inquiry: the ethical and political problem posed by the stranger is not whether we enjoy by having the stranger among us, but whether some among us can tolerate and enjoy being strangers. While we may enjoy discriminating, does the stranger enjoy being estranged? Having flagged this question, I now wish to bracket it momentarily. I will take it up again in the context of the work of Frantz Fanon, Homi Bhabha, and others, to argue that the stranger's enjoyment also depends upon the ironic conceit of membership. For what does the stranger want? The stranger's orientation to the collective is as ambiguous as the collective's is towards him or her. The stranger wants to fit in, while at the same time he or she doesn't want the particularity of his or her strangeness to be missed or overlooked.

In the sociological form of 'the stranger,' Simmel says, we find an example of the synthesis of the qualities attachment/detachment, or nearness/remoteness, that infuse every social relationship.[59] The stranger is 'the man who comes today and stays tomorrow, the potential wanderer, so to speak, who although he has gone no further, has not quite got over the freedom of coming and going (Simmel 1971, 143). The stranger is distinguished by his or her freedom. Although not wandering, or just passing through, neither is the stranger rooted here, native, tied to the land. The stranger is settled, but hasn't lost the potential to pack up and move on. The stranger shows us that freedom (freedom to enjoy) requires this synthetical paradox attachment/detachment, nearness/remoteness.

The stranger is an 'Other,' but a particular kind of Other: the Other amongst us. As 'the Other amongst us,' the figure of the stranger occupies a central place in the Canadian imaginary. The stranger figures prominently in the discourse of immigration (immigrants are 'strangers within our gates,' to cite the title of a landmark book on the issue) (Woodsworth [1909] 1972). In the discourse of the 'founding nations,' anglophones and francophones appear as 'strangers to one another.' White Men and Natives stand as strangers to one another also. In the recent controversy concerning the treatment of Canadians of Japanese and Italian descent during the Second World War, and more recently the harassment of Arab-Canadians during the Gulf War, the figure of the stranger is again central. Sometimes we recognize, as Simmel shows us, that we are all strangers; that all social relations are charged with a paradoxical simultaneity of closeness/remoteness. This paradoxical condition, for reasons of history and geography, is especially strongly felt in Canada (or so the story goes), and being able to negotiate this paradox in the antagonistic play of everyday life, while cultivating and displaying characteristic tolerance and unpretentiousness, is what makes us all Canadians. A recent excursus in this vein is the 1990 National Film Board production *In the Company of Strangers*.'[60] In the film seven elderly women are stranded in an old farmhouse when their bus breaks down during a trip into the Quebec wilderness. They work through their differences (racial, class, sexual orientation, etc.) and become united in a spirit of friendship that enables them to live enjoyably (catching trout with their pantyhose, and the like) until they are rescued and flown back to the nursing home.

The antagonistic aspect of the character of social relations, the fear and hatred of the Other and fascination and desire for the Other, as expressed in the dialectical play of theft of enjoyment, for example, is expressed with particular clarity in relations with the stranger. We are suspicious of the stranger because the stranger is not tied down, placing his or her commitment to the collective in doubt: 'Whose side will Arab-Canadians be on when the chips are down?' The specific character of mobility which Simmel says pertains to the stranger refers not only to the stranger's physical location but also to the whereabouts of his or her loyalties and values. The stranger is feared and disliked for his or her mobility when it appears as a dubious shiftiness, but conversely, the stranger's mobility also appears as a desirable freedom. The stranger is the figure in whom the desire for freedom is invested; the stranger brings into the constraining collective the promise of getting out. In the idiom of the airport paperback or the Harlequin romance, and in popular culture, the stranger invariably promises an ambiguous disruption. In the generic form the tall dark stranger moves into the tight-knit community, the beautiful daughter of the tyrannical landlord who is betrothed to the rich man twice her age falls in love with the stranger, the affair rocks the community to its foundations, they skip town to the big city, things return to normal in the community – though it is never quite the same as it was before the stranger came.

By not being tied down, by his or her specifically mobile character, the stranger shows us something of the space of enjoyment. The space of enjoyment is a space in which there is mobility, but a mobility within boundaries of attachment/detachment. The figure of the stranger, by his or her remoteness and detachment from us, reminds us of what we share, of what we are tied to. And we are tied: our enjoyment is bound to the symptom, as sinthome. The real sensuous character of the ties by which we are bound to the symptom as sinthome comes out in vernacular formulations of how the stranger doesn't 'feel the same way as we do' about these things; or of the reluctant emigrant who cannot bear the prospect of estrangement: 'the pain of tearing himself (or herself) away' from everything that must be left behind. The stranger, by his or her freedom from these bonds, brings to light our attachments. And also by virtue of his or her mobility, in so far as the stranger is close to us, the stranger brings us the promise of the possibility of a way-out-of-here, an escape from the ties that bind and the constraining force of our collective enjoyment.

Hitch-hiking west some years ago, I got a lift from Kenora to Medicine Hat in a big Freightliner truck. The conversation roved around, looking for points of identification: hockey, long distances driven without sleep, 'babes,' quantities of beer consumed at a single sitting, and, at one point, 'Pakis,' and the issue of 'how many of them are coming over here.' My host informed me how he 'hates those fucking Pakis,' and with great relish he spun out a long string of complaints about them. Then he told me, 'One of my friends at the depot is a Paki.' He told me about his 'friend' (who as it turns out is from Sri Lanka), how much he and the guys give him a hard time (but that it's all in good fun), how they go out for a beer together sometimes, how 'he's a real nice guy,' and how he (his Asian friend) 'hates those fucking Pakis too.'

The figure of the stranger whom we encountered in our conversation ('the babe,' but more particularly 'the Paki') was introduced as the resource through which my host hoped that we might recollect our shared membership. I was a student from Toronto (and from Ireland), we didn't have that much in common, we were certainly strangers to one another already. The figure of the third stranger, the stranger to both of us, we hoped, would recollect for us our common enjoyment. We were both white and we were both men, and Canada is a white man's country where we enjoy a high tolerance for beer and long-distance driving. The trucker's strategy for the recollection of membership, of our common collective enjoyment, differs only slightly from its construction by the refugee settlement host program as 'Show a new Canadian what us old Canadians are made of' – that is, have the stranger affirm the enjoyment of the collective.

But the Asian whom the truckdriver hated he also claimed as his friend, 'a real nice guy.' An explanation that is often offered for this paradoxical ambivalence is that, while the remote generalized Other might be hated, in the encounter with the embodied individual representative the Otherness is dissolved. In this formulation the problem is held to be ignorance; that is, racism stems from not knowing the Other, not having that intersubjective familiarity with one another whereby suspicion and prejudice are resolved. This formulation appears in the popular T-shirt slogan: 'Racism: 100 per cent Pure Ignorance.' And the liberal response to racial antagonism then is a sort of chaperoned mingling, within the terms of official multiculturalism, for example. But this may not be adequate, because it is not ignorance that is at the crux of racism, but enjoyment.

The figure of the stranger serves as a resource to facilitate the trucker's affirmation of a particular membership. To do this the stranger continues to be a stranger, both remote and close. The stranger stays strange. In the course of our conversation it transpired that the trucker didn't know much about this guy, even though he'd worked at the depot for about five years. He had never met his family, or been to his house. He scarcely knew him at all really, but still he was prepared to excuse him from his status as hated 'Paki.' So the liberal explanation of a shared intersubjectivity isn't sufficient. The trucker was still 100 per cent pure ignorant and 100 per cent racist (well, let's say 80 per cent, then!), and he was enjoying every percentile of it. The Asian was interesting to my host for very different reasons. The trucker's reason for calling the Asian his 'friend' was not because he knew him personally and thereby had his ignorance enlightened. He liked him and enjoyed being with him for precisely the opposite reason. He was friendly towards the stranger's continued strangeness. He valued his very strangeness. His co-worker's status as stranger served as the point around which the driver and his buddies could recollect their enjoyment.

The stranger brings us the gift of discrimination; the stranger gives us the means of being able to mark distinctions. The stranger gives us a glimpse of the near boundary of attachment in the space of enjoyment. He or she shows us the things (the symptoms) to which our enjoyment is attached as sinthome. And the stranger sometimes brings a bonus gift. My host assured me that this 'Paki' (his 'friend') 'hates those fucking Pakis too.' Whether he did or not (though of course it's extremely unlikely that he did) is beside the point, which is that for the trucker the stranger is the figure who not only brings the collective enjoyment of him and his buddies to light, but affirms or seems to affirm beyond all shadow of doubt the superiority and authenticity of that enjoyment by his alleged hatred of his own enjoyment.

The stranger's detachment from the collective means that he or she cannot and does not share in our enjoyment, our *jouissance*, in the same way as we ourselves can and do. The stranger somehow 'doesn't have a feel for it.' But the stranger's closeness to us ensures that he or she is not unaware of it. The stranger has an objectivity with respect to our enjoyment. The objectivity of the stranger is by no means non-participation, Simmel says, 'but is rather a positive and definite kind of participation' (1971, 145). The stranger's objectivity is a privileged position from which our enjoyment can be evaluated, and thus we can take the stranger out for beers sometimes, and invite the stranger to parties, and show the stranger our enjoyment, and let the stranger try out some bits of our enjoyment, without running the risk of the stranger stealing our enjoyment. Whenever the stranger 'gets into it,' he or she shows us how great it is and is cheered for it. When he or she makes a faux pas, or 'just doesn't get it,' the stranger shows us how wonderfully beyond or above him or her it is. So long as the stranger remains strange, his or her encounter with our enjoyment is affirmative and reassuring.

What is the ironic conceit that animates the encounter with the stranger and makes it enjoyable? It is easy to see the conceit in my driver's formulation of his relationship to the stranger in his workplace. Irony isn't much in evidence though, and in its paucity the stupid bigotry of conceit shows itself: 'our thing is so great ... see, even this other guy can see that.' 'Me and the rest of the guys, now we know how to have a good time, eh.' 'You and me, we understand one another; we know what we're talking about,' etc. But if we were having a good time, and if we were sure of what it was that we were talking about, we could run the stranger out of town, or at least run him out of our conversation, for his work would have been done. But instead we keep him there, and not locked in the stocks and pilloried, gratuitously pelted with the leftovers of our enjoyment, but as some kind of a 'friend,' in fact 'a real nice guy,' who comes from Sri Lanka, which is 'a pretty rough spot, man, I can tell you!' (Tell me what?) 'Stories I hear when we go out for beers with him sometimes.'

The ironic conceit is one of discrimination: that we are members and that the stranger is not; that we are not strangers to one another, whereas the stranger is strange to us. By the presence of the stranger we play with the ironic conceit that we can discriminate between members and non-members. But the stranger is also a member and his or her membership is a compliment to the collective. That is to say, by granting membership to the stranger, the collective compliments itself for its generosity (but it is the stranger who has given membership to begin with). And by the stranger's membership, by the identification with the stranger, the collective avoids claustrophobic mechanical solidarity. The stranger also gives us our own estrangement. This is the source of the erotic quality of the stranger. Everybody wants to sleep with the new kid in town because, through the stranger, the collective avoids incest, the enjoyment of which is also derived from the threat/promise of the stranger's miscegenation.

The Stranger's Enjoyment of Estrangement

The excess that the stranger wears, as a colour on her skin, as an accent on his speech, makes all the difference. But what is the excess? In Spike Lee's film *Do the Right Thing* (1989), Mookie confronts Pino with the paradox at the heart of his racism. Mookie asks Pino who his favourite singer is. Pino says that Prince is. Who is Pino's favourite movie star? Eddie Murphy. Who is his favourite sports star? Michael 'Air' Jordan, and so on. Mookie points out that even though Pino says he hates blacks, all of his heroes are black. Pino tries to explain: First, he says that they're not black, ... Then, he says, O.K., they're black all right, but they're more than black, they're almost white. Mookie, as the black guy working in the Italian pizzeria, the-Other-amongst-us, is also somehow more than black to Pino. Just as there is something more that makes the hero stand out, there is something more in the embodied stranger than is in the general category, something that makes him stand apart from the general category of Other. That 'something more' that is ascribed to the Other amongst us, that which makes Pino's black heroes almost white, is a bit of the self. The stranger is the Other whom we see as having some of our self in it. (Of course, what is actually operant here as the shared quality of the Other and the self is the lack in them both, in themselves, but that is not recognized; it is masked by the ideological fantasy of subjectivity.) The stranger then is the point at which the Other becomes what Homi Bhabha (1994, 102–22) calls the hybrid, the hybrid where the dualism self/Other breaks down.

In Bhabha's usage the troubled ambivalence experienced by Pino and my truckdriver is an effect of their encounter with the subversive power of the stranger's mimicry. The stranger is distinct from what might be called an itself that is behind its appearance. The stranger is not itself, because it has a bit of myself/ourself in it. By mimicry Bhabha means something like the confusing effect of the presence of the Other amongst us; being close to us and doing some things like us, while remaining remote from us. We are uncertain whether the mimicry is flattery or mockery, or both. For Bhabha, the persistent presence of the stranger shows us that 'fitting in' is not a question of harmonizing with a homogeneous background, but of being mottled against a mottled background. The effect of mimicry is a kind of camouflage. The stranger is simultaneously distinct and indistinct, exactly like the technique of camouflage practised in warfare. The stranger smeared with excess blends in against a symptom complex that is patchy and lacking, through which the void (the excess) beyond it peeps through.

The stranger – the Asian in Kenora – is a guerrilla (or perhaps secret agent or semiotic terrorist is a better metaphor), moving along the frontline of the symptom. His presence declares the zone of enjoyment safe and secure when he reassuringly affirms it, like a sentry, for the enjoyment of the trucker and his buddies. But the Asian's presence is always a reminder that this is a battle-zone. The ironic conceit of the trucker and his buddies is that all is quiet on the front and their enjoyment is safe. But by their treatment of the Asian as cannon fodder they confess that in order for their enjoyment to be lively, it must be endangered by something beyond the frontline. And this liveliness is given by the fact that the Asian is unnervingly not cannon fodder, for he embodies some of themselves, and they remain quite unsure of what he's fighting for.

The ironic conceit in the practice of discrimination facilitates our enjoyment of membership in two ways. By virtue of the remoteness of the stranger, we can arrogantly assert that 'We are Canadians, and he or she is not.' And/or, by virtue of the stranger's closeness, if we grant him or her the coolly abstract relation to us as other Canadians, we can derive the (perhaps more typical) unpretentious enjoyment of saying, 'I guess you could say I'm just an ordinary Canadian,' unmarked by the excess of the stranger. And yet, on the other hand, the conceit of membership is ironic. By virtue of the disruptive remoteness that the stranger brings amongst us, the assuredness of our similarity to one another is saved from taking on a mechanical oppressiveness, because it is also characteristically Canadian to unpretentiously enjoy one's membership in terms of sharing in the strangers' excess: 'I guess I'm just an ordinary Canadian, as much a stranger here as the next guy.' The stranger shows us how we are members, and by the very way in which he or she shows us – his or her remoteness from us – also shows us the lack in our thing; shows us that there could be more to it. Excess clings to the stranger, and that excess which the stranger brings amongst the members in his or her closeness to us shows us that there is something outside from which the stranger came and to which the stranger might move on, taking a member along, should one want to go.

The dominant collectivity enjoys its collective membership at the expense of the stranger, and it also enjoys an estrangement from itself by virtue of the stranger. But what then of the problem of the stranger's enjoyment? This also depends upon an ironic conceit of discrimination. The stranger enjoys being a non-member of the collective to whom he or she is stranger, and a non-member of the collective from which he or she came. The stranger's enjoyment also depends upon an ironic conceit of discrimination in the pursuit of a particular enjoyment in the space between the slippage of two particular enjoyments. We can see this most clearly when the stranger goes 'home.'

The returning emigrant is possibly the most typical case, but the stranger may be any one of us who has spent time amongst the Other (Mookie returning from working at Sal's pizzeria, for example, or for Frantz Fanon, in *Black Skin, White Masks* [1968], the Martinician returning to the islands from a sojourn in France). What happens to the stranger when he or she returns 'home'? When the stranger 'comes home,' the collective scrutinize him/her for traces of the Other that cling. They search for the change in speech and accent, particularly, for language is the house of Being, and gives away where one has been.[61]

When I visit Ireland, my friends listen for the smallest detail of my speech, pouncing on it gleefully: 'mailman? mail man!? It's the post man we have here, remember?' They want to see that I am different, how I've been changed, and at the same time they want to see that I haven't changed a bit. They want to pick off the bits of excess and find that I'm the same old me as ever I was, and that is reassuring for both of us, but the excess is never really dusted off, there is always something by which 'you would know that he's been away all the same.' They want to bring me for a 'real' pint of Guinness in the pub where we used always to be, because we both know that a real pint of Guinness is not to be had outside of Ireland. And then, they want to know, so what sort of a place is Canada anyway, and I want to know what's been going on since I left. And as soon as we begin to articulate a conversation about being in Canada and being in Ireland, we have to manage a delicate balance: I alternately praising aspects of being in Canada, complaining about others, marking the difference but being careful so as not to appear a loudmouth. They want me to show the excess without being excessive. And of course, for their part, they play a similar game about being in Ireland: 'Things are the same as ever here, you know yourself, nothing much happens around here, but a lot has happened all the same since you left, so-and-so got married, so-and-so's father died, and don't you remember so-and-so who's gone to Australia? Ah but sure you weren't around for any of that, and jaysus! you're out of touch.'

The stranger who returns home is 'a bit out of touch,' and this facilitates an enjoyment of recollection, of gathering up a shared membership with the stranger, but one discriminately marked as a membership of which the emigrant is no longer really a part. And I for my part enjoy the ironic conceit of being 'home,' I'm a member, but one who is somehow not really affected by the story of so-and-so's marriage, for what's it to me anyway, I've got my own life somewhere else. The stranger lives between two houses; of one, not fully in the other. In both houses the stranger enjoys being a member in the space cleared out by the ironic conceit of discrimination. The stranger enjoys fitting in, being a member in the new place, and back home, while being a bit of an outsider to both houses also. The stranger wants to fit in, but not to have the particularity of his or her strangeness overlooked. But there are, of course, degrees of estrangement and access to membership, and as a white anglophone immigrant to Canada I have little to complain about. What happens when the stranger is systematically estranged, rebuffed by the collective, by the hegemonic discourses of racism or sectarianism? The stranger cannot go home, for he or she no longer really lives there, and after all, this, here, is the stranger's house now, but he or she is being prevented from living in it. Now the stranger is thrown back on an expatriate community of strangers, who formulate an enjoyment of their collective membership as expatriates, giving birth to the distinct, particular cultures of immigrant communities. Part of the formulation involves a political struggle for equal access to the house, a struggle that in the process renovates and extends it, adding new living room to the space of enjoyment.

Here, with the question of the stranger's enjoyment, we should take the opportunity to explore the distinction between the political and sociological dimensions of enjoyment. It is patently obvious that the stranger's quest for a space for enjoyment in the face of hegemonic discursive practices that seek to exclude him or her from the new house has a political dimension. But that is not to assert, as Ernesto Laclau mistakenly does, 'the primacy of the political over the social' (1990, 33), to say that the quest for enjoyment is essentially political, that enjoyment can be reduced to its political dimension; that the ultimate character of social relations is their political character.[62] The search for a space for enjoyment is, I wish to argue, not guided solely by antagonism and will to power, but by sociability and will to enjoy – the will to come to terms with the Other(s) and live enjoyably with the collective in the face of the real.

The processes of collective identification of an expatriate community, their self-formation as a community, the elaboration and identification with particular symptom formation(s), may be, but are not necessarily, achieved by hegemonic articulation. That is, symptom formations may be political (hegemonic) constructs, but also, symptom formations may be generated through other forms of sociation, in which cases social solidarity is not immediately political, but would have to be made so by hegemonic practices. The playing out of collective enjoyment produces innumerable diverse symptoms (forms of sociation in Simmel's terms), not all of which are antagonistic or corrupted by the will to power. I think that it could be successfully argued that implicit in the elaboration of practices of enjoyment is nothing less than a claim to citizenship, the expectation that one's right to live enjoyably be recognized and respected, but this does not become political until hegemonic articulation makes it so.

Like Laclau and Mouffe, and Lacan, Simmel says that society doesn't exist, it appears only as forms of sociation.[63] But hegemonic projects competing in a field cross cut with antagonisms (Laclau and Mouffe 1985) is an inadequate representation of the plurality and character of these forms. We would want, I think, to recognize (let's say for example) curiosity, friendship, and sociability as aspects of the social and cross-cultural encounter. The encounter with alterity may be always lively, it may always concern enjoyment, but liveliness isn't necessarily agonal. It may be erotic, altruistic, imitative, playful, or accidental.

In other words, antagonism, even where generously theorized by Laclau and Mouffe as 'the impossibility of an identity of becoming positively, fully itself, due to its necessary relationality with other identities' (1985, 124–5), does not do justice to the enjoyment of sociation. In recognizing this we must try to develop an expanded picture of the economy of desire infusing the social encounter, in this case the social encounter with the stranger in Canada. We must see that there is more to the practices of enjoyment in identification with symptoms than a naked will to power and desire for mastery of the Other's excess, derived from a foundational existential terror. We should see rather a plural and polymorphous economy of desire in forms of sociation, and thus address social solidarity given by shared relations to symptom formations as both political and properly sociological phenomena.

Sharing Secret Enjoyment at a Party

Let us take this up in terms of a quintessentially Canadian encounter of strangers, the relations between Natives and whites. Here is a typical formulation of the encounter with the stranger, in this case a denunciation of the practices of the stranger who has invaded and taken over:

We have many particular things which we hold internal to our cultures. These things are spiritual in nature and they are for us, not for anyone who happens to walk in off the street ... I suppose it's accurate to say that such matters are our 'secrets,' the things which bind us together in our identities as distinct peoples ... [Secrets] are absolutely integral to our cultural integrity and thus to our survival as peoples ... obviously those who would violate the trust and confidence which is placed in them when we share some of our secrets ... misuse and abuse it for their own purposes, marketing it ... turning our spirituality into a commodity in books or movies or classes or 'ceremonials' ... the non-Indians who do it are thieves, and the Indians who do it are sell-outs and traitors.

Now, being spiritually bankrupt themselves they [non-Natives] want our spirituality, so they're making up rationalizations to explain why they are entitled to it. We are resisting this because spirituality is the basis of our culture, if it is stolen our culture is dissolved ... ripping off Indian spirituality is not a trivial or amusing matter, and it is not innocent or innocuous. And those who engage in it are not cute or groovy, hip, enlightened or any of the rest of the things they want to project themselves as being. No, what they are about is cultural genocide.[64]

What strikes me as particularly interesting in this articulation of the encounter with the Other is that the 'theft of enjoyment' is formulated in terms of secrets. Enjoyment is 'secrets' – the things we Natives have that the Other doesn't have. It is secrets that are at the heart of the economy of desire in the encounter with the Other. The strangers come to terms with one another through sharing one another's secrets. And note that the encounter is conducted in terms of *sharing* secrets. The desire is a desire for sharing secrets, selectively, at our pace, to see what it is that the whites will do with them.

The stranger does not cheat the Natives out of their secrets, or torture or bludgeon their secrets from them. The stranger becomes the thief of enjoyment by misusing the secrets that the Natives shared with the stranger, made him or her privy to. Theft of enjoyment takes the form of a betrayal of trust. For what do we risk, what is at stake when we share secrets? Trust, respect; you want to see what the Other will do with it. What is characteristic of the secret is that it cannot be kept, it must be shared with someone. You cannot keep a secret. If you're not dying to tell it, then it's not really a secret. It's only a real secret if you've really got to tell someone about it, but cannot, but tell anyway; then it becomes a secret, our secret. What about a deep dark secret, the traumatic kernel that is so secret it is even secret from ourselves? This is the real secret, that the other secrets dance around. The secrets are symptomatic of this secret. They protect it and hint at it. The secrets that we share we share as a test of membership. We are checking out what the Other might do with the real secret. It is in this characteristically social quality of the secret, the fact that secrets must be shared, that we can relocate sociability and the will to live enjoyably with the collective.

Simmel says that society (*Gesellschaft*) means 'party,' in the sense of a sociable gathering.[65] And *Gesellschaft* tells us that a party is a craft, a skilled practice, an art form if you like, whereby we produce a sociable gathering. Forms of sociation make up society (the party). There is no thing that is 'society,' as such but sociation makes it so. There are innumerable forms of sociation; gossip (the stock market of secrets), exchange, politics (antagonism), performance, conflict, erotic attraction, etc., etc., which contribute to the life of the party. These forms of sociation one might see as symptoms of a party, phenomena by virtue of which one might say, 'There is sociable interaction going on here'; they constitute 'signs of intelligent life,' if you like ('intelligent' because *Gesellschaft* implies a skilled practice). All of it together constitutes the ineffable thing, 'society,' which exists only in so far as people are participating enjoyably in its symptoms.

Is enjoyment of the party for 'anyone who happens to walk in off the street'? This is what is at stake in the encounter with the Other, embodied in the stranger, the other who is amongst us. This is the difficulty that immigration policy tries to deal with. It is not just anyone whom we will let come to our party. The stranger must make a commitment to contributing to the enjoyment, otherwise we won't share our secrets, so, 'bring your own beer,' pot-luck, or whatever. But this is the liberal model. The dialectical encounter involves subordination. The thief of enjoyment sometimes barges in off the street, guzzles the beers, and hogs the conversation, and nobody has a good time, including the bully. And sometimes (perhaps more often) the thief is the host, the mean, snobbish host who invites only very select guests; the overbearing host who instructs the guests on what they are to bring, limits the conversion, choreographs the whole thing like an obnoxious wedding consultant, and again nobody enjoys themselves. Or the host who invites according to the calculation of how much the host will profit, hoping that guests will bring more than they will consume.

We can trace a variety of hegemonic practices of oppression in contemporary Canada in this society-as-party metaphor. For the aboriginals the thief is the bully who barges in. The state might be the overbearing host, or the incompetent awkward host who ruins enjoyment by being undersocialized. (The state appears as the host who should get out more; the state doesn't know how to party.) We can also identify pockets of guests who are suspicious or hostile to the new arrivals, concerned that they will steal the limelight, disrupt the conversation, that there won't be enough food and drink to go around, that the newcomers will seduce the attractive guests, and so on. And we can also identify the loud guests who have been partying all evening (the dominant cultural groups), the cliques of 'in' people who insist that the newcomer tell everybody that funny story, wear that quaint dress, or sing that song we all know you people are famous for.

We can move through the party, participating as guests ourselves, overhearing snatches of the conversation, interacting, observing others interact. There are all sorts of dynamics going on, only some of which we can pick up on: ritualized greetings, introductions, recollections, story-telling, jokes, laughter, flirtations, hegemonic projects, persuasive arguments, schmoozing, wheeling and dealing, erotic encounters, casual interactions, serious discussions, small talk. There is an economy to the party, an economy of resources, a system of distribution, an economy of desire. People attend and participate in the party in a great variety of ways, with a lot of changing and varying agendas, which cannot be reduced to 'politics'; nor can the dynamics be reduced to antagonism. For example, could one think of enjoyment only in terms of antagonism? What would an antagonistic flirtation at a party look like? On the other hand, to play Laclau's advocate for a moment, one could imagine a hegemonic seduction. It might take the form of 'leading someone on.' Another hegemonic practice might appear as hogging the conversation, against which one could imagine someone objecting to the monopolization, and (counter-) hegemonically trying to change the topic, lead the conversation in a new direction.

While we are guests we are also theorists, interpreters of the symptoms of the party, bringing our interpretations back to the collective, our fellow guests. As interpreters of the symptoms of the party, reporting back to the collective, we rely upon, we trust, that the collective is interested, as we are, in looking out for the good of the party. We trust that there is a collective interest in keeping the party enjoyable. We rely on a collective understanding that the house of being shouldn't get trashed, and that guests who have come to the party in good faith and have made a commitment to contributing to the enjoyment should be welcome and allowed to feel at home, and not excluded from the conversation.

Conversation is the matrix of the common life of the party, the symptom of common enjoyment, and we rely on our shared interest in the conversation for the liveliness of the party, we trust that we share a common interest in keeping the party enjoyable. A political intervention then would take the form of leading the conversation so that it addressed some exclusion, corrected an imbalance that was souring it. This may require an interruption, an organized effort on the part of some guests to break the monopoly of the loud cliques. A hegemonic practice that loves the symptom would have to do this; to make a commitment and take a responsibility for deliberately changing the conversation for the good of the collective enjoyment. But this is not the only practice that loves the symptom. It is a no less sensitive and responsible practice, involving no less important a commitment, to do the small talk, make the introductions, and keep the thing light-hearted and friendly. The values that concern the party are not just power, but are rather the values of enjoyment. The economy of desire is not just desire for power, expressed in hegemonic practices, but desire in all its forms; desire for the desire of others, the desire for sociability.

PART TWO: POLITICS FOR AN ACCELERATED CULTURE

5

The Existentialist Ethics of the Canadian Party, Eh

During the winter of 1604–5, settlers on the Isle de Sainte-Croix endured terrible hardship. Thirty-five settlers died of scurvy, and others as a result of the bitter cold and a shortage of food and water. The following winter, matters had improved. The settlers moved to a new habitation, and to boost morale Samuel de Champlain established the 'Ordre de Bon Temps' (the Order of Good Cheer), the first social club in North America. A different member of the club was appointed 'chief steward' every fortnight or so, and was thus responsible for providing the feast and organizing entertainment for the other members. The chief of the Micmac regularly attended club gatherings. Each 'chief steward' sought to go one better than his predecessor, leading to quite extravagant affairs, considering the available resources and conditions. For example, Marc Lescarbot's play 'Le Theatre de Neptune en la Nouvelle France' was performed on several small boats by eleven settlers in November 1606 (Nader 1992, 2).

I have suggested that we can use the metaphor of the house party to explore the economy of desire in Canadian enjoyment. We can approach Canadian society as a sociable gathering going on, or happening, in language, the house of Being. I have also suggested that the living room of the house, the social space where enjoyment thrives, is a space created, cleared out, by ironic conceit, and that enjoyment consists of the multifarious and changing ways in which we play for the desire of the Other within that space. Furthermore, I have suggested that there is an assumption, normative/ethical in nature, which the guests at the party share, and that is that the party ought to be enjoyable. At the most elementary level, the ethical assumption is that the house of Being ought not to get trashed, lest the guests find themselves outside in the cold night of the real. Guests are required then to show that they want-to-be at the party. They must contribute to the life of the party by participating in the conversation of the party, by partying. They must show that they share with the others a commitment to sociability. And they must show this commitment to sociability in an idiom that is recognizable to the other guests: at a Canadian party, guests must demonstrate willingness to enjoy the endurance of lack of particularity by performances of tolerance and unpretentiousness. *Party on, Wayne. Party on, Others. Excellent!*

In what follows I want to develop and make explicit the ethical content of the problematic of national identity and national character. I want to draw out and develop the Lacanian ethical 'commandment,' to 'love thy symptom as thyself.' We want to know what the principles of a practice of loving the symptom might be, and whether or not they would constitute an adequate ethical framework for Canadians who want to be good. (And, perhaps, we are interested here, also, in at least the possibility of saying something about being good in a generalizable sense, by inquiring about what is good in a particular context.)

We are asking what someone ought to do if they want-to-be a good Canadian. How does 'loving the Canadian symptom' appear phenomenologically in the lifeworld? Can it be formulated in terms of a normative/ethical code by which Canadians live, or ought to live? For ethics is produced by and is subject to hegemonic articulation, so we are looking here at a discursive phenomenon existing in a field of contestation and antagonism. Ethics is something that some Canadians would wield hegemonically, demanding that some (Other) Canadians live by these standards.

I shall develop the Lacanian ethical commandment to 'love thy symptom' through Foucault's[66] work on the ethical practices of the care of the self and Heidegger's discussion of the ethics of *Dasein*, human-being-in-the-world.[67] In Foucault's archaeology of the technologies of the self, it appears that at some level the care of the self is closely tied to the care of the Other. To the ancient Greeks and Romans, for instance, to scrutinize the self and find the strangeness, that is, the lack, the otherness of self, and to face up to that otherness and come to terms with it, would be the precondition for living harmoniously with the Other.

According to Foucault, care/concern for the self/Other is not simply an attitude or an orientation, it is always a real activity; it means 'taking pains with oneself' (1988b, 5, 7). In Heidegger's view, 'care,' that is a 'solicitous being-with-the-Other,' is the basic ethic of *Dasein*. So a Heideggerian spin on Lacan's commandment might be 'Be careful of the Other (thy symptom) as thyself.' As we shall see, loving the symptom, being careful of the Other, and taking care of oneself, are formulated in a particular idiom in Canadian ethics. I shall explore the question of Canadian ethics by raising it in the only forum where it is sensible, Canadian *Dasein*, Canadian being, being Canadian at the Canadian house party. And the question that we will raise initially, to open some pathways towards the ground of Canadian ethics, is: What is it that is 'the life of the party'?

A Reading from the Book of Genesis

The Tower of Babel

1 And the earth was of one tongue, and of the same speech. 2 And when they removed from the East they found a plain in the land of Senaar, and dwelt in it. 3 And each one said to his neighbour: Come, let us make brick and bake them with fire. And they had brick instead of stones and slime instead of mortar. 4 And they said: come, let us build a city and a tower, the top whereof may reach to Heaven: and let us make our name famous before we are scattered abroad into all lands. 5 And the Lord came down to see the city and the tower which the children of Adam were building. 6 And He said: Behold, it is one people, and all have one tongue: and they have begun to do this, neither will they leave off from their designs, till they accomplish them in deed. 7 Come ye, therefore, let us go down and there confound their tongue, that they may not understand one another's speech. 8 And so the Lord scattered them from that place into all lands, and they ceased to build the city. 9 And therefore the name thereof was called Babel, because there the language of the whole earth was confounded: and from thence the Lord scattered them abroad upon the face of all countries.

Genesis 11:1–9

What is this all about and what does it have to do with Canada? It's about the impossibility of the phallic project. It shows how difference and confusion (the linguistic, polycultural babel) confounds efforts at transcendence, (completing the tower), *but the confusion is itself the very source from which the desire for transcendence springs.* It's about how the field of differences that is Canada, a field charged with antagonism and desire(s) for sociation, confounds the efforts to transcend the differences and constitute Canada, but how the failure to constitute Canada is the very thing that keeps the desire for Canada alive, and keeps us talking, conversing, wanting to transcend our differences despite the babel. It is this wanting-to-be, despite its impossibility, that actually constitutes Canada.

The people all spoke the same language. They desired the security of collective life, to dwell together on the plain, so they spoke with one another

and tried to build a place to live. 'Bricks' and 'mortar' represent the gram-
mar of the everyday language at their disposal, and, while they were all
skilled 'bricoleurs,'[68] their project was hampered by the problem of language: the slipperiness and context-dependent character of meaning. They
persevered, though, for they desired to make their name famous. 'Famous'?
That is, they felt that it was better to be recognized, familiar and reassuring
to one another, than to be scattered, estranged, and fearful. Through their
ability to communicate they formulated their desire, to build a 'city,' a
discursive structure, a community that would transcend their differences
and contain them all. And the city would be perfected by a tower, the top
whereof would reach to heaven. They would not only transcend the differences between themselves; in so doing they would transcend the difference
between heaven and earth, God and man, by virtue of their ability to signify
without ambiguity.

They desired to be equal to God, their common language and collective
organization enabled them to become so, they had begun already, and their
desire was such that they would not give up their designs until they had
accomplished them in deed. What would happen if the children of Adam
realized their desire and achieved transcendence? The game would be over.
So God confounded their language so that they would have problems
understanding one another and building the tower would be more difficult.
But not only that, they were scattered from their collective, off into all
lands, making differences between them that they would have to overcome
all over again.

The children of Adam sought to close the gap, to suture the social, to be
famous, fully recognizable coherent identities, Godlike subjects to one
another. And they had the means to do this, almost: language. Their motiva-
tion, the wellspring of their desire for transcendence, was the fear of being
'scattered': scattered to the real, to the 'many lands,' the field of the unknown, the abyss of infinite differences that is the face of the earth. And the
fear of the scattering is such that even though the task is monumental and
the mortar is viscous and slippery they will keep trying. But if they had
succeeded originally in reaching to heaven the story would have stopped
there. Hence the need for the babel. The confounded language and the
scattering means that desire is kept alive in the world.

What is the status of 'God' in this metaphor? Sartre provides one possible
answer.[69] 'God' is not an independent reality. 'God' is a name that conve-
niently designates the fulfilment that every human being seeks. The finite
existent desires to be God. God is an allusive/elusive ideal of unity. Because
of its allusive/elusive character, the unified ideal can accommodate an infi-

nite variety of particular imaginary articulations. This desire for unity cannot be fulfilled, for if the desire were fulfilled then the finite existent would cease to be, as it can only exist as wanting-to-be. 'God' designates the paradoxical character of desire for transcendence; that is, there is a direct coincidence of the cause of its frustration with the means to fulfil it. The fact of a plurality of existents frustrates the desire for transcendence; thus the Other is an obstacle to the fulfilment of existence, and simultaneously, as an interlocuter, as fellow bricoleur, the Other holds out the only promise to achieve fulfilment.

The 'life of the party' then is the Canadian babel, the collective desire to transcend difference, to achieve closure (unity) in spite of the confounding variety and polysemy. The unfinishable babel is the linguistic house of being in which the Canadian party is happening. And it is the unfinished, impossible character of the house and the fear of being scattered about the earth that is the basis of the collective desire to be, together. The enjoyment in the resolve to go on, in the face of the knowledge that to go on is impossible, futile, but that failure to go on would result in the even more unthinkable 'scattering,' is facilitated by ironic conceit, expressed in the friendliness to the possibility of going on in the ubiquitous Canadian idiom, 'eh.'

A Parable from the Modern Gospels

'The North is always in people's heads.'

Here and there, on some steep slope, the forest was gashed, and that was a symbol of Canada – the felled trees, the logs rolling into the water. We could see those orderly rafts, floating silently, like vast geometrical propositions, from the forest to the mills or to the harbours. The log rolls, the log piles of Canada, give to the inexhaustible savage landscape the first heartening signs of craftsmanship and the signs of civilization. One felt here the warning in rock and tree that one feels all over Canada when one turns north: do not go too far. In a step you will be in total solitude. And later, as you sit comfortably among the businessmen in a Vancouver club watching ships load wheat for China and Europe and timber from the Canadian forests, which supply nearly half our newsprint, your mind wanders off northward and you ask what people are doing two or three hundred miles away.

The answer is peculiar. To begin with, there are very few people. But there is an odd statistic claiming that Canadians make more phone-calls than any other people on earth. Up there then they are talking. Stay a few days in a forest cabin and you will remember only a few sounds; the scampering of chipmunks on the roof, and the day-long shrilling of the party-line. The Canadian is not a talkative man; but the shrilling bell attests that among the billions of trees, a human being exists, possibly alone.   *Reader's Digest*, 1965[70]

Canadians try to make their name famous in a rasping, hacking language that gashes the landscape, scratches vulgar marks on the wilderness, launches angular propositions to be pulverized and bleached. They sit in sober stuffed suits conversing in the coldly calculating register of dollars and cents. And the Canadian conversation is exclusively a man's conversation, at least this moment of it is. But for all its conceited triumphalism, its rapacious expanse and power, its business club comfort, the conversation is deeply troubled. The warning signs are everywhere that there is a vast 'outside' of it, symbolized here by 'the North,' by the 'billions of trees.' These hold the place in the Canadian imaginary of the Lacanian real, the infinite Otherness, a field of physical, psychic, and social differences that the hegemonic discourses attempting to constitute modern Canada have no mastery over. Canadians are scattered about the face of the earth, and the impoverished, inarticulate language(s) of modernization – domination of nature, rational instrumentality, economic calculability – are only 'first signs' of civilization.

What we might want to find in this 'language of the first signs of civilization,' then, are its desperations, fears, and anxieties. It's a language of loneliness, a language of solitudes, of alienation(s). The development of Canada has herded the children of Adam, shot them and starved them, forced itself upon them. It has dragged and enticed them from all over the globe and forced them to labour, fell timber, build railroads, till the land. It has thrown cultures, races, religions, and genders together, mixing the scattered elements in unprecedented combinations and quantities. It has brought the differences and inequalities, the innumerable discursive practices of the scattering – patriarchy, racism, nationalism, sectarianism – along also, preserving and rearticulating them in terms of its discourse, adding new stratifications: class scatterings according to their relations to the means of production, and a refining of already present lines of scattering through scientific classifications and legitimations.

But despite all of this, the modern Canadian subject in the *Reader's Digest* vignette reaches for the telephone. In spite of the dehumanizing scattering, in spite of the resulting aloneness in the vastness of the field of differences, in spite of, and because of, the being alone amongst the billions of Otherness, the Canadian reaches out for the party-line. The Canadian wants to transcend the difference and make some contact with the Other. Canadians are talking with one another. The presentness of the difference, the anxiety provoked by the aloneness in the face of the scattering, so starkly visible in modern Canada, is the source of the desire to transcend the difference and to come to terms with the Other, and together build a city in which we can all live enjoyably.

And what is it that we can say about this that is distinctly Canadian, what can we say that we could not say about, let's say, Australia, Brazil, the U.S., or Nigeria, about aloneness in the chaotic, buzzing billionness of Otherness of any modern society? The Canadian enjoys staying alone, enjoys enduring the scattering, while still venturing to speak with the Other. The Canadian reaches out for the party-line, participates in the conversation, but in a way that is mediated. Canadians are not verbose or effusive, Canadians converse politely. Canadians talk, but maintain a respectful, careful distance from one another. In the Canadian conversation there is a friendliness towards the space of openness between self and Other, a caring for the space, manifested in a quintessentially characteristic Canadian politeness.

It is not difficult to show that Canadian enjoyment is sustained in the mediated, distanced conversation. Arthur Kroker (1986) has shown that the Canadian contribution to the philosophical discourse of modernity has been a sustained reflection, by such writers as Grant and McLuhan, on the positive relationship between communications technology and social integration. Canadians are good with phones and spend a lot of time on them. Try calling one, if one isn't calling you. Canadians are world leaders in meeting and dating on the phone, and even having sex over the phone. But the distanced, mediated conversation, carried on via the phone or via politeness, might too easily be misinterpreted as coldness, aloofness, retentiveness, as a cultural hangover, inheritances from northern European WASPs. Or alternatively the mediation may be misinterpreted as a harbinger of a post-McLuhanesque dystopia, a spaced-out, cool, postmodern virtual-reality sensorium, where the interface with the machine replaces the face-to-face with the human.

A Sermon on the Apocalypse by 'the High Priest of Postmodernism'

Ecstasy is all functions abolished into one dimension, the dimension of communication. All events, all spaces, all memories are abolished in the sole dimension of information: this is obscene. Hot sexual obscenity is followed by cool communicational obscenity. The former implied a form of promiscuity, a clutter of objects accumulated in the private universe, or everything that remains unspoken or teeming in the silence of repression. However, this promiscuity is organic, visceral, carnal, while the promiscuity which reigns over the communications networks is one of superficial saturation, an endless harassment, an extermination of interstitial space ... so that what was once free by virtue of having been space is no longer so. The word is free but I am not. The space is so saturated, the presence of all which wants to be heard so strong that I am no longer capable of knowing what I want.

Baudrillard, 1988b, 24

According to Baudrillard, the individual lives in a terrific/ecstatic state of a forced extraversion of all interiority and a forced introjection of all exteriority. Hysteria and paranoia, the pathologies associated with the modern exacerbated staging and organization of the body, are superseded in postmodernity by schizophrenia, a state of terror due to the over-proximity of all things, 'a foul promiscuity of all things which beleaguer and penetrate.' This is the postmodern scattering: 'In spite of himself the schizophrenic is open to everything and lives in the most extreme confusion' (Baudrillard, 1988b, 26–7).

Postmodernity signifies perhaps an even wilder 'scattering' than ever before. For Foucault we are objectified and dispersed with an increasing systematics, rigour, and pervasiveness; then, with our subjectivity narrowed, limited, constrained, we are herded back again and put to work for utilitarian ends. Docile object bodies, we monitor ourselves and the other object bodies within a panoptical surveillant social order.[71] For Baudrillard, similarly, the re-collection, the implosion of the worlds of subject and object, is a continuation of the scattering, in so far as the stupefied masses do not, cannot, exist as a collective subject of active historical agency, or any longer as an object of manipulation (the object 'in itself' that wants to be, and fights to become, subject 'for itself'), but only as a 'black hole' that swallows up meaning.[72] The masses are no longer capable of collectively formulating their desire and of exercising historical agency, except only by the stupefied resistance of the 'great refusal.'

The Canadian in the cabin, amid the trees and the chipmunks, is jacked-in to the cyberspace virtual-reality shopping mall, grazing vacantly and being devoured himself in the information orgy. The wilderness (read: 'field of differences,' Otherness, Other Canadians) appears as simulacrum. The 'real world' of objects disappears. Nature reappears as Parks and Recreation centres, wilderness trips. Society becomes a vast 'theme park,' full of 'differences,' options of style more than matters of substance, multicultures to be encountered playfully. And certainly this form of life is apparent in pedestrian rainforest eco-tourism in Tofino, B.C., or in any July weekend in Muskoka, as the difference/distance between suburban Toronto and the cottage is filled in by McDonald's, Paramount Canada's Wonderland, and satellite TV.

The otherness of the Other is no longer really 'real,' not to be taken seriously. We interface with the Other world superficially, as an ecstatic, polyphonic sensorium of colour and sound on the street. We skim across it on a jet-ski, catch a glimpse of it in the rear-view mirror of the Asüna Sunrunner as we dash back to the city, searching desperately for the right music for the trip, to fill the space, because we have nothing to say to one another, because there is too much to talk about. 'There's some kind of constitutional referendum thing happening, it's everywhere. "Yes" or "No"? What's the difference? There's this about it, but on the other hand there's that! What can I say? What do I know? Only what they're telling me. It's all been said already. How can I decide? What do I care?! Gimme an "Ex" from the cooler, man, and shut up. I've had enough of this bullshit already!' The Canadian great refusal? Not. The <u>Canadian great refusal would be '... like,</u> <u>take off, eh.</u>' Even in the seemingly exasperated closure we can see the persistence of openness. It is an ironic expression of exasperation, one that awaits a rejoinder, not the speechlessness of the silent majorities, or the stony silence of indifference.

Baudrillard sketches a dystopian recollection of the scattering in the death/orgasm of the social, one possible future read from an already present, but one which – he says himself – is 'far from the living room and close to science fiction.'[73] The interstices haven't all been filled yet. The 'eh' tells us that (that they are still open). The 'eh' implies an anxiety (or antagonism) rather than an ecstasy of communication. The anxiety of the Canadian's 'eh' is provoked by the 'foul promiscuity,' the beleaguering of the subject by the dyschronous fragments of modernity. The schizophrenic world is one characterized by pastiche. Jameson argues that if postmodern pastiche is the cultural logic of late capitalism, then pastiche-making may also be the postmodern creative agency by which people regain historicity and produce meaning. Jameson envisages a project of 'undoing postmodernism by the methods of postmodernism: to work at dissolving the pastiche by using the instruments of pastiche itself to reconquer some genuine historical sense.'[74] 'Eh' announces, I think, that Canadians are actively engaged in such a project.

Postmodernism has brought us to the point at which we recognize the death of the subject, and consequently the impossibility of clarifying a stable, universal basis for intersubjective ethics. But I think that we can find traces of the possibility of ethics not grounded in transcendental, unified subjectivity, but rather in the wreckage of that subject, the split, incomplete, impossible subject who is condemned to work out its differences with the Other. This always incomplete, impossible working-out of differences is the open ground of intersubjective ethics, and the open ground where intersubjective ethics is practised in Canada is announced by 'eh,' which invites the Other to work things out.

Loving Canada, Caring for Canada

What is the openness that 'eh' cares for? How is 'eh' an ethical practice of loving the Canadian symptom? In what way can we formulate the ethical 'eh' collectively, as a caring politics that loves the Canadian symptom? We can develop these questions with Heidegger's help.

In *Being and Time* Heidegger argues that the moral practical dimension of being-in-the-world is 'caring' (1962, 225–30). *Dasein*, Being, is human-being-in-the-world, that is, necessarily, being-with-Others. *Dasein*, being-with-others, exists in many forms: being-for-another, being-along-side-another, being-against-another, etc. The *Dasein* of all these possible forms is that all Being is a being-with-the-*Dasein*-of-others as we encounter it within the world, and thus, says Heidegger, *Dasein* could be taken as 'solicitude.' *Dasein* signifies a relation with the Other that is anxious or careful. *Dasein* is a concerned, considerate, attentive orientation to the *Dasein* of the Other, careful of the Other, full of care for the Being of the Other, in the double sense of both giving care to the Being of the Other, and taking care of (in the sense of being wary of) the Being of the Other.

Dasein attentively maintains simultaneously a respectful distance from the Other's *Dasein*, and a friendly openness towards it, a concerned being-alongside it. The relationship with the Other 'is not one of grasping and pragmatic use, it is a relation of audition. We are trying "to listen to the voice of Being." It is, or it ought to be, a relationship of extreme responsibility, custodianship, answerability to and for.'[75] Note that for Heidegger, like Simmel, whom we have met above, the primary, constitutional relationship is considerably more complex than the word 'antagonism' conveys. 'Solicitude,' like Simmel's 'sociability,' strongly implies notions of friendliness, conviviality, and voluntary association with one another (Heidegger 1962, 182).

The crux of the matter of being-with-the-being-of-others is solicitude, that is 'caring' in the sense in which we have developed it. But we need to do some more work on caring. What do we mean by 'care' and 'caring,' this practice which, according to Heidegger, defines, or is essential to, *Dasein*?

More particularly, what is the particularity of Canadian *Dasein*, what does Canadian caring look like? It is those caring practices that are impregnated/informed/infused with an enjoyment of the endurance of lack of particularity, and values of tolerance and unpretentiousness; a being-in-the-world that is friendly towards these aspects of the Canadian conversation. Heidegger says that care means 'standing it.' That is, care is the practice of 'the Being of those beings who stand open for the openness of Being in which they stand, by standing it. This "standing it," this enduring, is experienced under the name of care' (Heidegger 1975, 271).

Care is 'standing it.' Care is akin to endurance/tolerance, but care qualifies endurance/tolerance significantly, for what does care say we endure/tolerate? Not simply the Other, or the bald fact of the existence of the Other, or the excesses of the Other's enjoyment, for that would amount to no more than a liberal stoicism. We must stand the excesses of the Other's being-in-the-world, put up with the noisy particularity of his or her annoying enjoyment. No. 'Care' as Heidegger conceives it is much more demanding. Care is 'the Being of those beings who stand open for the openness of Being in which they stand, by standing it.' At stake, in need of care, is the 'clearing,' the openness in the beings who stand open for the openness of Being. This is far from a spineless tolerance of all practices of being with the Other as equiventially deserving tolerance. This requires that we tolerate, endure, only those practices of being-in-the-world that stand open for the openness of Being, i.e., such practices as make living room for *Dasein*.

Care is a particular kind of 'standing it,' endurance/tolerance. Care is standing it, standing the openness (openness to the real) with the others who are standing it. It is a standing it in solidarity with the others who are standing it, thereby mutually maintaining it. To stand in solidarity with the others who are standing it is demanding, for it requires not simply empathy for the Other, but *identification* with the Other. Identification with the Other through the recognition of the Otherness of the self, i.e., mutual identification with the shared lack. Care is a very political practice, for if one cares, one stands with others mutually enduring the openness for Being, and mutually producing, clearing out, the living room of enjoyment.

Take, for example, recent events in Carmannah, B.C., or Temagami, Ontario, where urban environmentalists joined with Native groups to protest against the logging of old-growth forests. Protesters knew the many sides of the argument – that loggers' families need the work; that Native claims to millennia of tenure sometimes rest on spurious essentialisms; that suburban environmentalists have naïve and romantic illusions and nostalgic fantasies about both nature and Native culture; that the increasingly complex discourse on the environment is intimidatingly difficult to get a good handle on.

Whites and Natives, aware of the uncertainties and ironies underpinning their alliance, chose *nevertheless* to enter the dispute, to risk censure, estrangement, non- or misrecognition, prison. Why? To care for the environment by showing the antagonism underpinning Canadian modern practices of 'forest management.' What the protesters were committed to, aside from all the various, different, particular concerns that they brought to the roadblocks, was the disruption of the tranquillized obviousness, the indifference with which we accept as normal the social relations of commerce and nature, whites and Natives in Canada.

To care for is to withstand and endure our collective indifference to a modern Canadian history of the domination of nature and Natives. What is achieved by this enduring, this standing in solidarity at the roadblock, is a caring for Canada, an insistence that the question of Canada's future development, of our relations with nature and with Natives, be opened, questioned, changed.

A unique and peculiar Canadian idiomatic expression of the ethics of caring, possibly Canada's proudest contribution to the global moral heritage, is Greenpeace. The moral practical principle articulated and practised by Greenpeace is that 'individuals can influence the action of the most powerful by 'bearing witness,' that is by drawing attention to environmental abuse by their mere unwavering presence.'[76] 'Bearing witness' is standing, enduring the openness of the social by being an unwavering presence at a particular site of antagonism, insisting that we pay careful attention to social relations as they appear at that instance. The answer is not provided. The point is to insist upon the openness – to ask the question, by putting oneself at the epicentre of the atomic detonation, inserting oneself in the space between the harpoon and the whale, plugging the outfall pipe, interrupting the flow of the discourse of modernity by insisting that we look, and ask ourselves, 'What are we doing here?'

As the Greenpeace example reveals, a caring being-with-Others implies discrimination. Because being-with-(some)-Others is not just not-being-with-(some other)-Others, but *being against* those Others who are closed to the openness of Being in which they stand, whose being is not imbued with ironic conceit, and who therefore, by their closedness to the openness of Being would close it for others. But being-against some Others is not to say that one is somehow apart-from those Others, because while they may be closed to the openness of Being in which they stand, they nevertheless stand, as we do, in the openness of Being.

And so a careful politics of *Dasein* does not cut itself off from those Others whom we are against, those Others who are closed to the openness of Being in which they (and we) stand, but orientates in a caring way towards showing the openness of Being to the Others who are closed to it. Thus Greenpeace has developed in recent years to become more than a protest group. Increasingly, Greenpeace has entered into advisory relationships with both governments and industry around the world to engage in proactive dialogue in search of solutions and models of sustainable development. This emerging model of reflexive modernization brings with it new risks: risks of co-optation, the institutional containment and elimination of conflict in neo-corporatism.[77] Greenpeace now has to withstand and endure these forces and be careful of the space of radical democracy that it has opened up.

The politics of caring takes the form of engaging hegemonic and discursive practices that claim suture, that are hostile to openness. But caring politics would not engage them in terms of 'reverse' discourses (articulating a naturist ideology) 'counter-' or 'anti-' hegemony (the practices that get labelled 'eco-terrorism'), except as the initial move towards showing the contingency. There may then be a moment of (symbolic) violence involved in exposing the lack, a demanding of the discourse that it say what it really wants. A caring politics would insist on asking: 'What is it that you really want?'[78] What is the traumatic kernel that the discourse is a manifestation of desire to get away from?

Caring practices would aim to bring the lack in the discursive practice to light, not necessarily into a harsh, glaring light of real-ity, but in such a way that we get a glimpse of the lack, so that we are not subject to the desperation of the discursive practice, to its taking its claims to suture and mastery so seriously. Heidegger might say that a politics of caring is interested in 'tuning' closed discourses (that is, if you like, conceited discourses that claim to have successfully sutured the social) so that they correspond harmoniously with the openness of Being. Such a tuning might take the form of locating the point(s) of the discourse where the impossible effort of suturing is frustrating the desire of the discourse 'to be,' to become one with itself. The caring practice might then be to care for the desperation of the discourse that is faced with the terrible openness by standing the openness with it.

To move to a different register now, we may take for example the conceited discourses of xenophobic nationalism of either the Bloc Québécois or Reform variety. How might one engage these discourses in a solicitous – that is to say, caring – way? Is it impossible to be friendly towards these discourses? One would proceed by inquiring what is troubling these discourses, where are their points of desperation, anxiety, the points at which the suture is slipping, the points at which 'identification,' the stitching of the identity into the social fabric, fails. In terms of the closed discourses above, the troublesome figures are Homi Bhabha's 'hybrids,' Donna Haraway's 'cyborgs,' and Simmel's 'strangers.' Namely, the Vietnamese Quebecker, the Sikh Mountie, the ethnic who doesn't 'assimilate,' the visible Canadian, the Western francophone, and one would support their standing in the openness of Being by standing it with them.

How would one practise a caring politics by standing open to the openness of Being with the Other who stands in the openness of Being? Clearly, this is not a straightforward task, either to conceptualize or to practise! But it is only by such a tuning of the openness of beings to the openness of Being in which they stand that Laclau and Mouffe's radical democratic hegemonic politics is possible. For articulating links in a chain of democratic equivalences requires that the links are open at some point. If not, one would have to conceive of identities in terms of their requiring to be 'cut,' or 'broken' into, done some form of violence and then 'forged' or 'welded' together again. And here we may be in some danger of straying from democracy and towards some form of totalitarianism. So a caring politics would have to be committed to helping to find the openness in itself and in the Other, for it is in one another's openness that they can recognize their commonality and consent to work together. And furthermore it is in the openness which they recognize as their commonality that they recognize the openness of Being in which they stand, and can commit themselves to protecting the empty place of power as a requisite condition of the form of social organization complimentary to openness of Being, namely, radical democracy.

Care then is committed. It doesn't just let anything go. It is interventionist and proactive. It takes on the discursive practices that are inimical to openness, that have forgotten the melody and are discordant with the harmony of Being. Care is relentless in the pursuit of commitment to tuning to the harmony of Being. (Though, even if it is neglected, there is no real danger of closure, for the Other who has been shut out, closed out of the openness of Being by the closedness to the openness of Being of hegemonic others, will fight against that closure. So care depends upon the conceit of its necessity, while, ironically, openness would likely get on quite well without it: the repressed returns, the real returns to its place, the abyss starts to stare back.) Openness would still characterize politics if *laissez-faire* or arrogant selfishness were all that was practised.

By virtue of ironic conceit, care enters politically as good-hearted, friendly towards the thing in need of care. But the thing (the openness, lack) cannot be cared for, because the real thing would be far too terrifying and blinding to approach. We can only approach it through its symptoms. We can, for example, care for Being when it reveals itself in death, not by caring for 'death' per se, but only by those practices of commitment and intervention by which we take care of the symptoms of the dying human being, standing open to the openness of Being in which their being stands (now falters, on the threshold of non-being) by standing it with them. We can care for Being when it appears in the nation, not by caring for the nation per se (for where is it, where 'is' the nation?), but only by practices of commitment and intervention by which we take care of the symptoms of the nation (that is, the symptoms of the lack of the nation), those ways in which we perceive the horizon of openness where the potentiality of the Being of the nation is. And we take care of the symptom by standing the openness in solidarity with those others who are opening it by standing it: standing it in solidarity with the stranger, the cyborg, and the hybrid.

I think that we can locate in the 'eh' of the Canadian conversation a strong ethical commitment, a utopian moment that reaches out to the Other, openly and invitationally, an explicit acknowledgment of how Canada is unlimited, unfinished, and a commitment to keeping it unlimited. Now the 'unlimited,' the lack of limits – that is to say, for it amounts to the same thing, the lack of particularity (thus Canadians can enjoy the endurance of lack of particularity only by ensuring that Canada remains unlimited) – is reaffirmed by the idiomatic suffix 'eh.' The Canadian 'eh' is the key to understanding Canadian ethics. 'Eh' is the Canadian idiomatic way of designating *aporia*, the moment of discourse when interlocutors reach a gap, a doubt about what to do or say. *Aporia* is a state of 'being-at-a-loss,' as it were. It announces incompletion, and invites – requests – a helping hand, an answer, a continuation of the conversation.[79]

Why do I attach so much significance to this idiomatic suffix 'eh'? Because 'eh' is the return of the repressed in Canadian idiom. I think that in it one can locate a trace of desire for collective identity that persists against all the odds, as it were. Freud (1961, 78) says that civilization is possible only by virtue of the repression and containment of the drives of the id. But when we reexamine the genealogy of the modern subject with Foucault, it is clear that the 'good' drives and impulses, desires for community, for sociability, for living enjoyably with the Other, are also, and perhaps even more so, distorted and repressed in the subjectivization process. Perhaps one might even venture the hypothesis that the hostility towards the Other, the use of the Other as an object of gratification, derives not from essential drives, but is the historical result of the subjectivization process. Or rather, as we have seen in the case of Babel, the conditions of the impossibility of collective identity – all the forces that keep people apart – are the source from which this desire springs.

Foucault's analysis of subjectivization shows that the form that the care of the self takes is arbitrary, historically contingent, *contra* Freud, who says that it's got to be like this (the repressive hypothesis). Foucault shows us a field of 'what-might-have-been,' the promise of the possibility of an ethics of intersubjectivity grounded in care of the self. The 'eh' then is a return of the real as *aporia*, as a 'field of possibility' – the desire to work out the ethical practice of liberty, a desire for an openness in which this working out can take place. 'Eh' is the slip that signifies the return of something that is precisely the inverse of a 'drive' that would immediately realize itself; it is the return of the repressed real and consequently of the desire – a Canadian idiomatic expression of desire for identification with the Other as the only means to cope with the real.

I came to Canada between two 'No' campaigns. Shortly before I arrived, Unionists in Northern Ireland protesting continuing Anglo-Irish talks on the political future of Northern Ireland organized under the slogan 'Ulster says No.' Soon after I arrived, Canadians protesting the Free Trade Agreement with the U.S. spread their message on bumper-stickers, the American flag with a red maple leaf star, and the words 'No, eh.' These two 'No's' are very different symptoms of national identity. The people of Ulster (the majority of them, or at least some of them, speaking for the rest of the majority!) claimed to speak in unison, unequivocally, and to say with an absolute surety of closure, 'Ulster says No.'

Nobody in particular is identified in the Canadian case. There is no speaking Canadian subject, no 'Canada' equivalent to an 'Ulster' who is saying 'No.' And the Ulster 'No' is a final no. 'Ulster says No,' and that's that, period. You either say 'No' with us and confirm your commitment to us as an 'Ulsterman' (and Ulster women are 'Ulstermen,' naturally!) or you are an enemy to us, an Other opposed to us. The Canadian 'No' is of a very different character. Spoken with a Canadian accent, 'No, eh' becomes 'No way,' a fine example of the *double entendre* of ironic conceit. The statement is simultaneously a strong assertive nationalistic 'No way,' but simultaneously it's a 'No, eh'; a sort of 'No, but-that's-not-necessarily-the-last-word-on-the-issue,' kind of no.

'Eh' recognizes the unfinishable character of the conversation, and its reaction to the recognition of the openness, the unlimitedness, is not fear and loathing. On the contrary 'eh' is in a strong sense friendly towards the lack. It recognizes the lack, the impossibility of finishing, of having the last word, but rather than being intimidated or dumbfounded by this, it speaks anyway, ventures something at least, acknowledges its partiality, and invites Others to join in. 'Eh' sees the lack, then, not as an impossible obstacle, but as an unlimited opportunity, a promise of possibility that it can keep alive only while Others want to avail themselves of the opportunity also. 'Eh' invites anOther contribution because it cares that the openness be kept open. 'Eh' loves the symptom in so far as it is careful of the Other, committed to keeping the horizon open by saying 'eh' and inviting Others to join in the pastiche party.

6

Ars erotica, Ars theoretica, Ars politica.[80]

On the evening on which I first arrived in Canada in September 1988, I made a bit of a *faux pas*. I had taken the bus from Pearson airport to downtown Toronto, where I had made arrangements to stay temporarily with a friend of a friend. She was a student at the Ontario College of Art and shared a house with four other students in the Annex. They were having a party, not on my behalf, just a regular weekend party, twenty or thirty people, and a few two-fours of beer. I ditched my backpack upstairs, joined the scene, and was introduced around as 'a guy who's just off the plane from Ireland.' Small talk over a couple of Labatt's: 'Who do you know?' 'What are you doing here?' 'How long are you staying?' And, of course, 'So what do you think of Canada, eh?' To which I replied, naïvely, 'Well, how do I know that I'm not in the United States?'

It was, I felt at the time, a reasonable and innocuous question. I knew next to nothing about Canada, only some impressions I had picked up from the television show 'The Beachcombers' of lots of water and forests. I expected 'Mounties' and 'Indians.' I wondered whether my pathetic French would be of any use to me when I got there. But all I had seen on the bus ride were signs that spelled 'America': Buicks and Chevys and Mack trucks, a sprawling, ultra-new city, strip malls and skyscrapers, signs for Coors and Miller, and the guy who had asked me was called 'Greg,' or something, was six foot, blond and blue-eyed, and was wearing one of those jackets with leather sleeves and the logo of some university in cloth lettering on the back. I had never been to America either, but these were all signs of 'America' familiar to me from twenty-five years of TV in Ireland.

The conversation became a bit heated, in a polite kind of way, as I was advised in no uncertain terms that Canada was, make no mistake, a very different place altogether from the U.S. 'It's, well, it's cleaner, for one thing.'

'We're not loud and obnoxious like they are, for another.' 'Canada is like the U.S., run by the Swiss.' 'We don't have anything like their crime or race problems,' and so on. I wasn't fully persuaded then, but I have become convinced as time has passed, that yes, indeed, Canada and the U.S. are very different places altogether. The signs that seem to signify an absence of differentiation in massified postmodern North American culture must be read in the local dialect; there is an idiom that makes all the difference. But for the moment I want to concern myself with some aspects of the problem of 'blending' – and for the moment I don't want to pose this in the usual nationalist rhetoric of the absorption of Canada into the imperialist U.S. (it's just too bloody obvious!), but in the less loaded terms of a fading of differentiation, a loss of distinction between two cultures, that Canadians play a willing and active role in. (A bumper sticker has recently appeared that reads: 'My Canada includes Florida.') But where the lack of differentiation reemerged for me recently was with respect to making sense of the so-called Seattle sound, the 'grunge rock' thing, competing with rap as the predominant sound on North American airwaves over the last few years; suburban garage bands – Nirvana, Pearl Jam, Nine Inch Nails, Faith No More, etc.

The grunge aesthetic is about primal life being reborn in an exhausted, dead postmodernity. 'Grunge' is both the filthy polluted wasteland left over after the orgy of modernity, and the primeval muck from which new life emerges. The 'way cool' grunge look is waiflike, worn out, and recycled: scuffed workboots, blue jeans with no knees, a baggy plaid lumberjack shirt, a heavy wool sweater with serious holes, no jewellery, unstyled hair. The sound is heavy, dense, frenetic, hardcore punk meets heavy metal, morose, angry, and wildly energetic, and the lyrics express the existential angst of a generation coming of age in the anomic and nihilistic culture of contemporary North America. Grunge rock is an aesthetic expression of the edge of the suburban sublime. Grunge rock is a moment of a more general cultural phenomenon, expressed also in movies such as *My Own Private Idaho*, *Singles*, *Dazed and Confused*, and *Slackers*, but which has been brought into focus most clearly in *Generation X: Tales for an Accelerated Culture*, a novel by Douglas Coupland from British Columbia.[81]

I think that the trauma which is the motive force of grunge rock and the Gen.X subculture is the 'blending.' The lack of differentiation in massified postmodernity, which renders suburban life more or less indistinct from Scarborough to Seattle, deprives us of historicity (Jameson)[82] and leaves us with no particular tradition, no special way by which the world is given to us and meaningful action made possible (Mouffe).[83] Baudrillard offers the most extravagant formulation of this traumatic exhaustion: the death of the social, the implosion of the realms of subject and object, the end of the dialectical play between self and Other, replaced by a suspension in the ecstasy of communication.[84] In what follows I will explore Baudrillard's thesis, and suggest that the dialectic is not exhausted, that enjoyment is still grounded in working things out with Others, but that what postmodernism has taught us is that there is no sutured unity that grounds the social/political relationship. Postmodernism requires that we rethink the social relation with the Other, and refashion it more appropriately ambiguously. I will suggest that whereas we used to think of utopian intersubjectivity in terms of a metaphor of sexual union, we might now begin to rethink relations with others in terms of friendship.

In *Generation X: Tales for an Accelerated Culture*, Coupland explores the experience of postmodernity. Coupland's novel is a *bricolage* of anagrams and observations on contemporary culture, linked by a loose narrative concerning three friends. Andy, the central protagonist, does the introductions: 'Dag is from Toronto, Canada (dual citizenship), Claire is from Los Angeles, California. And I, for that matter, am from Portland, Oregon, but where you're from feels sort of irrelevant these days (since everyone has the same stores in their mini-malls ...).' 'Gen.X's,' even Canadian 'Gen.X's,' are from Baudrillard's America.[85] Difference is exhausted; borders and particularities have become sort of irrelevant, personal and political identities have become blurred, massified, and meaningless, and for that very reason (the scarcity of meaning) identities have become the sites of intense anxiety and antagonism. Coupland's heroes (heroic in the context of the odds stacked against meaningful action in postmodernity) are, in Baudrillard's terms, beleaguered with the obscenity of late capitalist culture, so they move to the sublime space of the desert to take stock of their situation. There, 'in search of the drastic changes that will lend meaning to their lives, they've mired themselves in the detritus of American cultural memory.'[86]

Refugees from history, the three develop an ascetic regime of story telling, boozing, and working McJobs ... They create modern fables of love and death among the cosmetic surgery parlors and cocktail bars of Palm Springs, disturbingly funny tales of nuclear waste, historical overdosing, and mall culture. A dark snapshot of the trio's highly fortressed inner world quickly emerges – landscapes peppered with dead TV shows, 'Elvis moments,' and semi-disposable Swedish furniture. And from

these landscapes deeper portraits emerge, those of fanatically independent individuals, pathologically ambivalent about the future and brimming with unsatisfied
longings for permanence, for love and for their own home ...

Coupland's book is intriguing and captivating for many reasons, not least
for its deliberate blending of Canada with the U.S. Andy, Claire, and Dag
are, in Jameson's terms, 'knee deep in the fragments of history,' and they
cope with this, regain some kind of coherent sense of history, by pastiche-
making (see Jameson 1988, 17–18). *Generation X* is a biting critique of
postmodernism/late capitalism, achieved by this Jamesonian practice. But
Coupland not only explores the recovery of historicity in pastiche, he also
shows the necessary limits to recovering historical coherence; the recovery
also of vanishing points in the imaginary, doorways to the real, as it were,
through which desire pursues utopian fantasy. The reinvention of vanishing
points, empty voids that seduce desire, little bits of the real that elicit the
production of utopian fantasy, is a profoundly radical move in the context
of an exhausted, fully transparent postmodernity, where there is 'nowhere
left to go,' as Hebdige says, 'but to the shops' (1989, 169).
    In order to get a sense of where Coupland suggests one might go instead
of to the shops, of alternative spaces in a seemingly exhausted postmodernity,
let's join Andy, Claire, and Dag at one of their favourite story-telling
locations, at the intersection of Cottonwood and Sapphire avenues in a
ghost town at the edge of the desert. The place is a 1950s 'new town'
development that flopped. Most North Americans (maybe especially Canadians) know of a place just like this, a ghost town in the middle of nowhere,
built on modern dreams of prosperity and happiness, near an emptied
mineral deposit perhaps, adjacent to a once-thriving industry, now fallen by
the wayside of recession or bypassed by technological development; towns
with optimistic and ironic names like Star City, Saskatchewan, and Ura-
nium City, Ontario, or Love Canal, New York, and with empty streets
called 'Progress Row' and 'Prosperity Boulevard.' Andy, Claire, and Dag
experience the location as a blank space at the end of a chapter, as an
exhausted space at the end of modernity, but simultaneously a space waiting
for a new narrative to be produced in.
    Claire tells the story of Buck the astronaut who lands in Texlahoma in the
suburban backyard of the Monroe family. He is trapped by Texlahoma's
gravity and cannot leave. Mrs Monroe invites Buck in and feeds him mush-
room soup, meatballs, and corn niblets, and they watch game shows on the
TV. Unfortunately, Buck develops space poisoning, and begins to turn into
a green-skinned Frankenstein monster. Mrs Monroe puts him to bed in the

basement rec-room. Her teenage daughters, Arleen, Darleen, and Serena, take turns taking care of Buck. Love blossoms, first with Arleen. Buck tells Arleen that the energy given off by a woman in love would boost his rocket sufficiently for them to take off. The drawback is that Arleen would die during take-off, but he could revive her shortly afterwards. Arleen says no, she won't go. Subsequently love blooms again, this time with Darleen, but she doesn't like the sound of having to die for a while either, and even though she loves Buck she cannot or will not go with him. Eventually Serena and Buck fall in love, and she will take the risk. They get into the rocket and, sure enough, lift off, and Serena fades out as they leave Texlahoma behind. Arleen and Darleen are sitting on swings in the backyard, watching the rocket disappear into space,

staring at the point where the jet's trail became nothing, listening to the creak of chains and the prairie wind. 'You realize,' said Arleen, 'that whole business of Buck being able to bring us back to life was total horseshit.' 'Oh, I knew that,' said Darleen, 'but it doesn't change the fact that I feel jealous.'   Coupland 1991, 45

To break the gravitational pull of the everydayness of Texlahoma requires desire. Buck is the stranger/monster/Other who can seduce that desire by his difference, offering a way out. Getting out means some sort of *petit-mort*, a short-term death of the social, a suspension of the weight of the symbolic order, and the promise of resuscitation, but will the symbolic order be reconstituted, can we risk the nothingness for the promise of something unknown? Arleen and Darleen can't, but even though they stay behind and reassure one another that there is no alternative, no possible life other than this one, no existence outside of the symbolic order as currently constituted, they are still piqued with jealousy and curiosity. Even though for them the social appears closed, sutured, it is opened. And what of Serena? Is there another form of life imaginable? What lies beyond the horizon of contemporary Texlahoma? Is the risk of taking off into the unknown worth it? Answers are invited, desire and fantasy are seduced by the window opened by the act of disappearance, the suspension of the symbolic order at the moment of the *petit-mort* structured in the narrative.

Andy tells the second story. It's about Edward, an intellectual, who lives alone in a grand oak-panelled room, lined with books, deliberately isolated from the outside world. Edward lives a dignified life at first, but gradually things begin to slip. He eats poorly, drinks too much, his pet dog soils the floor and becomes vicious, bugs and vermin crowd out from behind his books and crawl all over. Eventually Edward flees the room he had built for himself and where he has isolated himself for ten years, and finds that the rest of the world has been building something else:

a shimmering, endless New York, shaped of lipsticks, artillery shells, wedding cakes and folded shirt cardboards; a city built of iron, papier mâché and playing cards; an ugly/lovely world surfaced with carbon and icicles and bougainvillea vines. Its boulevards were patternless, helter-skelter and cuckoo. Everywhere there were booby traps of mousetraps, Triffids, and black holes. And yet in spite of this city's transfixing madness, Edward noticed that its multitude of citizens moved about with ease, unconcerned that around any corner there might lurk a clown-tossed marshmallow cream pie, a Brigada Rosa kneecapping, or a kiss from the lovely film star Sophia Loren. And directions were impossible. But when he asked an inhabitant where he could buy a map, the inhabitant looked at Edward as though he were mad.   Coupland 1991, 51

Edward gradually gets used to the place, and decides to rebuild his room in the middle of the crazy city, but it will be a very different kind of room. Edward was a modern intellectual, who held the chaos of the world at bay by the power of metanarrative – the books which lined his room, keeping noise and chaos outside – but his system of order broke down, it became decrepit and corrupt, and the bugs gnawed through the paper and scurried between the volumes. What can he do now? He vows to build a tower, but not a modernist phallocentric tower of Babel that seeks transcendence. His tower doesn't reach to heaven, but it would try to serve as a beacon to voyagers to the city. Edward would have a lounge at the top and serve cocktails, he would play jazz on a piano layered with zinc sheeting, and there would be a little booth that sold (among other things) maps. What Coupland is endorsing here and inviting us to imagine is the kind of map-making endeavour that Fredric Jameson recommends: 'a cognitive map which enables a situational representation on the part of the individual subject to that vaster and properly unrepresentable totality which is the ensemble of society's structures as a whole' (1991, 51).

Dag tells the third story. It's about 'mental ground zero,' the location where one visualizes oneself during the dropping of the atomic bomb, frequently a shopping mall. Dag says, Imagine that you're in the line-up at a supermarket. While driving there you got into an argument with your best friend. You'd been mouthing off, bleak tales about the state of the environment. Your friend got pissed off with your being so negative, you had a major argument that went nowhere. Anyway, you're in the line-up, your best friend outside in the car, both still pissed off about the argument.

There's a power surge, then failure. Through the window you can see vapour trails up into the sky, missiles from a base nearby. Then sirens, confusion, as it begins to dawn on people that a nuclear strike is imminent. Your best friend joins you at the line-up. And then ...

just before the front windows become a crinkled liquefied imploding sheet – the surface of a swimming pool during a high dive, as seen from below – And just before you're pelleted by a hail of gum and magazines – And just before the fat man is lifted off his feet, hung in suspended animation and bursts into flames while the liquefied ceiling lifts and drips upward – Just before all of this, your best friend cranes his neck, lurches over to where you lie, and kisses you on the mouth, after which he says to you, 'There. I've always wanted to do that.' And that's that. In the silent rush of hot wind, like the opening of a trillion oven doors that you've been imagining since you were six, it's all over: kind of scary, kind of sexy, and tainted by regret.   Coupland 1991, 64

Ground zero, the end of everything, becomes simultaneously the beginning of everything, the opening of doors to the unknown and unexpected, represented here by the homoerotic universe inherent in the ambiguity of friendship.

And here, in the ambiguity of the friendship relation, is another aspect of Coupland's work that is promising. In elaborating the relationship between his protagonists, Coupland explores the bond of social/political solidarity that sustains and develops their radical project to live meaningfully for one another amid the debris and open windows to the real. Andy, Claire, and Dag are representative subjects of the postmodern scattering. bell hooks (1991) might characterize them as 'yearning'; to come home, to live meaningfully and enjoyably together. On what basis can they (and the rest of us) come home, what grounds their developing solidarity?

Coupland suggests that it is a relationship of 'friendship.' Andy, Claire, and Dag are 'friends,' 'just good friends.' They enjoy a relationship of intimacy, but they are not lovers. They live closely with one another, share secrets, but respect one another's privacy. Their relationship is one that approximates Heideggerian 'solicitude.' They are careful of one another, in the double sense of both giving care to one another's Being, and taking care of (in the sense of being wary of) one another's Being. They are solicitous of one another's 'space.' But while they are not lovers, their relationship is enlivened with sexual possibility. There is a flirtatiousness in their playing for one another's desire.

Andy, Claire, and Dag live in what Baudrillard calls the 'post-orgy world'

(1988a, 45). Spent and over-stimulated to the point of exhaustion and boredom, they are refugees from 'the orgy of sex, political violence, the Viet-
Nam war, the Woodstock Crusade, and the ethnic and anti-capitalist struggles
too, together with the passion for money, the passion for success, hard
technologies, etc., – in short the whole orgy of modernity.' But the orgy is
over, Baudrillard says; we've done all of that. And this marks a new development in the field of sexuality. For now 'it is not sex one is looking for but
one's "gender" ... People no longer oscillate between desire and its fulfill-
ment, but between their genetic formula and their sexual identity (to be
discovered)' (Baudrillard 1988a, 46).

We should be clear what Baudrillard is talking about here as 'a development in the field of sexuality.' For Baudrillard, politics and Eros are interre-
lated and contingent discursive formations charged with a libidinal economy
of fear and desire stemming from the existential lack: fear of nothingness,
desire for unity/order. This economy of desire is expressed simultaneously
and recursively both sexually and politically: want-to-be loved and desired
by the Other, and want-to-be equal to the Other, free from the Other,
sovereign over the Other. Antagonism around identity heralds a cultural
development that is simultaneously erotic and political: Eros is politicized
and politics is eroticized in a new configuration. What is this new configuration? Baudrillard says that in postmodernity the signs of difference are
tending towards zero, and with the loss of difference – the implosion of the
worlds of subject and object, the closure of the interstices – seduction/desire
becomes exhausted as an intersubjective and political dynamic. With no
Other to seduce desire, desire now plays with itself; that is, increasingly,
desire is played out in a desperate search/production of 'identity' to sur-
round its lack.

It seems to me that if one considers left and radical democratic politics
during the recent past, one can readily discern some of the changing politi-
cal/erotic discursive formations that Baudrillard is alluding to. The political/
erotic configuration emerging in the 1960s 'New Left' was a promiscuous
politics of communion with the Other. The new left imaginary was animated by a metaphor of sexual union. New left meant free love: political
promiscuity, marriages, swinging, and cross-fertilization, Marxists with feminists with blacks with gays with 'Third Worldists' with greens and peaceniks;
a political vision most clearly expressed perhaps in the slogan 'Make love,
not war.'

The utopian horizon was that of the liberation of desire, lifting repression, permitting the coming-into-being, the realization of the authenticity
of the human being of women (negated by patriarchy), of blacks (negated

by racism), of workers (negated by capitalism), of gays and lesbians (negated by heterosexism), of the human family (negated by imperialism and the nuclear threat), an ecstatic 'coming together,' a climactic revolution, a releasing of the previously alienated and repressed. But as many have noted, the enjoyment which the encounter promised was marred by Marxist phallocentrism. Foucault, for example, formulates the conjuncture as follows: 'what exactly was taking place? An amalgam of revolutionary and antirepressive politics? A war fought on two fronts: against social exploitation and psychic repression? A surge of libido modulated by the class struggle? Perhaps. At any rate it is this familiar, dualistic interpretation that has laid claim to the events of those years' (Deleuze and Guattari 1983, xi–xii).

The utopian vision in this political/erotic configuration is currently in deep crisis. This is most emphatically confirmed, as Žižek (1996) shows, by events in Eastern Europe, where the liberation of desire, the lifting of systems of repression and the breaking out of enjoyment, emerges not as the forms of a new community of lovers but as forms of xenophobia and neofascism.

Foucault had already noted, with reference to the sexual revolution and gay politics, that the aspiration towards liberated desire does not automatically produce ethics. Rather it only poses more urgently than ever the ethical question of the 'good life,' demanding, as Foucault says, an ongoing deliberate practising of liberty. Foucault sees in the proliferation of new social antagonisms 'a movement toward political struggles that no longer conformed to the model that Marxist tradition had prescribed. Toward an experience and a technology of desire that were no longer Freudian ... the combat had shifted and spread into new zones' (1988b, 4, 5). It is in these new zones that Laclau and Mouffe hope to articulate their project of radical and plural democracy.

The difficulty facing a project of radical democracy, outlined by Laclau and Mouffe for example, is one of bringing together a passionate community in the context of AIDS and a new regime of safe sex. Radical democracy requires a passionate and open-minded coupling of subjects, a skilled and creative recursive intermingling, an immodest but respectful exploration of the social body, a usurping of the forbidden and taboo, a celebration of miscegenations. Hegemonic politics implies a cultivation and harnessing of desire, a tall order in a culture of monogamous safe-sex politics. The political/erotic discursive configuration that is fading and exhausted is one of sexual union. The configuration that has emerged in the postmodern scene is more celibate and careful. Hegemony now has to take the form of a kind of courtship. Others need romancing, they/we need to take one another out to dinner. A radical democratic hegemonic articulator needs to think about dressing to please the Other, developing a charming and suggestive conversation.

Contemporary politics, such as Butler's 'strategic essentialism,'[87] and Haraway's 'affinity with cyborgs' (Haraway 1991), begin to imagine at least these courtship practices. Laclau and Mouffe's 'equivalence' formulates the ideal relationship: not simply an alliance between parties, but 'a relationship which modifies the very identity of the parties engaging in that alliance,' and they formulate the riskiness of the dating game: 'total equivalence never exists; every equivalence is penetrated by a constitutive precariousness ... the precariousness of every equivalence demands that it be complimented/limited by the logic of autonomy' (Laclau and Mouffe 1985, 183–4).

Baudrillard's hypothesis is that seduction of the Other no longer characterizes the political relationship, and desire now becomes self-centred. It seems indeed that the postmodern erotic/political discursive configuration gives expression to the 'solitary vices': virtual sex and virtual politics in the sterile world of cyberspace; tattooing, piercing, and bodily mutilation; identity obsessions, ethnic cleansings. Or, another variation, excess appears as puritanism, a zealous and self-righteous political correctness.

In the context of this culture of excessive solitude, the question is how it is possible for a passionate collective to pursue radical democracy. After the orgy is over, we are left looking at one another, a little flushed, a little shamefacedly perhaps. The risky relationship is the conduct of the agreement to 'be (just) good friends,' the political relationship that emerges in the postmodern morning, the political relationship that restrains itself, that orients to the Other in a spirit of self-limitation, politics that commits to a friendship with the Other without the explicit expectation of sexual union (but which would nevertheless keep an open mind on the matter).

Radical democracy, I want to argue, might find its new enjoyment in friendship, in the riskiness of the friendship relation animated with enough sexual tension to keep the parties interested in one another. The enjoyment of radical democracy is contingent on commitment to the openness and caring that friendship demands, in the solicitude that the risk of friendship implies.

What is in friendship that would sustain a radical and plural democracy? In *Lysis*, Plato's dialogue on friendship, the dialogue concludes in *aporia*. Socrates concedes that 'neither the loved ones, nor those who are loved, nor those who are like, nor those who are unlike, nor those who are good, nor those who are akin ... if nothing among these is a friend, I no longer know what to say' (paragraph 222e). What is brought to light during the course of the dialogue with Socrates is that friendship is dynamic and unstable, but what gives friendship its particularity is that it is characterized by a commitment to transcend the instability for the parties' mutual benefit. Friendship is grounded in the lack, the uncertainty, the need for Other, and thus friendship, being grounded in our feeling of lack or imperfection, is closely akin to erotic love in that it is characterized also by openness, vulnerability, trust – the absence of fear of power.

Friendship desires the good; friendship desires to be free of lack, want, need: the imperfections in which desire – desire for friendship – is grounded. Friendship desires to transcend desire. Thus friendship is endangered by desire. Friendship free of desire and lack is an impossible ideal. So friendship remains an unstable, dynamic relationship between oppositional Others, who, recognizing their lack, attune to the Other concernedly in order to transcend the destructive force of desire, while keeping desire alive all the while.

Friendship implies the recognition of One by Other as equal in his or her humanity. To do so the parties must transcend their oppositional social roles as master and slave. They must escape the trap of the antagonism of their dialectical relationship to one another. The aim of friendship seems to be the establishment of a state of equality, of give and take, an equality of openness and power, a process of dynamic readjustment that aims to transcend games of power and replace them with concernedness and solicitude, whereby oppositional Others come to attune to one another in terms of mutual and shared responsibility for self and Other.[88]

Underpinning the heightened existential anxiety of generation X and all of us who are suspended in the ecstasy of communication is the troubled relationship with the Other, a relationship of antagonism, of irreconcilable ambivalence, charged with fear/desire, love/hate, which we must try to transcend as best we can by solicitude and audition. But

The drama of the interpersonal is played out, so to speak, in the tension of relation and distance. Sometimes the Other slips into the distance, the genuine relation is lost or fails to be actualized, and the 'I-it' supervenes. But even when the relation is established some distance must remain. People are too ready to think of the interpersonal relation in terms of union. But a true relation preserves the Other in his otherness, in his uniqueness, it leaves him room to be himself, so to speak.

Macquarrie 1978, 110

It is in these terms that we need to rethink multiculturalism in Canada. How do we articulate the principles of friendship as the basis for a principled relation with Others?

PART THREE: AN EROTIC POIESIS OF
CANADIAN FRIENDSHIP

7

Eroticizing the Wilderness

According to Bataille, 'poetry leads to the same place as all forms of erotism – to the blending and fusion of separate objects, ... the sun matched with the sea' (1986, 25). This matching of sun and sea appears in Canadian culture as the synthetic moment of friendship in an erotic quest for a continuity of being with the Other. We can trace this reconciliation of polarities in the eroticization of nature in Canadian poetry and in the landscape painting of the 'Group of Seven,' where there is a reconciliation of voluptuousness (physical excess) and the sublime.

Nature is constructed as the locale for erotism in the Canadian imaginary. 'Nature' is paradoxically that place in the symbolic order where the symbolic order is lifted and suspended, permitting enjoyment to break out: 'There are strange things done in the midnight sun / By the men who moil for gold; / The Arctic trails have their secret tales / That would make your blood run cold.'[89] The extremity of Canadian nature necessitates erotic activity as a survival strategy. 'Bundling,' for instance, refers to the practice of sleeping together during winter in order to maximize body heat, a survival tactic – sleeping alone, one would freeze to death – and a long-standing Canadian tradition of articulating enjoyment and endurance.[90] In Canadian literature and film, isolation in nature gives rise to fornication, and particularly incest. A typical example is Yves Simoneau's 1986 screen adaptation of Anne Hébert's *Les Fous de Bassan*, a portrayal of the economy of desire in a small, isolated fishing community. Most of the characters are blood relatives, who spend all of their time thinking about, staring at, and lusting after each other. The pastor (whose barren wife no longer wants to have intercourse) lusts after Nora, who lusts after Stevens, who's sleeping with Maureen but whose love for Olivia remains unrequited, etc.[91]

In the dominant (patriarchal) narrative of Canadian identity, nature seduces: forests, gold, oil, and natural resources are articulated discursively in feminized, or at least sexualized terms: virgin forests, gold fever, the lust for the motherlode and the associations that go with it; the brothels and whores of Moose Jaw, Edmonton, and Dawson that are part and parcel of the rush to the west and the north. They were part of the lure from the beginning. This is especially clear with regard to the fur trade, particularly beavers – and notice how the quest for beavers has entered the imaginary: 'beaver' is Canadian nerd slang for the female pudendum. Interestingly, the beaver has associations of industriousness, and teeth, *vagina dentata.* The erotic allure of Canadian nature is especially risky. The 'pussy,' the counterpart in American vernacular, has associations with comfort and domestication, signifiers of a more confident, more totalized patriarchal civilization.

The rather peculiar idiom of Canadian erotic fantasy can be heard if one listens to how people talk about flies and mosquitoes and blackfly season, and how they deal with them at the cottage or on the canoe trip. Flies are all part of the enjoyment/endurance of it. 'Of course there were flies, man, I tell you, I never seen them as thick as they were last weekend, those blackflies, they're miniature buzz saws, take a chunk outa you.' 'Yah! You heard about that child in Sudbury that was carried off by the mosquito, eh?' People have their own secret ways of dealing with them, mixtures of lotions and creams, 'eat lots of garlic and they won't touch you, sours the blood'; and of course there are many Canadians who endure the bites because 'you just gotta put up with it, eh.'

A bunch of us went on a canoe trip in Algonquin Park a few years ago. At one point during the trip we came to a fork in the river. Erik and I took a canoe and went down one stream to scout ahead. Gradually our stream petered out into a shallow lagoon, but we could hear heavy water up ahead. We left the canoe and waded through the water to see if we could portage to the main channel. When we climbed out on the bank again we saw to our horror that our legs were covered with slimy black leeches. Aaaggggh! Disgusting! Brushed them off desperately. Terrible anxiety about whether any had made it up the legs of my shorts, God forbid!! Later by the campfire, and weeks later sitting around in the pub, recounting the highlights of the trip, the story about Erik and Kieran and the leeches is one of the central nodal points around which the narrative of the enjoyment of the trip and of our shared friendship is recollected.

Erotism then is precisely our enjoyment of the sensory dimension of *Dasein,* the sensory experience of continuity that we articulate symbolically, linguistically, in our story-tellings, that constitutes our shared experience of the symptom as sinthome. Erotism is the ground of the social, for it's not the individual physical sensory experience but rather our shared collective articulation of physical sensory experience as meaningful, as our shared enjoyment, that gives us the *feeling* of Being: of being somewhere, being something in particular – for example, of sharing the feeling of being Canadian friends.

What is the character of the transgressive enjoyment in nature? Carnivorous lust, the slavering, fat-tongued creatures excited by the scent of blood, the blackflies and leeches, ravenous, blind things burrowing and sucking voraciously, these give embodied form to the desire of the Other to incorporate us, to literally eat us up. The Other (nature) reveals itself – its enjoyment – to us in such monstrous forms: we desire that it desire us, showing us our enjoyment by its threat to steal it from us, so that we, in turn, desire its excess all the more, so that nature (Otherness) appears as the engorged organic world on which our enjoyment feeds. This is the reciprocal economy of desire of being in Canada.

The monstrosity of nature is brought to light in transgressive erotic encounters, and although, as we shall see, we are more haunted by a lack of ghosts than by their presence, there are at least two ghostly monsters in the Canadian imaginary: the Wendigo, a monster borrowed from Native lore, and the Werewolf, a monster brought from Europe, residing mainly in Quebec, and particularly in the Ottawa valley.[92] Wendigos and Werewolves are various figures of lycantrophy, the transmutation of human into animal. The human loses its soul to nature, loses control of desire, and carnal enjoyment, animal erotism is unleashed. The Werewolf and the Wendigo are aspects of the same monster, the human reabsorbed by nature, reminding those on the human side of the threshold of the precariousness of *Dasein*. Erotism is the cottage window open to the full moon through which terrible seductive monsters come to haunt and excite sleeping Canadians.

Frye's Haunted Canada

To explore these themes of Canadian erotism further, I will revisit a classic essay by Northrop Frye: 'Haunted by a Lack of Ghosts: Some Patterns in the Imagery of Canadian Poetry' (Frye 1977). In this brilliant essay, generally representative of his work on Canadian identity, Frye argues that it is the lack of a symptom which is terrifying in Canada. Gods, ghosts, and spirits are absent in Canada. We modern Cartesian egoists didn't bring any with us; we Christians and scientists killed off any that were here. Without a symptom we are exposed to the real, a vast nothingness, external to us, the land of Canada Frye likens to 'leviathan,' a dark monster that has swallowed us, with which we have no way of relating:

the leviathan is the monster of indefinite time and space surrounding us on all sides; we are all born inside his belly, and we never escape from it; he is the body of death from which we cannot be delivered. The Christian, Baroque, Cartesian attitude that the white invaders brought from Europe helped to ensure that in Canada the sense of being imprisoned in a mindless emptiness would be at its bleakest and most uncompromising ... the ego's one moment of genuine dignity is the moment either of death or some equally final alienation.   Frye 1977, 37–8

This external leviathan has haunted Canadians, eliciting historically a poetry full of solitude and loneliness. More recently, Frye says, we see poetry inspired by the internalization of this leviathan, as we discover our guilt. We killed off the gods and spirits, we are the ghosts in the Cartesian machine that we built for ourselves. Here Frye is echoing Max Weber's diagnosis of the malaise of Modernity; that we are haunted by the ghosts of dead religious beliefs, and now we seek re-enchantment (Weber 1986, 182). Modern Canadians are nostalgic for spirit, haunted internally by its absence, and we turn to Others (Natives, newcomers, nature) (again) in a desperate guilty quest for it.

Frye identifies three aspects of the colonizing culture. First, there is the monotheism of Christianity: all the gods that had been discovered in nature were devils, and relations with them idolatrous. It followed that religions like those of the Natives had to be extirpated. Second, there is the baroque sense of the power of mathematics, the results of which can be seen in the grid patterns of our cities, in the concession lines in the rural areas. And finally, there is the Cartesian egocentric consciousness, the feeling that man's essential humanity was in his power of reasoning. Together these fundamental aspects of modern culture, given free rein in Canada, contribute to a consciousness of nature as a territory but not as a home. Nature constitutes an alien field of Otherness which we define ourselves as being-against, rather than being-with. Thus the most characteristic feature of Canadian culture according to Frye, a thesis which he makes more explicit elsewhere (Frye 1971), is the 'garrison mentality.' What Frye misses, however, as do many others ploughing the same furrow (Gaile McGregor's *Wacousta Syndrome* [1985] is a noteworthy exception that begins the formulation developed below), is that fear and trembling in confrontation with the alien leviathan of nature is only one moment in what is in fact a much more deeply ambivalent relation. For we also enjoy the terror of nature. It makes us horny.

The collapsing of Native culture and nature, and then the systematic subjugation and destruction of both, leaves us haunted by guilt. The negation of the Other, the annihilation of Native culture (life/being), its reduction to the status of object immersed in organic life equivalent to rocks, lakes, and trees, leaves no subject to offer recognition to the imperial master but merely a world of objects.[93] The master then, by negating and objectifying the Other, objectifies himself and leaves himself lacking subjectivity. Frye cites George Grant's *Technology and Empire*:

That conquering relation to place has left its mark within us. When we go into the Rockies we may have the sense that Gods are there. But if so they cannot manifest themselves to us as ours. They are the gods of another race, and we cannot know them because of what we are and what we did. There can be nothing immemorial for us except the environment as object.   Frye 1977, 28

Accordingly, Frye says that 'we are the ghosts, Cartesian ghosts, caught in the machine that we have assumed nature to be.' Having no way of relating to another people's gods, and discovering the lack of our own, we find nature assuming terrifying dimensions, and we must accept her vengeance, stoically. Canadian heroism, Frye observes, is tinged with futility, and withdrawal becomes a more characteristic response than commitment. Again, I'm not convinced that it is so much a matter of stoic withdrawal, which carries in Frye's formulation very melancholy overtones. I would read the characteristic manifestation of Canadian heroism as being tinged with enjoyable resignation, finding comfort in the fulfilment of a familiar expectation of an inevitable failure. Canada is indubitably 'the land of the one-legged hero.' It is not just Terry Fox, but all heroes, that are seemingly destined to be found lacking: Ben Johnson, (twice!), the U.N. 'peacekeepers,' the soldiers 'armed for life,' as the current Armed Forces recruitment slogan has it, who shoot and beat to death Somali civilians under their protection. Are we shocked, or surprised? Is there a feeling of public embarrassment? Of course not. Canadian heroes are supposed to let us down.

When we try to make atonement and recover subjectivity, Native culture is a pool from which we draw resources to reformulate our relations with Native/Nature/God. It is through becoming Native – that is, literally, by being 'born again' – that 'settler' Canadians can find salvation, imagine themselves as no longer immigrants, but as becoming indigenous, recreating sensibilities appropriate to people who really belong here. But this process of rebirth is charged with ambivalence and ambiguity, as it remains undecidable to what extent the process involves the continuation of an imperialistic appropriation of Other, or a self-sacrificial giving ourselves over to the

Other for deliverance. Frye cites British Columbia 'gone Native' poet Susan Musgrave:

Sometimes an old man
whispers down the smoke hole,
Sometimes an old woman
furrows in the wind.
My skin is thick
with the dark seed
of their coming –
the blade of a fine axe
wedged between my eyes.

Musgrave, in Frye 1977, 41

Musgrave articulates the ambivalence of desire for reconciliation with the Other: that her white identity be violently sacrificed, so that the Other, and she herself reborn as Other, might relive in continuity in her embodiment, an embodied continuity that, while she desires it, still makes her skin crawl. Musgrave's 'going Native' in search of the rootedness that gives meaning to her enjoyment of being Canadian, and her ambivalence towards it, reflect the popular ambivalence towards enjoyable mingling evident in so-called 'ethnic' neighbourhoods of Canadian cities: the ambivalence of people who like to shop in Kensington Market, listening to the many rich and exotic accents, savouring the aromas of Caribbean roti and Ecuadorian fruit, but who are upset that the Asian family who've moved into their building always seem to be cooking and now the whole building smells of cumin.

Recent Canadian poetry, according to Frye, is still trapped in Cartesian dualism: 'the nostalgic and elegiac are the inevitable emotional responses to an egocentric consciousness locked into a demythologized environment' (Frye 1977, 33). Even when it is self-critical and reflexive, it cannot formulate a new relationship with estranged nature, at least not yet:

Winnipeg, what once were you? You were,
Your hair was grass by the river ten feet tall,
Your arms were burr oaks and ash leaf maples,
Your backbone was a crooked silver muddy river,
Your thoughts were ravens in flocks, your bones were
    snow,
Your legs were trails and your blood was a people
    Who did what the stars did and the sun ...

Then on top of you fell
A Boneyard wrecked auto gent, his hair
Made of rusted car door handles, his fingernails
Of red Snowflake Pastry signs, his belly
Of buildings downtown; his arms of sewers,
His nerves electric wires, his mouth a telephone,
His backbone – a cracked cement street. His heart
An orange pendulum bus crawling with the human fleas.
Of a so-so civilization – half gadget, half flesh –
   I don't know what I would have instead –
   And they did what they did more or less.

Reaney, in Frye 1997, 30

Idealized nature, raped by the machine. Here is the modern monster, the 'auto gent.' But the poet, James Reaney, can only see the monster two-dimensionally, as Frankenstein's terrible, rapacious, and vengeful invention gone out of control. The poet articulates himself as an impotent and innocent bystander. It is an unethical position, an inability and a refusal to take responsibility. The unleashed power of modernity is brutally overwhelming to Reaney. He doesn't take responsibility for power relations in which he himself is implicated. He can only indulge in a demonization of technology and modernity. Now, not only does nature stand alienated from the Canadian imagination, but so too modern culture appears as externalized and hostile. While the poet might articulate a reflexive, responsible relationship to both nature and culture, he glimpses this relationship only vaguely: the postmodern promise of the monster as cyborg, half gadget, half flesh, 'I don't know what I would have instead.' He can't have nature back (she was only ever a nostalgic fantasy anyway), but as yet he can see no value in the cyborg.

Frye then suggests at least one dimension of a manifesto for Canadian poetry: 'the poetic impulse is imaginative ... and its most direct product is mythology, which is essentially the humanizing of nature' (Frye 1977, 34). Poetics is the practice of humanizing our relations with Others, and at a conjuncture where modernity has become an alien Other world of gadgetry and rapacious invention we need to humanize culture as much as nature. The first step in attuning to the Other is perceiving Other as erotic being. We are interested here, for the moment, in the eroticization of nature in the Canadian imaginary, but we should keep in mind the question of the eroticization of the world of gadgets and inventions.

Alienation in modernity is crucially tied to the coldness of the machine, its frightening lack of visceral carnality, its mechanical invulnerability. We have Woody Allen's neurotic relation to vibrators: Allen says that he cannot be intimate with something that has 'General Electric' written on it. On the other hand, the promise of enjoyable erotic relations with the machine is a sci-fi staple – witness the allure of Rachel the replicant in *Blade Runner*, the erotically charged relationship between Sara Connor and the Terminator in *T2*, or the celebrated moment in 'Star Trek: The Next Generation' when Data, the android, informs Tasha that yes, he is 'fully functional,' and has been programmed with ninety different modes of pleasuring. One of the most adventurous excursions in this dimension in Canada is Atom Egoyan's film *Speaking Parts*.[94] In a perfectly Canadian idiom, Egoyan's protagonists enjoy a long-distance relationship, masturbating for one another via video-phone. But Frye's call for a Canadian project of mythologizing – and, as I have suggested, it's not just a question of mythologizing nature but modern culture also – has been most creatively taken up in terms of an emerging cyberpunk imaginary, articulated by William Gibson from his suburban Vancouver rec-room.[95] Gibson says:

Well, 'Technology 'R' Us' at this point! What I find alarming is people who say, 'Technology, Bill. Good or bad?' As though we could put it back in the box! We're such fabulously artificial creatures that we live four or five times longer than we do in the wild ... I'm always amazed that anyone could say [he mimics a German accent, noting that its the most technological of people who ask most often] 'Can ve not go back to Nature?' Well, I guess you can, but you won't like it.   1993, 21

Humanizing the Other, that is living as human beings in the world of being constituted by being with the being of Others, be the being of the Other organic, technical, or, ever more so, a hybrid, cyborg being with indeterminable boundaries, depends upon its eroticization by a process of mythologizing; attuning with solicitude to its erotism. Check out this early excursus by Isabella Valancy Crawford:

In this shrill moon the scouts of Winter ran
From the ice-belted north, and whistling shafts
Struck maple and struck sumach – and a blaze
Ran swift from leaf to leaf, from bough to bough;
Till round the forest flash'd a belt of flame
And inward lick'd its tongues of red and gold
To the deep, tranced, inmost heart of all.
Rous'd the still heart – but all too late, too late.

Too late, the branches welded fast with leaves,
Toss'd, loosen'd to the winds – too late the sun
Pour'd his last vigour to the deep, dark cells
Of the dim wood. The keen, two-bladed Moon
Of Falling Leaves roll'd up on crested mists
And where the lush, rank boughs had foil'd the sun
In his red prime, her pale, sharp fingers crept
After the wind and felt about the moss,
And seemed to pluck from shrinking twig and stem
The burning leaves – while groaned the shudd'ring wood.[96]

Frye says of this poem: 'Nature here is not a Cartesian extension in space, but a field of conflicting energies which are seemingly just about to take on the forms of mythological beings.' But somehow, Frye says, 'it doesn't come to life, and we are pulled around to death and winter again' (Frye 1977, 35). I would say that it is much more alive and sexy than that. What we can see here is the cycle of nature charged with erotism: seduction, desire, games of flirtation, a little s/m even, an orgy of the elements – the hot tongues of sunlight, the sun pouring his vigour into the dark forest, the coy resistance of the leaves and the rank lush boughs to the sun's red prime. But resistance to seduction is (inevitably) too late, too late, as the (female) moon takes over, and her probing fingers of winter find their way to the moss, as the wind undresses the trees, and the wood shudders in ecstasy.

Frye's interpretation, which focuses on the return of winter as death, seems to confirm Margaret Atwood's observation that Canadians are inclined to interpret symbols in the bleakest possible manner. He sees death rather than sexiness, but a frosty, tingling erotism could be evoked by 'the pale fingers feeling about the moss.' But Frye is on the mark to note the connection between Crawford and the Group of Seven, the eroticization of nature as part of a coming to terms with it. 'Crawford has done in words what Tom Thomson was later to do in his art: evoking a dissonance of colour that seems like an autonomous force of life itself bursting through the tree trunks, the sumac, and the sky' (Frye 1977, 36).

The Group of Seven's Spirit of Canada

The heroic modernist act of Thomson and the Group of Seven was self-consciously to set out to express the 'Spirit of Canada.'[97] They began by violating the convention of pastoralism, imported from Europe, which was properly the art of what Frye calls a 'garrison mentality.' Pastoralism responded to the enormous externality of Canadian nature by denial of its Otherness; by representing it as pasture and farmland, familiar and domesticated. So the first move of the Group of Seven was to violate this symbolic order of bourgeois Canada by disrupting its fantasy construction of a domesticated and civilized nature and allowing an enormous mass of stuff, all that had been repressed and painted out of this picture, to rush back in. Critics were outraged, renaming J.E.H. MacDonald's works 'drunkard's stomach' and 'Hungarian goulash.'[98] Note the return of the repressed in the art critic's voice; the connotations of the hateful excesses of the lower classes, the drunken masses, and the racist fear of the Eastern European hordes. In the unconscious of the Canadian bourgeoisie of 1910–1930, poverty, popular communist sedition, and ethnocultural Otherness are the equivalents of the alien leviathan of nature: all of this is now protruding horribly from the walls of respectable salons and galleries.

Where does the Native figure in this explosion of the real into the Canadian imaginary? A recent commentator charges Thomson and the Group of Seven with 'the erasure of the Native presence from the Canadian landscape' (Bordo 1993, 1). While he may sound 'politically correct,' this commentator is utterly mistaken. Before the Group of Seven, Natives figured prominently in Canadian art, but primarily, if not exclusively, in representations of the 'noble savage,' the primitive of European invention, being no more than 'whatever we wanted it to be.'[99] In Canadian art Natives were pastoralized and domesticated, sheepishly gathered around the settlements, or trotting like faithful dogs at the heels of Wolfe and Champlain.[100] At other moments they appear as majestic as mighty trees and eagles; tall, broad, steely-eyed, and plumed. And in other representations, as stealthy and dangerous, prowling the forests like wildcats, senses bristling, bows poised.

But in all of this the Native is safely integrated in the imagery and text of Western civilization. Thomson and the Group of Seven do not erase the Native; on the contrary, they erase the image and the text in which the Native had conventionally been contained. They disrupt the integrity of the fantasy of civilization and in effect set the Native free. The Native, no longer confined by pastoralist romantic representation, bursts into the gallery, and into the drawing-room also.

The viewer is now confronted with the radical absence of a subject (Native) that was previously felt to be securely located and identified. The Native again becomes troubling, insisting that we radically alter our perspective, that we look more carefully, for the Natives are not as we thought they ought to be. This insistence that we 'look again' in order to see the

Native presence is what is at issue in Jackson's wonderful *trompe l'œil* where a party of Natives appear as almost indistinguishable from the landscape. The achievement of Thomson and the Group of Seven is that they restored to the Other its otherness, presenting us the opportunity of renegotiating our relationship to it.

This moment of opening a window to the real is characteristic of the Group's early work, and also perhaps of Thomson's in particular: the rage of brilliant colour, the flashes of light, the density of the forests, the dark, profound lakes, roaring rapids, wind-warped pines, the never-ending horizons, the vanishing point drawing the eye to an ever more distant vanishing point in infinite regress. But we're not simply left with this, affronted by what some experienced as an ugly glimpse of the Canadian real. We can reestablish a relationship with the excess, the Otherness of nature, in so far as Thomson and the Group eroticize the physical excess of nature and thereby reconcile the sublime and the beautiful.

The Group's work is characterized by the representation of the physical excess of Canadian nature as 'voluptuous': alive and carnal, wet and fecund, ample and powerful, dark and profound, intimate, seductive, and yet austere and unfathomable. J.E.H. MacDonald and A.Y. Jackson's works move towards harmonizing these polarities, but Lawren Harris's work expresses best of all the Group's project to attune to the spirit of Canada.

Harris attunes to the spirit by attending to the body of Canada. From the profusion and density and texture of the Group's earlier work, Harris begins to bring into view the eroticized body of Canada. In *Beaver Swamp, Algoma* (1920) and *Above Lake Superior* (1924) we see a progressive reduction in the spectrum of colour and an increasing definition of form; a dark, ponderous, pregnant mountain, foregrounded by birches so polished and graceful that they recall nude bodies. Then, in *Lake and Mountains* (1928) we see an unmistakable female form of m(Other) nature, giant breasts, curvaceous contours, a wet vaginal opening in the dark body of the land, through which a shaft of light illuminates a dwarfed phallic tree in the foreground. Canada's Otherness comes into view, vast and awesome, shaming man's puny intrusion, but yet intimate and seductive, promising the possibility of enjoyment together. This moment, when the sublime and the beautiful are reconciled as an infinitely undecidable horizon of suture, where the character of the relationship between One and Other appears as a dialectical problem, requiring a constant working out, shows us a glimpse of the spirit of being in Canada.

And one further digression, as a segue from art back to poetry and to Frye: lest it be thought that the erotic mythologizing of nature is just a feature of the modern Canadian canon, a WASP masculinist thing, let us take a sample from the contemporary postmodern smorgasbord; 'Salmon Run,' a piece by Japanese Albertan feminist poet Sally Ito, who formulates the enjoyment of being in Canada in a now familiar idiom:

Sometimes in the night
I find you spawning in my bed.
As if the sheets were the last wrinkling folds
of the stream that is to claim your life.

Hilderly and Norris 1988, 62

Ito continues in this vein of reversed anthropomorphism, dreaming of enjoyable identification through the dissolution of her identity in the infinite, timeless stream of Nature. In 'the incessant thumping' of the salmons' tails in 'the frenzy of mating,' Ito dreams of recovering a lost unity, a sense of oceanic oneness. She desires that we be re-collected and recalled from the scattered paths of our individual migrations to a primordial womb, as the salmon, by some mysterious natural calling, is brought back to the very spot from which life began.

And so, back to Frye! Frye's formulation of the leviathan in the Canadian imagination, nature as a monster that has swallowed us, is brilliant, and certainly this is one of the chill wellsprings of an ascetic culture of solitude, loneliness, and despair. Frye cites Margaret Avison's poem 'Identity' as exemplary. In this poem Avison articulates the lonely isolation of Canadian identity, singular and naked at the icy pole, pried loose from all covering and warmth.

But there is something going on here which again Frye misses, an obscene enjoyment, a particularly Canadian enjoyment, enjoyment of endurance of lack of particularity. The solitary ego, pried loose from being-in-the-world, can define its identity in naked, stoic, splendid isolation. But while this may be seen as expressing loneliness and despair, a pure lack of enjoyment, it is, I would argue, equally a celebration of an enjoyment of purity and unpretentiousness. For if there is existence at the icy pole of solitude, then existence at the icy pole must be enjoyable, for to live at all is to live enjoyably.

I think that Frye doesn't see how we live enjoyably in the belly, by ironic conceit. Our enjoyment of endurance of lack of particularity is clearly evident in Avison's articulation of identity. Without particularity, without the covering wings of symptom, soul pried loose, etc., we still have a singular presence at the icy pole: we have the pure, singular particularity of the lack of particularity. There is an arrogant and hypocritical pretence in this claim to icy, solitary, pure unpretentiousness; a crypto-fascist purification by trials of icy endurance, like an ice-brewed beer: cold, pure, clearly CanAryan.

Sacrifice, Torture, and Canada's Body

We organize our desire for community in the face of nothingness outside the belly, we achieve community by making sacrifices to leviathan that bring to light our continuity, sacrificial practices by which we define ourselves to ourselves by the leviathan's sublime externality. But there are two leviathans in play here: nature – the land of Canada – which takes its sacrificial victims as it wants them, as we want it to want them and according as we give ourselves to it – Tom Thomson, smothered by Algonquin; drowned fishermen and ski-dooers; frozen Arctic travellers; crashed highway drivers lulled to sleep by the enormity of distance; decapitated by moose reclaiming the highway or by black ice that insists on slowness rather than our arrogant speed. And there is Thomas Hobbes's leviathan, the symbolic order of Canada, through which the collective seeks to govern the land of Canada – the leviathan that manifests itself in the institutions of parliamentary democracy, the law, the welfare state, multiculturalism – and this too demands sacrifices. And what sort of sacrifices do we make to it to remind ourselves of continuity under it?

The sublime externality of the law is crucial here. Canada is legislated into existence. Canada exists by law. What sustains us as a unified society is our shared relationship to the law. The glorious aspects of the Canadian leviathan are its laws: peace, order, and good government. The figure of the Mountie is the sublime face of the law. Legal rationality is invested with a sublime status in Canada in the figure of the Mountie. The Mountie always gets his man, the law must be obeyed, because it is the law. Why are the Mounties mounted? The disciplined animal (nature, Frye's external leviathan) is the very basis of peace, order, and good government.

Canadians sacrifice particularity to the law – the particularities of ethnicity, identity – and the law gives it back to us, official multiculturalism and individual and collective rights, guaranteed by the Charter of Rights and Freedoms. The law negates all particularity, all are equal before it as subjects, but as citizens the law gives us back particularity (absolutely) as individual and collective rights enshrined by the charter, and delivered by the welfare state. It is through the sacrifice of individual particularity to the law that we can 'die as egos and be born again in the swarm, not separate and self-hypnotized, but individual and related.'[101]

Again, what is crucial here is the law, because multiculturalism is official. New York, London, and Rio de Janeiro are just as multicultural as Toronto, Montreal, and Vancouver, but it's not official there. The chaotic mingling of scattered Others in the new Babylon here in Canada is approached in terms of an injunction to 'mix enjoyably,' it's the law here. But enjoyment has to be transgressive, it must break the law (hence the obscene enjoyability of racism, the boys in the Klan and the Heritage Front sure have a good time!). So official multiculturalism, while it commands us to 'mix enjoyably,' some-how maybe promotes the opposite: preserve particularity, don't mix, don't lose your particularity.

The law needs to do both simultaneously, it needs to negate particularity, and at the same time it needs to preserve and reproduce particularity. So official multiculturalism then is inimical to the enjoyment of multiculturalism in some ways. But on the other hand, if we consider official multiculturalism in terms of the alternatives that it replaces – official racism, apartheid, exclusionary immigration laws, which we have had (and still have) plenty of experience with in Canada – we see it in better perspective.

Official multiculturalism is our current Canadian version of the Tower of Babel, a discursive effort to transcend the scattering, a legal discourse that tries to constitute the law, the voice of the collective. Official multiculturalism represents our best democratic effort (to date) to write the script for the city in which we can all live enjoyably. But the law is flawed. Official multiculturalism is always incomplete, multiculture defies legal designation and bureaucratic administration. Official multiculturalism is a discursive framework that tries to address the problem of discontinuity and scattering, conceitedly expecting to solve it despite the reminders that the problem is apparently insurmountable – by the return of the repressed antagonism; by, for example, the violent destructive sacrifices periodically offered by per-petually reemerging extremists, such as the Heritage Front and Ernst Zundel.

Paradoxically, and tragically, it is the returning of this antagonism that is the source of the desire to keep on working it out. It is in its self-acknowledged imperfection and incompleteness that the strength of official multiculturalism actually lies. 'All things considered ...' Marshall Berman concludes, 'as the twentieth century schleps to a close, official multi-culturalism in our cities would be a sign of great achievement.'[102]

Perhaps Newfoundland poet E.J. Pratt's epic work about the Jesuit mis-sionaries and the Iroquois, *Brébeuf and His Brethren*, can develop the problem of multiculturalism. The poem focuses on the relationship between the Jesuit priests and their Iroquois torturers. Peter Buitenhuis notes: 'The ultimate meeting of minds of Jesuit and Indian comes not on the question of belief, but on the common ground of physical endurance' (Staines 1977, 52). The sacrificial death through torture brings to light the continuity between the radically alien Others, Jesuit and Indian. It brings to light their continuity in their shared relationship to a particular symptomatic configuration of enjoyment: that of enjoyment and endurance. They share a valuation of tolerance.

Now this may be crucially significant: the meeting ground of identities is not their capitulation to one another, but the process of bringing to light their relation to a shared nodal point. In Brébeuf we have an extreme example, but could we think of multiculturalism in similar terms? One can maintain particularity, so long as one demonstrates a shared relationship to enjoyment of endurance, but in demonstrating this relation the continuation of the torture is inevitable. We must test the limits of endurance, and thus torturous synthetic frontier effects of assimilation will characterize the development. Then the question becomes whether we can tolerate the torture of lack of particularity that we both lose when we subject our identities to the infinitude of the difference in the Other, as commanded by the law, official multiculturalism. Can we tolerate the monstrous hybrid, the polyglot Frankenstein, made of bits of the bodies of Other cultures? Is official multiculturalism itself the elusive ghost, which is nothing because it is everything?

In *The Body in Pain* (1992), Elaine Scarry argues that whenever the normative world of a community survives fear, pain and death in their more extreme forms, that very survival is understood to be literally miraculous both by those who have experienced and by those who vividly imagine or recreate the suffering. The miracle in question here is the miracle of the social, constituting the collective in their relation to symptom as sinthome; the feeling of being-one-with-one-another, as a community of survivors of pain. While Natives, Quebeckers, and many other communities in Canada have no scarcity of martyrs, victims, and casualties, Canada itself has a scarcity of people who shed their blood; people who put their very lives on the line for *Canada*.

Or has it? The uniqueness of the Canadian experience is that it is Canada itself that is constituted symbolically as the body in pain; the lack of the body, the body that exists as the body that is being coerced torturously into being, that is not yet born and that is always in danger of dying. The tortured body of Canada is something that only begins to materialize against the background of a practice (or the ominous threat) of torturing the body, tearing it apart; the threat of dismemberment represented by separatism: Bloc, Reform, Native self-government, the torturous fragmentation of identity politics and political correctness.

The paradox of official multiculturalism is that it is the 'terrible world' produced by the torturer and the tortured – a world that simultaneously seeks to end the torture by extracting the 'Truth,' the secret that would unite us – that would close the narrative and give us Canada 'once and for all,' as it were. But the truth is that there is no Truth. (The secret of theory, as Derrida says, is that there is no Theory.) Thus there is always a new threshold of pain, something else to be given up, a further addition to the narrative, yet another moment of assimilation, that reveals yet another frontier of antagonism. What emerges from this unending painful process is the cyborg body of Canada, a body that emerges as the normative universes of wholeness are destroyed, as the worlds of various identities are betrayed. This process, through which torturer and tortured become one, is agonal and interminable.

8

Shit with the Bear. Bear Your Friend

Casual sex in America means having sex with a stranger, but casual sex in Canada means sleeping with a friend.

Canadian joke: How do you get the Canadians to get out of the hot tub? Say, 'Would you all get out of the hot tub, please?'

A fellow expatriate, from the U.S., said this to me once about casual sex and friendship in Canada, and it hit the nail on the head somehow. And yet while this seemed promissory, another expatriate warned me that Canadians are humourless as a rule, and don't get jokes at all. That humour and comedy need to be exhibited and explained to Canadians seems all but confirmed by the recent opening of a museum of humour in Montreal, but yet the one about the hot tub was told to me by a Canadian, and it never fails to get laughs, especially from Canadians.

Canadians deal with sex and humour in ways that are very particularly Canadian. Sex and humour are perhaps the grounds of enjoyment *par excellence*, in so far as these are the frontiers of our encounters with one another that are most explicitly charged with desire and endangered with excess and risk. Sex and humour both depend on excesses of the parties, excesses that call for desire to be deployed artfully, so that the practice is enjoyable, and the result is pleasurable or funny, or both. Both sex and humour risk everything in transgressive encounters with Others. Sex and humour risk offence and alienation, rendering the sexual partner or the subject of the joke ludicrous or 'gross,' obscene or excessive. But the risk is taken, because on the other hand there is the hope of enriching and deepening the enjoyability of social relations.

By paying close attention to the idiom of symptoms of the antagonism of sexuality and comedy in Canada, we will be able to see the particularity of the symbolic order of Canada: the articulation of enjoyment with endurance, and endurance of lack of particularity; the elevation of values of tolerance and unpretentiousness; the ironic conceit that makes living room for enjoyment; the organization of desire for reconciliation with Others in terms of an ethic of a mediated openness, disclosure, demonstration of vulnerability, an invitation to attunement and pastiche enunciated by the 'eh,' and the cultivation of the grounds of friendship, the basis of a Canadian principled relation with Otherness.

I have a lot to unpack here, and I'm not going to be able to show everything at once, but I do want to show all of the themes I have addressed so far appearing in the fields of sexuality and comedy. I will try to collect these themes and conclude with a discussion of the principles of friendship as they appear in Canadian culture. I will draw upon Georges Bataille's work *Erotism* to show sexuality and comedy as arenas where transgression, violation, and sacrifice are employed to bring 'continuity of being' to light. The bringing to light of continuity of being Heidegger calls 'poiesis,' an artful, poetic practice. Poetry leads 'to the blending and fusion of separate objects. It leads us to eternity, it leads us to death, and through death to continuity. Poetry is eternity; the sun matched with the sea' (1986, 25).

So I am interested in the continuity of Being in Canada, what Keith Spicer referred to as the poetry of the nation. What do we do to bring continuity between scattered Others to light for ourselves, so that we share experiences of being Canadian? We are interested then in seeing the artfulness and poetics of Canadian friendliness in the erotic and humorous practices of everyday life. I began by tracing the particular phenomenological manifestations of this quest for continuity with the help of Frye's exploration of the Canadian poetic imagination, and then examined a moment of reconciliation, a glimpsing of continuity, in the work of the Group of Seven. I will now show a changing configuration of social relations, from a utopian aspiration of sexual communion with Other to a more ambiguous and open friendship with Other in Marian Engel's now canonized Canadian erotic masterpiece, *Bear* (1976). I will then examine Canadian comedy in order to see how we demonstrate to Others our openness and vulnerability, which invites attunement.

In *Erotism*, Bataille says that 'we are discontinuous beings who perish in isolation in the midst of an incomprehensible adventure, but we yearn for our lost continuity' (1986, 15). This nostalgia is responsible for erotism, that is 'assenting to life up to the point of death.' This unrelenting erotic quest for continuity is manifested in three forms; physical, emotional, and religious. All erotism is animated by the desire to replace isolated discontinuity with a feeling of profound continuity. Erotism, grounded in nostalgia for a profound continuity of being, is Bataille's formulation of desire for collective enjoyment.

We can see the basic unity of forms of erotism in sacrifice. Religious erotism is concerned with the fusion of beings with a world beyond everyday reality, and the significance of sacrifice is that it brings continuity to light through death. Not only in death – continuity found in not-being, the religious community united in death – but also in the living, existent, being-in-the-world which the death of the sacrificial being brings to light. Continuity of being-in-the-world is brought to light by the putting to death, the ritualized violation of continuity.

Religious erotism might appear to be qualitatively different from physical and emotional erotism in so far as it seeks continuity of being beyond the world of everyday reality through sacrificial death, but sacrificial death is also a central aspect of physical and emotional erotism, for sacrifice more generally refers to the ritualized violation of taboo. There is a strong link between the act of love, being in love, and sacrifice, Bataille says, for sacrifice is like erotic activity. Physical and emotional erotic activity dissolves the separate beings that participate in it. 'We suffer from isolation in our individual separateness. If only you possessed the soul of the beloved one, your soul, sick with loneliness, would be one with the soul of the beloved. One would kill, or kill oneself, for this unity. The aura of death in erotism is what denotes passion' (1986, 20). Erotism involves risking death in search of continuity of being, as we shall see in Marian Engel's *Bear*.

Stripping naked is a decisive action in erotism, according to Bataille, as it reveals a quest for a continuity of being beyond the confines of self. It produces a feeling of obscenity, a deliberate loss of scene, a rendering each other transparent in the erotic encounter. Obscenity refers to the uneasiness that upsets the physical state associated with self-possession, with the possession of a recognized and stable identity. When we enter relations nakedly we lose possession of recognized and stable identities. We are vulnerable and uneasy. How do Canadian friends or even lovers orient towards one another in terms of 'stripping naked'? Stripping naked can be a simulacrum for killing, but we must think of this act more broadly as a metaphor for exposing ourselves to one another. Being naked is a question of disclosure, demonstrating vulnerability, showing an open moment towards which the other might attune. This may be best seen in Canadian comedy. We will see how Canadians do nakedness by tracing self-disclosure as the central element of Canadian comedy.

The business of erotism then is 'to destroy the self-contained character of the participants as they are in their normal lives' (Bataille 1986, 17). In so far as erotism requires the destruction of self-containedness of existence in order to bring continuity of existence to light, every manifestation of erotism is kindled by elemental violence. In essence the domain of erotism is the domain of violence, of violation. 'The whole business of erotism is to strike to the inmost core of the living being, so that the heart stands still. [A] basic violence [that] leaves us gasping' (Bataille 1986, 17). Erotism refers to practices that violate our complacency with everyday normalcy, that evoke in us what Heidegger calls a 'radical astonishment' (Steiner 1978, 31), moments at which we glimpse the traumatic kernel of enjoyment, our shared relationship to symptom as sinthome (Lacan), that elusive implosion of subject and object to which ecstasy aspires (Baudrillard) the moments in the phenomenology of spirit where we experience the '"I" that is "We" and the "We" that is "I"' (Hegel). Such moments appear following violent death, especially ritualistic sacrifice. 'A violent death disrupts the creature's discontinuity; what remains, what the tense onlookers experience in the ensuing silence, is the continuity of all existence with which the victim is now one' (Bataille 1986, 22).

Continuity of being is not a state or a condition that can be achieved, nor would we desire the establishment of a stable state of continuity of being, for such a state could only mean death. In erotism our discontinuous existence is not condemned to death, it is only jolted. It has to be jolted and shaken to its foundations. Continuity is what we are after, but generally only if that continuity which the death of discontinuous beings alone can establish is not the victor in the long run. 'What we desire is to bring into a world founded on discontinuity all the continuity such a world can sustain' (Bataille 1986, 19). What are these moments when Canadians experience a profound continuity of being? The continuity that erotism brings to light is something that we can only experience fleetingly, in the extraordinariness of the ordinary and the everyday. As Hegel says, 'the Spirit is a bone.'[103] We have to glimpse the spirit of Canada in the bones of Canada.

Bear

There is no better way to know death than to link it to some licentious image.

de Sade, in Bataille 1986, 11

Bear is a story about an archivist/historian who spends a summer in a house in the forest in northern Ontario, cataloguing a library bequeathed to the historical institute for which she works by the Carys, an Anglo-Canadian colonial family. She shares the place with a bear, whom she initially fears, whose companionship she then enjoys, and with whom she eventually develops an intense and sexual relationship. *Bear* explores, through the development of this relationship, a woman's journey towards emancipation and strength, found in a sense of a shared community, a solicitous being-with-the-being-of-others.

I think that in order to understand Engel's book we must think of the bear here as a figure representing nature, and thus in the Canadian imaginary as a stand-in for the figure of the Other more generally. The bear is a radical archetype of the Other, and bestiality an extreme formulation of miscegenation, or otherwise transgressive encounters between different identities. There are three dialectical moments – thesis, antithesis, and synthesis – in Engel's account of relations with the Other in *Bear:* these show the utopian desire for union, for a consummated suturing of the social relation with Other; the antagonism defying this and making it impossible, but the possibility nevertheless, of an intense, intimate relationship, which, I am suggesting, is best formulated in terms of friendship.

In the beginning the heroine lies naked by the fire with the bear and encourages it to lick her, but the bear loses interest. Later, she enjoys regular cunnilingus with the bear, and the bear, she thinks, is into it too. But she wants to consummate their relation in genital intercourse. She tries this, but it ends in failure and danger as the bear scratches her and she fears for her life. The bear might kill her, knowingly, unknowingly, she cannot tell, and that shows the limits of the desire for unification with the Other: there is a point at which unification is discovered to be impossible because the Other always remains opaque. The third moment is the renegotiation of the relationship. She stops trying to fuck with the bear, but still has the bear with her all the time, plays with the bear in a sexually charged manner, and then they part, still friends, Canadian friends, intimates with discreet distance between them.

We will explore this dialectical development of their relationship more carefully in a moment, but there are some aspects of the novel which also merit attention. First, the locale – the forest, the wilderness, the north, provides the context for transgressive erotism. The north is where the symbolic order of civilized Canadian society is lifted. The north is the real to the symbolic order of Canada. Socially isolated, in the woods, the meticulous librarian (civilization, culture) yields to erotism in nature. This blurring of the culture/nature boundary is facilitated by the bear as a monstrous figure, 'phasing' – as it were, anthropomorphosing, a (m)animal, de-monster-ating the arbitrariness and permeability of the nature/culture bound-ary, and the ambiguity, fear, and hatred/love and desire which characterize relations with Other.

As she works through the library, the heroine finds 'with a quite surpris-ing frequency,' as Freud might say, bookmarks and marginal notes on relations between bears and humans – throughout history, in mythology, on their sexual anatomy, etc. These notes constitute a returning of the re-pressed, her (and our) unconscious desires for unity with the Other. She begins to perceive the human/animal boundary as arbitrary; the bear ap-pears as not unlike humans, but yet radically different, and the different identities are antagonistically interdependent. The monstrous Other is al-ways seen like this; alike/unlike, all that separates identities is cultivated pretence and conceit. Attuning to the Other being requires the sacrificial violation of the pretence and conceit of convention, thereby exposing the moment of openness in the categorical identities.

Another facet to which we will attend is the contrast between the protagonist's erotic relationship with the bear and her sexual intercourse with the neighbour who runs the store across the lake. She and Homer, the neighbour, are drawn together by their shared circumstances as people at the threshold of the north, the real. Their sex is casual, necessary, and enjoyable, but lacking erotism. Given the isolation and the circumstances, sex is performed as a friendly service for one another, a neighbourly thing to do for a friend. The really erotic encounter is with the bear, the figure of the stranger, the migrant to the land of human sexuality, and while the erotic encounter is a desiring quest for continuity with Other, a quest for unity/continuity that inevitably ultimately ends in failure, the synthetic moment of the encounter is the generation of friendship.

Early in the narrative, the librarian begins to move beyond her initial suspicion and fear. She discovers that the bear is house-trained: he comes inside and shuffles around harmlessly, sleeps by the fire while she is work-ing. The incongruous juxtaposition of the animality of the bear snoring loudly in the colonial living room constitutes one of the tensions which Engel plays with: the tension between pretentiousness, associated with bourgeois metropolitan culture, and the transgressive violation of the pre-tences of bourgeois culture by unpretentiousness, associated with nature, the north, in its particular embodiment in the bear.

The house, the librarian says (and of course we should read this as referring to the 'house' of Canadian society) is 'an absurdity; too elaborate, too hard to heat ... To build such a place in the north ... was colonial pretentiousness' (Engel 1976, 36). But clearly she is delighted by the luxury and comfort and the (very bourgeois) privacy of the place also, and is thrilled at the idea of spending the summer there. This ambivalence regarding the pretensions of culture versus the freedom of nature emerges more explicitly later, when, as she works on cataloguing the library, she finds a biography of Beau Brummell. As she browses disapprovingly through a pretentiously written book on a man famous for his pretentiousness, the bear sleeps by the fire.

The fire blazed. The bear slept wheezily, occasionally winking his fireward eye. She grew warm, kicked off her shoes, and found herself running her bare foot over his thick, soft coat, exploring it with her toes, finding it had depths and depths, layers and layers.   . Engel 1976, 56–7

The richness and texture of the bear's presence compares favourably with the biography and its subject, Brummell; the book she finds 'pompous and speculative, badly researched, unindexed' (56), and Brummell, the dandy, a ludicrously superficial man, as opposed to the thick, deep, layered quality of the bear.

The Beau was dominating duchesses. The Beau was on the make. How she disapproved of him, how she admired him. His egg-like perfect sense of himself never faltered. To circumstances and facts he never bent ... Cornet Brummell who would not go to Manchester (not on liberal grounds, refusing to quash a popular riot, but because gentlemen do not go to Manchester), who would not touch reality with a barge-pole, who invented the necktie and made it fashionable to be clean ... really!

She looked up at [the portrait of the house's owner] Cary and down at the bear and was suddenly exquisitely happy. Worlds changed. Two men in scarlet uniforms, two men who had lived well; neither rich or highly well born, both she was sure, in the end, ruined. She felt victorious over them; she felt she was their inheritor: a woman rubbing her foot in the thick black pelt of a bear was more than they could have imagined. More, too, than a military victory: splendour.

Engel 1976, 57

The development of the relationship between herself and the bear, their learning to like one another and live harmoniously with one another, is connected with transgressing and transcending pretentiousness, finding something beyond the 'military victory' of bourgeois culture over nature; the splendour of unity. At this moment she is playing with a utopian fantasy of continuity with the Other. She wants to lose herself from the conceit and pretence of civilization and find herself in the depth and layers of the Other.

She despises the conceit of culture, an absurd edifice set against nature, signified here by the ostentatious house and the account of Brummell's outlandish conceit. She fantasizes that she might transcend the restraining conventions of a bourgeois conceit of culture that ends in ruin, and instead enjoy transcendence in a splendid continuity of being-with-the-other. But she is an archivist, perfecting history, a suturing technician, working, not unlike Brummell, to get an egg-like perfect sense of self. She despises Brummell for this, and yet her own enjoyment is directly tied to it. She can never get away from her ambivalence towards her inherited culture, she shares in Brummell's pretension, but she is pretentiously unpretentious – a cultured and professional woman, but one who can rough it in the bush; a friendly, neighbourly type, but one who pulls rank of class and status to (initially) suppress Homer's sexual overtures. She enjoys her pretentiousness by an ironic conceit – that she is not pretentious.

She cannot disassociate herself from Brummell and lose herself in nature; it is clear also that she wouldn't want to.

The rain made her want to urinate. She went downstairs and found, as she had expected, a rose-painted, lidded chamber-pot in the bedside table. And used it gratefully. Resisted, then, the urge to crawl into her sleepingbag and put her hands over her ears. The bear, she thought affectionately, is in his sleepingbag with his hands over his ears. He has no middle-class pretensions, no front to keep up, even to himself. She went into the kitchen and began to make a pot of soup.

Engel 1976, 62

She is intimately bound to nature, the otherness in her, her animal embodiment, appearing here as the urge to urinate, the carnal pleasure of excretion. And she is a cultured being, the rose-painted, lidded chamber-pot, which she expects to be in its place, a symbol of cultivation overlaid on defecation; containment, masking of the other excess, which is in us and of us, excess which we must put a lid on and contain if we are to enjoy the conceit of civilization.

She anthropomorphizes the bear and naturalizes herself. She formulates their bond in terms of her fantasy of their shared relation to sinthome, their shared sensory enjoyment – the pleasure of snugness, listening to the sound of the rhythmic plutter of rain outside, the comfortable self-touching – but they are separated and differentiated by cultivation, by middle-class pretensions. She must urinate in a pot and cover it; her fantasy of the bear is that he is free in nature, despite the fact that he is chained in an enclosure behind the house. But this fantasy is utopian. Not only is the bear not free, he is subject to human culture, and directly to her. And he is not free in nature either: a bear is compelled to conform to animal excretory rituals. Furthermore, she all the while has a secret, excess enjoyment inaccessible to the bear: the human, cultured enjoyment of making soup in the kitchen.

Their relationship develops and deepens as more and more boundaries are transgressed, as she pursues her fantasy of a relationship of continuity with the Other.

She had never embraced him upright. It was hot and strange. She swayed against him. She put her head on his shoulder. He stood still, very still. He did not know what to do. ...

He did not reciprocate her embrace. He stood very still as she moved her body as close as possible to his. Then he yawned. She felt his great jaw moving down against her face. ...

The bear went down on all fours ... The bear lay down, his ears pricked to half-animal sounds. She let him rest a moment, then lay beside him. He excited her. She took off her clothes. He began his assiduous licking. He licked her armpits and the line between her breasts that smelled of sweat. ... Sometimes the bear half-ripped her skin with his efficient tongue, sometimes he became distracted. She had to cajole and persuade him. She put honey on herself and whispered to him, but once the honey was gone he wandered off, farting and too soon satisfied.

'Eat me, bear,' she pleaded, but he turned his head wearily to her and fell asleep. She had to put a shirt on and go back to work. Engel 1976, 114–15

Seduction of, and attunement with, the Other can be a trying and frustrating business, fraught with misunderstandings and intentions at cross purposes. The 'other worlds' of the various identities – nature (appetite, sleep) and culture (shirts, work) – continually reclaim them.

To return to de Sade's question: how do we know death, and thus continuity of being, by the licentious image of the bear licking the librarian's vulva? The moment of transgression where the symbolic order is violated, the social ceases, the subject 'risks death' – that is, risks alienation from the symbolic universe: can the act be accommodated within the symbolic order of the collective of which she is one? Will the Other offer recognition? Death is at stake with the violation of the symbolic order, her transgressive stepping outside of the boundaries of normal convention, her deliberate exposure of herself to the risk of alienation from the collective. She risks her own life, literally – for life is the recognition of life by the collective. She risks the loss of the symbolic universe in her quest for continuity of being with the Other; she enters what David Cronenberg, in his interpretation of

William Burroughs's *The Naked Lunch*, calls 'interzone'[104] – the terrain where she is no longer securely a member of 'normal' society – and neither can she be sure of recognition from the bear.

But how is this a unique and peculiar Canadian act of transgression/risk? There are two aspects of this particularity. The first is the particularity of the idiom of the symptom: that in Canada it is nature, the bear, the wilderness, that holds the place of the real. And secondly, particularity is given by the groundedness of enjoyment in the endurance of the lack of particularity: that the bear cannot offer recognition, yet the librarian perseveres, derives her enjoyment from enduring repeated misrecognition.

Her desire for unity between them is a consuming passion:

She knew now that she loved him. She loved him with such an extravagance that the rest of the world had turned into a tight meaningless knot. ...

... loved him with a clean passion that she had never felt before. ...

... She felt him to be wise and accepting. She felt sometimes that he was God. He served her. As long as she made her stool beside him in the morning, he was ready whenever she spread her legs to him. He was rough and tender, assiduous, patient, infinitely, it seemed to her, kind. ...

... There was a depth in him she could not reach, could not probe and with her intellectual fingers destroy.   Engel 1976, 117

This is a crucial moment of their relationship in terms of the progression of Hegel's 'Lordship and bondage of self-consciousness': she posits the Other as self-consciousness redoubled (Hegel 1977, 112), as a subject equal to herself, capable of surviving her desire to negate him, a subject like herself with an unreachable depth. and it is this recognition in the Other of the quality of excess, which appears as unreachable depth (and simultaneously as incompleteness, lack) that keeps being together enjoyable, playful and passionate, independent and reciprocal. This is the synthetic moment of sexually ambivalent friendship. She is intimate with the Other, but preserves the Other in his Otherness.

She lay on his belly, he batted her gently with his claws; she touched his tongue with hers and felt its fatness ...

... this was an enormous, living creature larger and older and wiser than time, a creature that was for the moment her creature, but that another could return to his own world, his own wisdom.   Engel 1976, 119

But this is also the threshold moment where she pursues her desire for their unity to an unattainable and frustrating utopian unity; from the open-ended, playful intimacy of friends to the consummate unity of lovers. The supreme unity that she seeks is such that the progeny of their union would be 'twin heroes that would save her tribe,' that their union would heal the great Cartesian wound, the tyrannical modern dualism culture/nature, subject/object. In the quest for this unity, the fun goes from their play, the fun of friendship is lost to the consuming desire to negate the antagonism of their difference and become one.

She lay, naked, panting, wanting to be near her lover, wanting to offer him her two breasts and her womb, almost believing that he could impregnate her with the twin heroes that would save her tribe. But she had to wait until night fell before it was safe to see him.

... She took him to the riverbank. They swam in the still, black water. ... They were serious that night. They swam in circles around each other, very solemnly. ...

She sat up. The bear sat up across from her. She rose to her knees and moved towards him. When she was close enough to feel the wet gloss on her breasts, she mounted him. Nothing happened. He could not penetrate her and she could not get him in.

She turned away. He was quite unmoved. She took him to his enclosure and sent him to bed.

...

The next day she was restless, guilty. She had broken a taboo. She had changed something. The quality of her love was different now. She had gone too far with him.

Engel 1976, 121–2

What has she broken, why does she feel guilty, what is at stake in the transgression of the taboo against bestiality? She has sought a continuity of being, a bridging of the gap between discontinuous, discrete beings, which was impossible, impossible because she misrecognized the subject. Subjects are not discrete self-knowing and knowable identities, who understand one another's intentions, who are, or can be, of one mind. 'Nothing happened.' 'She turned away. He was quite unmoved.' At the very moment when she thought she could bridge the gap, she experienced the profound distance separating one from the Other. Bringing to light this absolute limit of the social, an intolerable antagonism that her desire for totality and continuity revealed by its inevitable failure, is what she feels guilty about. By transgressing the taboo she has blown the conceit of an ultimate continuity of being, a nostalgic and desperate conceit that is hard to relinquish, for later she tries one last time with the bear.

We will look at that encounter in a moment, but not before seeing her atonement for her transgression by engaging in friendly, dispassionate sex with Homer. Homer's very name tells us what he is symbolically: he is 'home.' She and Homer are already 'at one' in so far as they share a membership in being Canadians at the threshold of the north. They recognize a continuity between themselves in the face of the real – the isolation and loneliness of the wilderness. Furthermore, the continuity between their identities is something that Homer constantly affirms against the Otherness of the bear. Homer repeatedly reminds her that the bear is a wild animal, and never to lose sight of that fact. But desire is, precisely, desire to lose that 'fact' and find continuity.

In the failure to receive recognition from the bear as another self-consciousness equal to her and of one mind with her, the failure of the risk of her transgression, she is confronted with the 'fact' of a radical break in the continuity of being. And for her sin – her losing sight, her sacrificing of her identity, her risking symbolic death, alienation from her shared membership in Canadian (human) society by her miscegenation – she must make atonement, at-one-ment; she must reestablish her being 'at-one' with Homer. And for this she must make another sacrifice: she must sacrificially renounce her erotic quest for continuity of being with the bear if she is to receive recognition and be reintegrated in Canadian society.

'Hi.'
'Long time no see.'
'Been on a work-jag.'
'Thought you might get bushed.'
'I brought you a drink.'
He grinned. 'Cups?'
'I've got one in the glove-compartment.'
'Me too.'
... When half the bottle was gone he plucked her sleeve and took her into a decayed bunkhouse. Unbuckled his belt. As she did hers. They stood half-undressed before each other. He grinned. 'Can't do too long without it, can we?'

There were no preliminaries. He had a good long prick and he used it ... it was good to have that enormous emptiness filled, but she felt nothing with him, nothing.

When he was finished he said thank you. Then they dressed.
'You keep the rest of the bottle,' she said.
'No, you. It's easier for me to git.'
'Well, okay. You can stop by for a drink some time.'
'Sure will. Thanks.'   Engel 1976, 126

Sexual intercourse with Homer is ritualistically casual; they go through the motions of fucking while being friendly and polite with one another. But the encounter is dispassionate; a necessary ritual intercourse between friends to remind one another of their shared membership in the face of solitude and isolation, tinged with the same well-mannered desperation of personal ads: 'Str. w.m. sks F 20s (any race) for hot afternoon encounters, clean, sincere, discreet. reply box.#.etc.' Such encounters are symptomatic of the problem of Canadian unity in general: independence, solitude, reconciled with desire for unity, achieved by institutions of mediation (politeness, discretion, telephones, beers), marred by the risk of lack of passion and scarcity of feeling, making the shared house of Being a 'decayed bunkhouse.' What saves the encounter and keeps Being alive is the 'really' erotic promise of the Other; the bear, the surprise of 'any race,' 'bi curious,' or some such vanishing point.

Following her act of atonement with Homer, the heroine returns to the island and sits by the fireside with the bear again. She has reconstituted her shared membership through Homer, filled the enormous emptiness which the failed encounter with the bear had left her with, but without the promise of a transcendent continuity which the bear had promised she feels nothing with Homer. At first it seems that she is resigned to the impossibility signified by her failure with the bear, but that is not the case. She refuses to give up on her desire, and risks everything again, and it is through her refusal to relinquish her desire, by risking everything in transgression (alienation again from her social membership, numbing misrecognition by the bear), that she eventually achieves a moment of transcendence.

'It's over, now,' she told him. 'It's over. You have to go to your place and I to mine.' She sat up and put her sweater on.

He sat up across from her, rubbing his nose with a paw and looking confused. Then he looked down at himself. She looked as well. Slowly, majestically his great cock was rising.

It was not like a man's, tulip-shaped. It was red, pointed, and impressive. She looked at him. He did not move. She took her sweater off and went down on all fours in front of him, in the animal posture.

He reached out one great paw and ripped the skin on her back.

At first she felt no pain. She simply leapt away from him. Turned to face him. He had lost his erection and was sitting in the same posture. She could see nothing, nothing, in his face to tell her what to do.

Then she felt the blood running down her back, and knew she had to run away.

Engel 1976, 131–2

It is the fact of the unknowability of the Other, the fact that she could see nothing, nothing in his face to tell her what to do, that she knows that she must run away. The Other always remains, at some point, ultimately opaque, an impenetrable, dark object that denies recognition and assimilation and incorporation into the identity of the one. The otherness of the Other then is restored to the bear by this second failure, but not only does this restoration of radical otherness not eliminate the possibility of their relationship, it actually enriches it, restores to it antagonism, dynamism, and uncertainty. For the following day:

She sat beside the bear for a while, reading. Last night she had been afraid that the smell of blood on her would cause him to wound her further, but today he was something else: lover, God or friend. Dog too, for when she put her hand out he licked and nuzzled it.

Something was gone between them, though: the high, whistling communion that had bound them during the summer.   Engel 1976, 134

So the high, whistling communion, the extravagant, ultimately frustrated desire for continuity, is quieted, but by the return of her desire to herself she is enriched:

What had passed to her from him she did not know. Certainly it was not the seed of heroes, or magic, or any astounding virtue, for she continued to be herself. But for one strange, sharp moment she could feel in her pores and the taste of her own mouth that she knew what the world was for. She felt not that she was at last human, but that she was at last clean. Clean and simple and proud.   Engel 1976, 136–7

Here we see an excellent example of what Hegel calls Being coming to know itself from its reflection in the Other (1977, 111). She comes to know not that she has become fully 'human,' understood conventionally as a unified, totalized identity, but that she is clean, clean and simple, clean of that fantasy of complete identities, a fantasy of an achievable state of continuity amongst discontinuous beings, and simple in the knowledge that the world is for enjoying the elusive synthetic moments of discovery of the self and the Other; the discovery of the Other in the self and the self in the Other, and taking responsibility for the artful conduct of relations with Others who are always, necessarily, simultaneously, lovers, gods, dogs, and friends.

The story concludes when the bear is taken away to stay with an old Native woman, Lucy, who had previously looked after him. Lucy's son arrives with a boat to collect the bear, and tells the librarian that Lucy hopes she made friends with him. 'Oh, I got on good with him,' she says 'He's a fine fellow' (Engel 1976, 138). And this exchange, Lucy's hope that they made friends, the librarian's affirmation that they got on good, and were fine fellows – fellow beings – gives us the key to the beginning and the end of the character of relations with the Other: friendship. At the beginning of the story, Lucy offers some advice on attunement and making friends with the bear:

> 'Good bear,' she said. 'Good lady. Take care of bear.'
> 'I don't think I really know how to take care of him,' she said, modestly citified.
> ...
> ... 'Good bear,' she said. 'Bear your friend.' ...
> ... 'Shit with the bear,' she said. 'He like you, then. 'Morning, you shit, he shit. Bear lives by smell. He like you.'   Engel 1976, 48–9

The culture/nature boundary is crossed already: they are both interpellated by Lucy as 'Good': 'Good bear,' 'Good lady.' The good is served by their attunement to one another. Note the use of 'like,' meaning 'similar to,' and 'affectionate/friendly to.' 'Like [similar to] you, he live by smell.' Freud says that smell is the most repressed of the human senses; when we were on all fours, noses and genitals were on the same level.[105] The adoption of an upright posture required the repression of this sense most closely linked to erotism. The first step to reenter this erogenous zone we share with the Other requires a ritual transgression of taboo, a sacrificial destruction of the pretences of convention – shitting with the bear in the morning. It is by the ritualized violation of the system of taboos (laws) by which society is hegemonically ordered and organized that we get to 'be like' – similar to – and 'like' – be friendly towards – the Other.

Transgression of taboo, of course, is not limited to defecating with bears in the forest, but as we will see below, may be practices of everyday life in modern multicultural Canada.

9

The Comedic Fundamentals of Canadian Enjoyment

But if the truth of the subject, even when he is in the position of master, does not reside in himself, but as analysis shows, in an object that is, of its nature, concealed, [then] to bring this object out into the light of day is really and truly the essence of comedy.
Lacan 1978, 5

Les Anglais pensent seulement au cul.
Graffiti in toilet of Ottawa bar

The 'object' to which Lacan refers, he proceeds to explain, is the fundamentum, literally 'the bottom parts,' the pudendum, the 'naughty bit'/ 'dirty bit' ('naught' = 'zero,' 'dirty = profane excrement), the 'hole,' the lack of integrity, the coincidence of lack/excess. Canadian comedy seeks to expose Canada's bottom, its laughable part. What comedy does is to 'moon' Canada. Mooning is the fundamental comic act, the fundamental subversive act; it shows the lack in the symbolic order by reflecting the lack back to the gaze of the Big Other. How is mooning subversive? It lets the gaze fall on the arse, offers the arse for recognition, so that the master too, the gazer, is rendered an arse. He becomes literally the 'butt' of the joke. Mooning Canada is saying 'I know Canada lacks, my own lack mirrors it,' and this comic mirroring of the lack is enjoyable (announced by our laughter) because now the comedic Canadian is no longer alienated from Canada, but identifies with it as also lacking. A sense of humour – our recognition of the comic – allows us to escape alienation.

Another act of exposing the fundamentum (pudendum) is 'cocking a snook.' The gesture is expressed in different idioms in various cultures. The typical Western usage is the open palm extended from the thumb resting on the nose, accompanied by wiggling the fingers, protruding the tongue, and expelling the breath to mimic flatulence. Directed towards the Other's gaze, it reflects an exaggeration of the size (the elongated nose) of the Other's 'phallus' (i.e., His Word, His Law), but it exposes the phallus of the Big Other as impotent, as powerless despite its great size; for all its grotesque enormity, its engorged arrogance, it is no more than a flaccid windbag (signified by the wiggling fingers and accompanying sound effects).

The most familiar contemporary form of cocking a snook is the 'crotch grab and thrust,' a gesture with which many Rap artists punctuate their performances. In the context of the defiant aesthetic developed by Public Enemy or Niggas With Attitude, for example, the gesture is directed at the gaze of white hegemony. It says, in effect, 'All of this, all of your civilization, your world dominance, your power, can be reduced to this – this purely phallic project.[106] I've got your number. You suck. You're a mothafukka.' Michael Jackson, an artist who has made the crotch grab and thrust virtually his personal trademark, has a particularly interesting and subversive usage. Jackson is a disturbing and alluring cyborg in so far as he resists categorization. What race is Jackson? What gender? Jackson's crotch grabbing is transgressive, it affronts us and enthrals us precisely because he draws attention to our uncertainty and anxiety about the phallus. Maybe Jackson actually doesn't have a phallus, in which case he is mirroring the lack of the Big Other's phallus, and thus the Father's law: His naming and policing of the categories of race and gender is without foundation, and we are simultaneously freed and freaked out at this possibility.

In Ireland when we are talking about enjoyment we use the term 'the crack.' A crucial dimension of our national thing is 'the crack.' Irish people are always 'looking for the crack,' 'having a crack,' talking about 'the great crack we had last night,' and so on. The most common salutation is: 'How's the crack?' To which 'The crack is mighty' is an appropriate retort. The 'crack' is the flaw in the symbolic order, the fundamental lack in the Big Other, the king's profane arse as opposed to the king's sublime head which signifies the law. And it is 'a mighty crack,' big enough to accommodate enjoyment.

In the Irish case, in so far as the dominant humours, the ruling conventions, are Catholic, it would of course be the pope's arse that must be brought into the light of day – hence the profusion of jokes and lewd yarns concerning nuns and priests, and the public delight in the discovery that a bishop has an illegitimate son in the U.S. An interesting aspect of this incident is how the authority of the bishop, while seemingly erased by the fact of his fornication, is in fact preserved by a joke that appears to mock his lack. 'What does it take to get the pants off a bishop? A good yank.' Here the bishop appears not as a licentious fornicator, but as one tempted and seduced, by an excessive and forceful 'yank'; a 'good yank,' though, who has done Irish Catholics a favour by giving them some respite from the might of the bishop's phallus, now revealed as rooted in the profane. The bishop's authority is erased momentarily by his being 'caught with his trousers down,' but his authority is simultaneously restored by shifting the burden of responsibility from him onto the Other who does us a favour, the 'good yank.'

There is a passage in Joyce's *Ulysses* that illustrates this poetic art of opening a crack for enjoyment. The moment is located structurally at a point in the novel where Joyce's hero, Leopold Bloom, a Jew, is entrammelled in the symbolic order of Irish Catholic National Socialism. The incident occurs in the street between two bars, sites of enjoyment both constituted and endangered by these hegemonic discourses. Bloom has just left a bar where a group of men were passionately singing a nationalist/Catholic ballad/hymn called the 'Croppy Boy.' The ballad tells of a youth on his way to fight in the rebellion of 1798 who stops at a church to make a confession lest he be killed in the combat. He relates his puny little sins (good Catholic Irish lad that he is) and concludes, 'I bear no hate against a living thing / but I love my country above my king.' A sin of grave consequences for the hapless youth, for it turns out that the 'priest' is actually a British captain who has heinously murdered the true Irish priest. The would-be patriot is promptly arrested and hauled away to die, a martyr for Irish Catholic nationalism, an even more purified and elevated status than that of a rebel with blood on his hands.

Later Bloom is in another bar where he meets 'the Citizen,' a lout who spouts nationalist cliché and socialist rhetoric, but who, it becomes clear, is a narrow-minded xenophobe and rabid anti-Semite who makes thinly veiled threats to Bloom. How does Joyce/Bloom make room for enjoyment in this oppressive context? Between the bars, on the street, Bloom pretends to be looking in a shop window, a ruse to avoid a woman with whom he's had dealings. His eye falls upon 'a gallant pictured hero,' a portrait of yet another patriot, Robert Emmett, and underneath, his last words from the scaffold. Bloom reads:

... When my country takes her place among
Prrprr.
Must be the bur.
Fff. Oo. Rrpr.

Nations of the earth. No-one behind. She's passed. *Then and not till then.* Tram. Kran, kran, kran. Good oppor. Coming. Krandlkrankran. I'm sure it's the burgund. Yes. One, two. *Let my epitaph be.* Karaaaaaaa. *Written. I have.*
Pprrpffrrppffff.
Done.   Joyce 1961, 291

Joyce punctuates the glorious patriotic rhetoric with farts. The sublime is profaned. Bloom's breaking wind literally blows apart the quilting points of Catholic Irish nationalism. The fat balladeer and the oafish 'Citizen,' who embody all that is grotesque and menacing, stupid and small-minded, fundamentalist, xenophobic, and physically threatening, now appear as comical blustery windbags, and the hegemony that they represent becomes tainted with the odour of stale stout.

Freud says: 'Caricature, parody, travesty (as well as their practical counterpart, unmasking) are directed against people and objects which lay claim to authority and respect, which are in some sense sublime. The degradation of the sublime allows one to have an idea of it as though it were something commonplace, in whose presence I need not pull myself together, but may to use the military formula, "stand easy"' (1981, 261–2). Comedy violates the Law of the Father, but doesn't erase it, for what it seeks is the living room in which to stand easy, not the abyss in which things would fall apart. Comedy must acknowledge the Father while exposing his crack.

An underlying sensibility of ironic conceit that allows us to 'stand easy' in the face of the authority of the Father is evident in carnival, Bakhtin says. 'All the symbols of the carnival idiom are filled with ... the sense of the gay relativity of prevailing truths and authorities' (1984, 11). Carnival laughter is utopian because it is universal in scope, it hopes to include everyone. The people's ambivalent laughter 'expresses the point of view of the whole world. He who is laughing also belongs to it.' Does this apply to Joyce's hero? His carnivalesque transgression is private. We snicker with him secretly. Is the possibility of festive, collective, carnivalesque laughter denied by modern hegemonic formations, such as sectarian nationalism?

Bakhtin would say yes. He repeatedly bemoans the passing of the festive laughter of carnival. Speaking of the poverty of the carnivalesque in modernity, he says: 'The satirist whose laughter is negative places himself above the object of his mockery, he is opposed to it. The wholeness of the world's comic aspect is destroyed, and that which appears comic becomes a private reaction' (1984, 12). But I would argue that what Bakhtin fails to take into account here in his critique of the absent and privatized nature of the carnivalesque in modernity is that the carnivalesque now takes different and diverse forms, from graffiti and subcultural style to the institution of the comedian and the role of popular literature, mass media, and television, in uniting the collective(s) in carnivalesque conspirac(ies). Joyce collects his readership, the 'Kids in the Hall' collect another, in our shared capacity for irony in the collective unconscious. But quite apart from this, which I will leave undeveloped for now, there is also evidence that the carnival is alive and well in Canada.

An example of the everyday comic art of carnivalesque self-parody is provided by the people of Leaf Rapids, a small town in northern Manitoba.[107] The community holds an annual 'beach party,' in February! (in the minus thirties and forties). The 'beach party' is held in the community centre, the heating is cranked up to July temperatures. The theme of the party varies. In 1993 the theme was 'Bondai Beach, Oz. style.' In other years Leaf Rapids has had 'Fort Lauderdale' beach parties and 'Caribbean' beach parties. Everyone in town, including the Mounties and the bank manager, plays a role. One of the highlights of the 1993 party was a relay race. People dressed as kiwi fruit rolled other kiwi fruits around the hall; the relay was taken up by 'sharks,' people with large dorsal fins tied to their backs, who swam (crawled on their bellies) around the hall. 'Roos took over from the sharks and bounded around the hall in sacks to the finishing line.

The people of Leaf Rapids make enduring winter enjoyable by a carnivalesque parody of themselves and the humours to which they are subject: the bad humour of Big (m)Other Nature and the bad humour of envy of the enjoyment imputed to Others. The bad humour of nature, which prohibits enjoyment, is transformed in the carnivalesque inversion. But by a parody of themselves? Yes, not Australians, for what they're playing up for laughs is the Canadian beach party. At the lake in the summer, Canadians play at being Australians and Californians: windsurfing, jetskiing, wearing the hottest beachwear, having the right shades, getting the perfect tan, addressing one another as 'dude,' cruising in the convertible with the top down and some brewskies in the cooler on the back seat. Canadian 'beach' culture, on the lakeshore, is already a parody of 'real' beach culture that Others – in Australia, Florida, the Caribbean – are assumed to enjoy, that Canadians self-consciously borrow from to produce 'our' version of a Canadian beach party.

'Humour,' according to Samuel Johnson, is 'the ruling passion' (the bad humour, or good humour as the case may be, of the Father) that keeps us in 'a state of ritual bondage,'[108] i.e., our slavery to the conventions of His house and His humours. The dominant humour has society in thrall to its obsession. The tragedy is that action is impoverished, becoming merely the repetition of the humour for no reason other than the repetition of the humour. 'Humour' refers to the hegemonic order. One could formulate the problem of the discourse of political correctness and official multiculturalism in these terms: that is, the tendency towards enslavement to the conventions of a bureaucratic methodologism of categorization (see Bordo 1990, 133–56), whereby the ethical purpose of collective emancipation through equalization amongst diverse identities becomes lost to the purpose of demarcating and identifying the contents that constitute the particular categories. We are becoming subject to the bad humour of the people whom Foucault refers to as 'bureaucrats of the Revolution and civil servants of Truth.'[109]

The action of comedy moves towards breaking the absurd or irrational law of the humour. 'A sense of humour' is sensing (the lack in) the dominant humour. Frye says that comedy begins with the recognition that the hero's desire is prohibited by the law, appearing from this aspect as absurd, cruel, or irrational.[110] The process of comedy takes the form of overcoming obstacles to the hero's desire. The obstacle is the Father's humour – His will, His law, or a substitute for the Father, some form of authority that prohibits the hero's enjoyment by obstructing his desire. And comedy climaxes in uniting as many as possible in a new society. The Father is not killed, or His law erased. Rather his humour is transformed and the opposition resolved, and the audience recognizes the unity in enjoyment of the comedic society as having been the desirable state of affairs all along.

Comedy is the exposure, with varying degrees of artfulness, of the lack in the Father's humour. Laughter is the moment of hesitation/trepidation, suspense/release, that announces, signifies, our recognition of the lack not as an obstacle to going on enjoyably, but as an incentive, an opportunity to recollect our shared enjoyment. The joke, like the souvenir, tells us that the Big Other is not so powerful as to prohibit enjoyment, but that He offers us security nonetheless. Laughter shows our *relief* that this is the case, that there is room to go on enjoyably. (Our relief that the comic didn't turn out to be tragic, that we didn't kill the Big Other, leaving us exposed to the void.)

One possible hypothesis on Canadian humour, then, would be that Canadians don't tell jokes because there is nothing serious and tragic enough to cause a need for jokes. In so far as it may be fair to say that Canada is a humourless society, this is because the phallic signifiers that quilt the symbolic order are weak already – the figure of the dashing/flaming Mountie, or the flaccid Fathers of Confederation (there is no really substantial member in Canadian history, it took a bunch of them to father the nation, and none of them had even a particularly memorable style!). Perhaps there is no dominant humour that we are in thrall to, so the Canadian sense of humour is gentle, proceeding by exposing the comic's lack first, as if to permit Canada to not be alienated from its citizens.

Canadian Comedy

Let us take some examples of comedy in Canada that show us the humours that we are subject to, our sense of the 'crack' in these humours, and how we open spaces for shared laughter, friendship, and enjoyment for one another.

Mike Myers identifies a crucial wellspring for Canadian comedy: 'Americans watch T.V. Canadians watch American T.V.' (1993, 5). Canadian comics do their best work in the U.S., the object domain outside that really constitutes Canada, that which Canada is Not (Not!). And here names like Leslie Nielsen, Dan Aykroyd, Mike Myers, and John Candy provide ready examples. Ottawa's Dan Aykroyd gives us a good example of comedic subversion of servitude to the hegemonic humour of 'mass consumption.' His 'Saturday Night Live' 'Coneheads' are space aliens living in suburban New Jersey, who in an effort to blend in try to conform to the convention by mass-consuming (they eat mountainous plateloads of waffles and bacon and eggs for breakfast, swallow submarine sandwiches whole, and drink beer a six-pack at a time). They expose servitude to the convention by overdoing it. The Coneheads bring the lack in the symbolic order of consumer society into view.

The integrity of the symbolic order of suburban life, its constitution as an enjoyable and meaningful form of life, depends upon the conceit of 'consumer choice,' 'discernment,' 'taste.' The Coneheads show that it is precisely these that are lacking, and that suburbanites simply do mass-consume compulsively, mindlessly, slavishly. But of course we are all – including suburbanites from New Jersey – protected from this scathing critique of mass society enough to permit our laughter, because the Coneheads are still aliens from outer space, stranger Others, who simply don't get our enjoyment, they haven't quite got the art of being in suburbia. In so far as they have, and obviously enjoy our enjoyment, they reaffirm for us that in fact we are cultivated and creative in the arts of consumption.

While Aykroyd's comedy speaks to a North American sense of humour, it's especially an opportunity for Canadian laughter. Canadians are subject to the bad humour of envy of the imputed enjoyment of even more excessive mass consumption in the U.S. For Canadians know that it's really only Americans who over-consume so shamelessly. Not! (Canadians generate more waste per capita than any other industrial society, including the U.S.)

Consumerism for Canadians can still be a source of enjoyment, because *we* still have taste. (Not!) Aykroyd shows Canadians the lack in the envious humour we are in thrall to, and in so far as we identify with the Coneheads' estrangement from America (Aykroyd is playing on another Canadian comic figure of alienation, the 'Canoehead'), we are laughing at our envy of American enjoyment.

Another obvious but excellent example is provided by Paul Schaffer, Dave Letterman's band-leader straight-man. Schaffer, who is originally from Winnipeg, appears as the consummate Canadian. Dave sets him up, again and again, and he falls for it. He can enjoy/endure the arrogant American, tolerate the whole thing, while staying unpretentiously in Letterman's shadow. But simultaneously he plays a subversive comic role, showing that there is nothing behind Letterman's conceit and hysterical chatter, a nothingness declared by the instrumental 'dah – dahaaa's,' frisky riffs, and anti-climactic drum rolls. Shafer exposes the nothingness behind the symbolic order of that object domain that is the cause of Canada's desire, and by exposing its fundamentals, its flaccid phallic signifiers, its lacks, he enables Canadians to love their symptom – all that is not-American – as themselves.

The Monty Python Incident

The CBC began transmitting 'Monty Python's Flying Circus' in autumn 1970. The show quickly developed a cult following, particularly amongst students and the young. 'Middle Canada,' however, took offense, at 'poor taste' and 'lack of respect for revered British cultural institutions.' One incident in particular was pivotal. I am referring of course to the (in)famous lumberjack song. In this sketch, a manly lumberjack in check shirt and fur hat sings about the *jouissance* of the Canadian woodsman. He is supported by his woman at his side, and by a chorus of Mounties resplendent in their scarlet tunics. The song begins with a celebration of the forest: the smell of freshly cut timber, the crash of mighty trees as they are felled into the rushing rivers. The lumberjack extols the virtues of the unpretentious Canadian, who enjoys enduring the simple, hardworking life – 'I sleep all night and I work all day / I chop down trees, I eat my lunch ...' – and so on. The Mounties sing a chorus of approval: 'He's a lumberjack and he's O.K. ...' Gradually the lumberjack's song begins to move in a rather different direction. The manly woodsman tells us about his very unofficial *jouissance*, one that radically subverts the master signifiers of the Canadian symbolic order. The lumberjack sings that he likes to skip through the forest, wear women's clothing, and hang around bars. The Mounties have some difficulty singing along to this, and as the lumberjack continues, describing his predilection for wearing suspenders and brassieres, they leave the stage in disgust.

In January 1971, in response to the 'Lumberjack Song' (among other things), the CBC dropped the series. At McGill University in Montreal, the 'Rassemblement pour Conserver Monty Python' (RCMP, the initials of the Royal Canadian Mounted Police) was founded, and in temperatures of minus twenty, two hundred protesters assembled outside the CBC offices, doing 'silly walks' and singing the 'Lumberjack Song.' Similar demonstrations were held in Toronto and Winnipeg (see Hewison 1981, 15).

The CBC, Canada's 'ideological state apparatus' (Althusser 1984, 109), was concerned with the hegemonic articulation of a true, good, and beautiful Canadian symbolic order, quilted with figures of manly lumberjacks, fair and buxom Canadian women, and constant, ever-loyal Mounties. The elevation of such figures in the hegemonic project of Canadian nationalism necessitated the denigration of their counterparts in the fading symbolic order of the British Empire, so the CBC readily embraced Monty Python's cocking a snook at the Father in its portrayal of nerdy accountants, stuffy petty bureaucrats, cross-dressing judges, inane royalty, etc. – staples of the Flying Circus's repertoire. But the CBC could not find comic at all a ludicrous representation of figures which they were attempting to elevate to the status of sublime objects: the true Canadian man, the beauty of Canadian womanhood, and the good law embodied in the Mountie.

For the mandarins of the CBC with the official mandate of fostering Canadian nationalism, the Pythons proved too hot to handle. While they fitted with the objective of establishing some distance from the Father's (British imperial) humours, their transgressions against them were too violent for nostalgic Anglo-Canadian sensibilities. But more important, the Pythons were also subverting the new Canadian phallic project. While the state cannot tolerate the profaning of the sublime objects that stand for the Name of the Father (transvestite lumberjacks and foppish Mounties), 'ordinary Canadians' can, because they can enjoy/endure the lack of particularity, and they enjoy by transgressing the law, which they nonetheless continue to pay homage to by ironic conceit. Canada needs sublime figures like Mounties and lumberjacks, but not if they are only sublime – the stoic, hardened woodsman, melancholy in his solitude in the primeval forest, the stiff, earnest Mountie, who promises/threatens relentlessness, to always get his man. The sublime object is only tolerable if we can sense its lack.

But what at one point seemed oppressive and in need of comedic subversion we now relate to nostalgically. No one in Canada experiences him- or herself as subject to the British monarchy any more, and neither do we really feel subject to the nationalist phallic project of the Canadian state and its ideological apparatus as it was twenty-five years ago. Thus the Queen and the Mounties aren't good targets for comedy any longer, and we relate to the cartoon hero 'Dudley Doright of the Mounties' as kitsch. If we want to see what we are in thrall to today, what humours we are subject to and how comedy gives us some respite from the law and seeks to renegotiate our relationship to the Father, we need to look at current comedy.

A hint of the target for subversive Canadian comedy came to me from a conversation with a Toronto Blue Jays fan.[111] He told me that American baseball players visiting SkyDome frequently comment that 'it's a class place,' and that Toronto Blue Jays fans are a 'class act.' By which they mean, as they go on to explain, that the fans are well behaved, and that they applaud, as in *clap*, to show appreciation for good play, as if they were at a theatre, not a ball game. The downside is that the fans are too restrained, and managers have had to request (on the giant TV) that they be more exuberant and show the players that they are enjoying themselves. With this in mind the example we will examine here is a 1993 skit from 'The Kids in the Hall' that reworks a classic 'Keystone Kops' routine with our servitude to the Canadian humour of politeness and good manners as the target.

As I recall it, the scene is as follows: A 'Husky' truck stop in rural Ontario. Enter three men, obviously escaped cons, since they are dressed in prison clothes. Customers glance at them momentarily, and then resume eating. Cons take a seat, wait their turn, place their order, with 'pleases' and 'thank yous,' smiling and nodding. Everything proceeds according to Canadian conventions of politeness as if nothing were out of the ordinary. Enter two Ontario Provincial Police officers, who take a table alongside the escapees. Cops call for waitress, place their order, commence eating. Cops and cons notice one another. Cons begin to eat faster, cops eat faster too, racing to finish first, but yet trying not to gorge themselves rudely or cause a mess. They are both equally subject to the conventions of polite restaurant etiquette. Cons finish first, call for the cheque, cops are also calling for the cheque. Cons get cheque first, pay, tip, and leave. Cops get cheque. One cop goes to pay, the other cop says that it's his turn to buy, as first cop paid for coffee and doughnuts earlier. Second cop insists. First cop agrees to leave the tip, and so on. Cops pay, smile, leave. Cops and cons dash to their respective cars. Cons burn off, cops take off in hot pursuit. Cons stop to get gas. Cops join the line-up behind them. Smiles. Banter with the attendant.

Pay and thank him. Cons get into their car and burn away again. Cops do the same routine, get back in their car and resume the chase. Cops and cons scorch down the highway, across the provincial border. Both cars screech to a halt, cops and cons get out. Cons cock a snook at the cops. One cop says to the other: 'Well, it's up to the Mounties now.' Ends.

In Canada all parties are in servitude to the humour of politeness: conventions of 'correct behaviour' that prohibit enjoyment – getting service first, running out without paying, stuffing one's face, and so on. Politeness, being bound by the conventions of 'correct behaviour,' 'good manners,' is a trope for our servitude to political correctness, official multiculturalism, and peace, order, and good government. We are all bound by this law. The cops' enjoyment is equally restrained and prohibited by these conventions; the object of their desire, consuming coffee and doughnuts at the truck stop, is stolen not by the presence of the Others, the cons, but rather by the prohibition on catching the escapees while they are involved in their enjoyment (eating their lunch). The enjoyment of both cons and cops is infringed upon by their servitude to the same law of politeness. They can neither escape nor arrest, nor eat as they wish, unless they follow the conventions correctly.

And yet it is precisely because both are subject to the same law that enjoyment is permitted. They cross the provincial border and that marks a new jurisdiction, a new category. Respect for the categories of identification and the jurisdictions that go along with them is what permits and assures enjoyment. The cons escape, not to freedom, but to enjoy being pursued further in their quest for an impossible freedom. And the OPP cops get to resume their enjoyment; 'It's up to the Mounties now.' The OPP can get back to enforcing the law within their jurisdiction, and patrol the doughnut houses of the nation.

Comedy achieves continuity of enjoyment, so how then is comedy transformative and emancipatory? The moment of comedic violation shows us the humours we are subject to, the conventions that restrain us. Its double action shows us the lacks in the humours, and simultaneously shores them up. The action of comedy then is a 'breathing': opening and closing gaps in the symbolic order, collecting enjoyment in a fresh synthesis. Comedy's relation to official multiculturalism and to political correctness then would have to be similar. It would not aim to erase the law, to be politically incorrect, to be anti-affirmative, to devalue diversity, to insult the Other, but rather to bring the lack in the law into view, so that we are not subject to its lack of irony, so that we experience it as 'lightened up,' so to speak, to provide room for the laughter of a wider comedic society.

The Friendly Character of Canadian Comedy

Bakhtin tells us that there is an aspect of carnivalesque inversion when people form friendly relations with one another: 'They address each other informally, abusive words are used affectionately, and mutual mockery is permitted' (1984, 16). Let us consider the relationship between comedy and friendship in Canada.

God is bored one day, looking down from Heaven, not that much goin' on, eh. Sees this guy in a small fishing boat off the east coast. The Newfie is rowin' away, and singin' to himself: 'I'se th' bye tha' bilds de boat / an' I'se th' bye tha' sails her / I'se th' bye tha' catches th' fish / an' brings 'em home to Liza.' God decides to do an experiment on the guy, eh. Zap! Snaps his fingers, takes away half the Newfie's brain. The guy stops rowin,' scratches his head, and then starts up again, rowin' away, singin' eh; 'I'se th' bye tha' bilds th' boat ...' 'Hmmm,' says God, waits for a minute, and snaps his fingers again. Zap! Half of the rest of the guy's brain, gone, eh. The Newfie stops, eh, and then takes off again: 'I'se th' bye ...' God is blown away! Awesome! Snaps his fingers again and the rest of the Newfie's brain gone. Totally! Guy just stops for a second, and then takes off again, singin' 'Alouette, gentille alouette ...'

Ha ha. Double whammy. But here's a good rejoinder, from Quebec:

When Anglos say that they want to sleep with you, they're serious!

Here's one for all of us:

Why did the Canadian cross the road? To get to the middle.

And here's a funny byte of Canadian idiom. 'Coyote manoeuvre': When you would rather gnaw your arm off than wake up the person with whom you've spent the night. (A coyote caught in a trap will, reputedly, gnaw off its leg to escape.) An example of the usage: 'I was really hammered at Chuck's party and scored so and so. Jeez, did I want to pull a coyote manoeuvre on him or her, or what, eh.' There is something endearingly Canadian in this articulation of a familiar trauma. Although the person is repulsive, and you are embarrassed, you are too polite to wake up, or disturb, him or her. And the joke is on you, the coyote, waking up with the ultimate hoser or the homely ditz, a reflection on the perversity of your desire, your crude lack of artistry and taste; they're innocent.

The first two jokes collect a shared enjoyment at the expense of Others; the latter two are more characteristic examples of Canadian comedy, I think. Making fun of ourselves, self-disclosure, and self-deprecation are hallmarks of Canadian comedy. Stephen Leacock is the classic example. Leacock's writings are personal reminiscences – 'The Boy I Left behind Me' (1946), *Sunshine Sketches of a Little Town* (1912), 'My Remarkable Uncle' (1942). His comedy depends on self-disclosure, showing a disarmed vulnerability, openness, not offensive to an Other, but rather self-deprecating, in the hope, I would argue, of facilitating attunement.

The 'uncle' piece is perhaps especially interesting, because the uncle is the promoter of grandiose enterprises, and this makes him the subject of our shared laughter. The uncle is the subject through whom Leacock sacrifices unpretentiousness (simply, the uncle is pretentious), and we, the rest of us Canadians, find ourselves, our continuity, in our shared laughter at him. But the uncle is a subject to whom Leacock is closely related, an Other who is kin to us, so that we and Leacock are implicated in the uncle's schemes, and so our laughter is at ourselves when we glimpse the conceit of our unpretentiousness. In much of Mordecai Richler's work – for example, 'The Art of Kissing' – we can see the same device, that his comedy is seldom at the expense of others; rather, it is usually anecdotal and autobiographical and at his own expense, initially. Then, in so far as we find ourselves in the situation that he discloses for us – familiar traumas and enjoyments of adolescence – we find ourselves identifying with Richler and laughing with him at ourselves.

The initial move of disclosure is the Canadian idiomatic expression of the utopian moment of comedy: comedy tries to collect the widest possible membership in festive laughter in a new society. And disarming self-disclosure is not just the hallmark of the 'classical' stuff. Margaret Atwood and Max Braithwaite employ the same tactic too. Portraying the ordinary Canadian as goofy and vulnerable, and thus open to audition, ready to make friends with others and share enjoyable membership, is also the central device in films such as *Roadkill* and *Highway 61*, and TV's 'The Kids in the Hall.' We've heard from the Kids already, so let's take an example from Bruce McDonald's 1990 film *Roadkill*, and show a connection between the valuation of 'clarity' (which of course bears a strong family resemblance to unpretentiousness) and the Canadian comedic device of self-disclosure.

Clarity is an important value in the Canadian symbolic order: 'clear water,' 'true north,' 'prairie light,' the insistence by Molson's that their beer is 'clearly Canadian,' and so on. Here clarity relates to the visual: what is Canadian comes clearly into view in these phenomena. Clarity is also, perhaps even more closely, related to communication and audition – the call of the loon, the crystal clarity of the long-distance telephone. Clarity is opposed to pretence. There is nothing behind clarity, nothing hidden or covert. In communication with others in Canada, what is valued primarily is clarity. Interestingly, this is perfectly sensible in Habermas's schema, as validity claims of sincerity, truth, and normative appropriateness are contingent in the first instance upon the clarity/comprehensibility of the utterance exchanged between the interlocutors (see 1976 or 1984). Bilingualism, or accented speech in general, in so far as it appears to the non-bilingual as a hindrance to clarity, is initially, in and of itself, a source of antagonism.

The value of clarity is central to the discourses of political correctness and official multiculturalism. Political correctness is an effort to 'correct' language, to achieve clarity, to eliminate ambiguity, to rid language of its excess, its cloudy equivocation, its pretence to neutrality while masking sexism, racism, etc. But now consider how political correctness has become a comic topic, and necessarily so: as it becomes convention, it becomes part of the formidable power of the Big Other, prohibits enjoyment and thus needs resisting. Clarity is central to the discourse of official multiculturalism in a similar way, with the emphasis on 'distinctiveness' – that Canada is a community of communities, each piece of the mosaic with its own distinct particularity, or a tossed salad, each component clearly identifiable, preserving its unique flavour, and so on.

The valuation of clarity appears in Canadian friendship and interpersonal relations in our insistence on verbal articulation, 'talking about it,' disclosing ourselves, while maintaining discreet distance and respecting personal space, and in our renowned politeness, the clear rules of personal etiquette and good manners to which we are in thrall. All of this as if there were a real ground to the social which correct(ed) language could represent, as if there were a true self to disclose! Despite this naïveté, however, we should see the good will in these phenomena; in these phenomena desire is oriented towards the good of recognizing the Other, respecting the Other's particularity, of living harmoniously with the Other; the desire to hegemonically articulate a version of the good society – the Habermasian 'ideal speech community,' perhaps – and to articulate the authentic being of the subject. The problem arises, unfortunately, when the value of clarity becomes institutionalized in a juridico-bureaucratic system, such that the subjectivities (identities, cultures, enjoyments) become objectively and rigidly categorized.

Comedy responds to the problem of the bureaucratic juridification of the value complex of clarity/frankness/politeness/unpretentiousness in official multiculturalism and political correctness by showing that the impossibility of clarity provides us with occasions for collective laughter. A classic comedic device is to show the vortex of misunderstanding that ensues when people set out to be perfectly frank with one another; the descent into farce of the drama between people who begin with good intentions – who presuppose the conditions of an ideal speech situation, as Habermas says we always implicitly do.

Farce shows that intersubjectivity is always and inevitably at risk of misrecognition; that we are never certain of what the Other wants of us, no more than we are ever certain of what our own desires are. We can never fully articulate or make transparent the grounds of our interaction. Universal pragmatics notwithstanding, the standards of ideal speech presupposed in interlocution cannot prevent the farce from developing, but can only help us to unravel it retrospectively. Comedy responds to the discourse of political correctness by showing the irony in the fact that by its efforts to make things clearer it actually risks rendering things nonsensical – for example, in formulations like the following:

At my school we no longer say that students are 'lazy.' We say that they are 'motivationally challenged.'

In an effort to counteract 'baldism' in society we now refer to such individuals as 'follicly disadvantaged.'

In this context of comedy's transgression of the conventions that govern our enjoyment, check out this scene from *Roadkill*. The heroine from Toronto is stranded in the boondocks somewhere near Sudbury. She is befriended by a likable goofball. He introduces himself as a serial killer – someone who kills several people, but in sequence, not all at once. He assures her, however, that he thinks of her as a friend, not a victim.

Clarity of communication, no matter what the topic, is the key to friendship. What is really important to Canadians is that we disclose clearly to one another who we are and where we're coming from. The would-be serial killer (he hasn't actually killed anyone yet) wants to be clearly recognized, and there are just two paths to recognition in Sudbury, he says, 'hockey and serial killing, ... and I've got weak ankles.' The danger/risk of lack of friendly recognition – sleeping alongside the elephant, as Pierre Trudeau put it, or being alone on the tundra – is a quintessentially Canadian problem, exaggerated for the sensitive hoser when hockey – the particularity which we allow ourselves – is denied him. He turns to serial killing, the degenerate art form of postmodern North America: inscribing seriality without teleology, pattern without beauty, and meticulous order without utopia. And of course, true to the form of Canadian heroism, he isn't up to the task and ends up being killed himself.

But the really important point here is that the object of comedic subversion in this example is our servitude to the normative conventions of being frank/clear/polite/unpretentious, for it is on these values that the reification of categories of subjective identities in official multiculturalism and political correctness is grounded. In this example, what is being exposed for our collective enjoyment is the absurdity of the supposition, the supposition on which political correctness and multiculturalism are based, that if we can clearly identify ourselves to one another, that clear definition of the category alone will constitute sufficient grounds for our friendship.

There is nothing about the man's clear identification and categorization of himself, in and of itself, that constitutes sufficient grounds for friendship, any more than there is in the bureaucratic inscription, by official multiculturalism and political correctness, of clear categories to contain Canadian multiplicity that would constitute the grounds of Canadian community. In fact, such efforts at clarification may well be inimical to friendship and community, in so far as friendship is grounded in the risks and enjoyments of the parties 'working out' their common world together. Friendship comes to light through the mutual discovery of commonalty that transcends originally obvious differences, not by declaring the absolute particularity of original difference and committing oneself to the preservation of that difference as the goal of social relations.

But what I don't want to lose in this example is its continuity with the self-disclosure and demonstration of vulnerability that I think is the Canadian idiomatic expression of comedy's utopian moment: its desire to unite all of us in laughter. The sensitive serial killer is ultimately likeable because he is naïve and vulnerable. We imagine that we could actually become friends with him because he shows us the moment of openness in what would seem at first to be a categorical identity that would prohibit attunement.

We will need to keep this in mind when we think about the subtleties of a comedic response to multiculturalism and political correctness. The problem is that we need to violate the juridico-bureaucratic conventions by which Others are scattered and kept distanced from one another in contemporary Canada, while simultaneously endorsing and shoring up these laws. The task is extremely difficult, for political correctness and official multiculturalism aren't embodied in some subject-made-sublime-object in the same way as the Mountie embodied the good law and thus provided a clear target for comedy. Now the law of political correctness and official multiculturalism is embodied, but its embodiment coincides with the embodied Other; the Other-as-object-of-denigration. Unlike the Mountie or the Queen, the Other who now embodies the law of official multiculturalism is still a vulnerable subject, so that in transgressing the law we run the risk of offending and hurting the Other.

Others are rarely the butt of Canadian jokes; we make fun of ourselves, of our alleged mediocrity *vis-à-vis* Others. Take Mike Myers's comedy on Saturday Night Live: 'Wayne's World' is a portrayal of the enjoyability of the utter banality of suburban Scarborough. Dieter of 'Sprockets' is inspired by a German waiter/actor(!)/poet(!) in a Queen Street café frequented by hipster intellectuals and culture vultures. Mike Myers plays up a Germanic stereotype of urbane sophistication, repressed perverse sexuality, mechanical anal retentiveness, and cosmopolitan pretension, the excess of which is a foil for our ordinary, Philistine 'vanilla' Canadian unpretentious enjoyment.

The German is safely 'an Other that can take it.' The symbolic order of Germany is extremely powerful and secure: Aryan, masculine, modern, it instils fear in us and commands respect. Mike Myers can mock the German Other as petulant, uptight, and fundamentally weird, alleviating our deep-seated and historically well grounded fear of his power, but there is no real danger of insulting and alienating this Other because we are still respectful and friendly towards the qualities of industriousness, rationality, and success that we impute to this Other. Myers isn't being unfriendly to the German Other; in fact by playing up the lack in an Other that could otherwise seem tyrannical he cultivates the basis for friendship. In Dieter of 'Sprockets' the joke is on us as much as it is on the German, because in laughing at Dieter's excess we are laughing at our own lack. Canadians have always been self-conscious about the alleged lack of depth and sophistication of our culture compared to Europe, and attunement is evident somehow, I think, in Queen Street clubs that are packed with 'Sprocket' wannabes.

Canadians deprecate themselves, but don't understate difference. Difference is presumed to be volatile, the practical joke is uncommon, and frankness (which again bears a strong family resemblance to unpretentiousness) is valued in our dealings with one another.

Think of the ad for the 'Coffee Crisp' chocolate bar. An Anglo-Canadian man is sitting alongside a woman of obvious though unspecified ethnicity. They are on a first date perhaps. There is a polite, tension-laden gap between them. As they are having coffee she says to him, with a strong accent: 'So how do you like your coffee?' He says: 'I like mine crisp,' and has a little chuckle. She gives him a puzzled, uncomprehending look, and he tries to let her in on his little joke: 'Coffee crisp. Get it?' (showing her the chocolate bar) 'I like my "coffee crisp."' She looks at him quizzically, not getting the pun, or finding it silly but unfunny, or probably both. He is embarrassed, looks a bit sheepish, confused, stuck for words, as he sees that puns don't work outside of a fairly limited language game. There is a moment of confusion and uncertainty as he tries to come to terms with the gap, and then he laughs, at his conceit, at his presuming that the Other would get it; how perfectly foolish, he laughs at himself. The woman, also confused and upset momentarily, laughs also, at her failure to get it, seeing the limit of her language game.

The utterly insignificant, silly pun exposes some *aporia* for them both, but they find in the exposure of this vulnerability an opportunity for shared laughter. What comes to light is the good of the comedic possibilities in encounters between differences. The Coffee Crisp ad shows how multiculturalism makes comedy difficult, but at the same time it provides new opportunities for laughter (and maybe a richer laughter than the silly pun could provoke). The joke falls through. The lack of understanding is unnerving, it shows that we cannot share the joke, but when we get over the discomfort we are excited by the prospect promised by the failure of the joke: the challenge, what can make the multicultural date enjoyable rather than uncomfortable, is the realization that we have a lot to discover about one another. What is brought to light by this poetic moment captured in the ad is that multiculturalism demands commitment to audition, and with this comes the beginnings of friendship, perhaps.

10

Socializing with Cyborgs: In the Restaurant at the End of the Trans-Canada Highway

What Does Canada Want?

'What does Canada want?" It wants what we impute to it by fantasy. In the fantasy of Canadian nationalism Canada desires closure; Canada desires a sutured self-consciousness, self-certainty; Canada desires to be Canada. That is, of course, we desire that Canada desires closure, we desire that Canada desires to be Canada. But our desire is formulated within a context of ironic conceit, such that the sutured Canada also desires to be open. In the fantasy construction of the desire imputed to Canada, Canada desires to be constituted, sutured, definite, but it also desires to be open, lacking. It desires that the suturing – as suturing always is anyway – be unsuccessful, or only partially successful, that the gap not be closed, that the wound from which desire for Canada springs not be definitively healed. The fantasy takes this form because we are never sure of our desire, and so the desire of Canada (desire imputed to Canada to reciprocate our desire) is just as ambivalent as our own desire. The Other, Canada, precisely because of its detachment, the omniscience and omnipotence that we impute to it, is the ironist *par excellence*, and we are the victims of its irony, because we cannot ever know what it wants; its desire is insatiable and perpetually evasive.

Hegel says that 'to enter the native land of truth is to recognize that the object of consciousness is consciousness itself.'[112] Or, put another way, that truth coincides with the path towards truth. In terms of our concern here, this means that Canada is the path towards Canada. What is truly Canadian is the phenomonality of the spirit which we encounter on the path towards Canada – the peculiarity of the symptoms of Canada, the unique idiom in which our collective desire for Canada is expressed in the organization of enjoyment.

Desire is what brings consciousness towards consciousness (and Canada towards Canada). Consciousness experiences the world through desire, i.e. pure animal hunger. Desire desires to incorporate the Other, to literally eat it up, to make externality internal, to negate the independent reality of the Other. Desire seeks to overcome the externality of reality, negate it, but in so far as desire succeeds in completely abolishing what is Other to it, negating the external reality of Otherness, self-consciousness (desire) returns to itself, and voraciously negates itself. The problem thus confronting self-consciousness is that it must simultaneously consume and preserve the otherness of the Other: it must negate the Other, without obliterating it. In fact, while negating the Other, it must also accomplish preserving the Other in its otherness. That is, it must cancel the opposition between One and Other while preserving the difference. Self-consciousness must have its cake, and eat it too.[113] How can this impossible bargain be struck? By a 'reduplication of consciousness.' Consciousness must engage with anOther equal consciousness, because the only kind of object that can withstand negation of desire is another self-consciousness. Self-consciousness is only possible if there are Other self-consciousnesses. For Canada to be Canada, it must have Canadians, who are Canadian, so that Canada and Canadians recognize themselves in and of one another.

The desire of Canada is insistent and can be explicitly formulated. 'England expects that every man shall do his duty,' Nelson told his sailors at the Battle of Trafalgar. 'England expects ...' The leader articulates the desire of the abstract empire. What does Canada expect of us? We can formulate this explicitly also. Desire is for the desire of the Other, a desire that we impute to it by fantasy: precisely, we desire that Canada desires us, and Canada desires that we desire it. In post-colonial Ireland, Father-of-the-Nation Eamonn deValera used to say, 'When I want to know what Ireland wants I look into my own soul.' The secret of the leader is to recognize the circularity of the dialectic of desire for identification around an empty place, and to enter that void and fill it by the articulation that 'I,' 'We,' and 'The Nation' are one. And clearly if the lack in the leader isn't somehow apparent, if we cannot see that this articulation is contingent and unstable and that the occupation of the place of power is temporary, then fathers become tyrants.

Canadian leaders have historically been faced with a difficult problem in achieving this articulation and persuasively presenting themselves as embodying the soul – the spirit – of the nation, even temporally. Up to the present, the vast majority of national leaders have straddled the anglo/franco frontier, Pierre Trudeau perhaps most successfully. He holds a place in the symbolic order of contemporary Canada as the archetypal Canadian political leader precisely in so far as he successfully embodied/failed to embody the soul of Canada: his necessary pretence of embodying the spirit of the nation simultaneously violated the value of unpretentiousness, negating his own claim to embody the spirit.

Jean Chrétien provides another good example. In the run-up to the 1993 election, his years of experience and accomplishments in politics placed him head and shoulders above other Canadian party leaders and contenders for the prime ministerial office, but this was offset by his facial disfigurement and his strongly accented English. The Tory election campaign ads that intimated that these 'embarrassing defects' made Chrétien unsuitable for office completely backfired, not only because it was an extremely 'impolite' and thus a very un-Canadian tactic, but also because precisely these evident physical manifestations of lack assured Canadians that Chrétien was eminently suited to be the Canadian leader.

A further nuance, of course, was that Kim Campbell and Audrey McLaughlin (leaders of the Conservative and New Democratic parties), as women attempting to articulate themselves as phallic signifiers of Canada, were themselves much more profoundly 'disfigured' than Chrétien could ever be.

But despite Chrétien's election success, it becomes more and more difficult to occupy the empty place of power in Canadian democracy: no one can claim to embody the proliferating antagonistic different identities that constitute the Canadian body politic, and consequently the body tends towards dismemberment. The present manifestation of this in the parliamentary strength of the Bloc Québécois and the Reform party is only the tip of the iceberg of a much more profound grass-roots separatism based on a micro-politics of antagonistic identities. And it is in this context of the lack of radical democratic leadership, the absence of a new hegemonic project, that we see that political life in Canada today is dominated by pathologies of bureaucratization and juridification, expressed idiomatically, at the levels of institutions and formal organizations and in the lifeworld, as what Bordo refers to as the tyrannical 'methodologism of political correctness' (1990, 135, 138).

Canada desires particularity, but for the particularity of Canada to be recognized above and beyond the diversity, it must produce this diversity as independent self-consciousnesses (ethnicities, identities, regional particularities), and simultaneously it must negate them, incorporate them, assimilate them. And Canada desires that the particularities desire their incorporation, that they give themselves over to Canada, that they subject their particularity to the infinity of the difference. And for the particularities to constitute themselves as particular self-consciousnesses, as 'ethnics,' 'distinct,' or by virtue of whatever sign 'special,' they have to impute to Canada a particular self-consciousness that desires to negate their particularity, that desires to eat them up. They can constitute their particularity only in terms of resisting that desire and fighting to the death for the preservation of their particularity. For if we give in to the desire of Canada, surrender to it, we are swallowed up, lose our particularity, and Canada no longer desires us. Deprived of recognizable, desirable particularity we suffer the radical alienation of mass society, like Andy, Claire, and Dag or the Scarborough grunge rockers, kicking and screaming to assert a new and meaning-giving particularity.

The desire of the Other is desired, not simply to have it, but because it is desired by Others. Canada desires that Canadians see themselves as Canadians, because Others desire that Canadians see themselves first as Anglos, Quebeckers, Chinese, etc. That is, Canadians desire that Canada desires Canadians to see themselves as Canadian, for in order for Canada to exist as a self-conscious collective consciousness it must capture the desire that otherwise local particularities would get. But in order for Canada to constitute itself it must preserve the local particularities that compete with Canada for the desire of their members. In this way desire is kept alive, its object is always ahead of itself.

Hegel asks: 'What is Spirit?' It is that which lies ahead of itself. It is '"I" that is "We" and the "We" that is "I."'

What still lies ahead for consciousness is the experience of what Spirit is – this absolute substance which is the unity of the different independent self-consciousnesses which, in their opposition, enjoy perfect freedom and independence: 'I' that is 'We' and 'We' that is 'I.' It is in self-consciousness, in the Notion of spirit, that consciousness ... leaves behind it the colorful show of the sensuous here and now and the nightlike void of the supersensible beyond, and steps out into the spiritual daylight of the present.   Hegel 1977, 110–11

The spirit of Canada is not the colourful diversity, the bald fact of polyglot difference. Nor is it the void, the lack at the heart of the sensuous here and now. It is the '"I" that is "We" and the "We" that is "I"' that is synthetically produced by the antagonistic playing for desire amongst the diverse Others across the lack, the very particular character of the symbolic order that we produce for ourselves and to which we impute desire for us to go on producing, in short, our symptoms, which we love as ourselves.

But the symptom formation is constitutionally unstable. For self-consciousness arises from the fundamental insecurity of the reciprocity of the Other's desire. Does the Other desire me? Am I sure that the Other will return my desire? The troubled liveliness of this insecure reciprocity of desire for recognition we have already seen in Marian Engel's *Bear*. Let's recap briefly. The problem of the desire of self-consciousness is: 'How do I recognize the Other being as self-conscious? How do I know that I am being recognized by an equal self-consciousness, by anOther self-consciousness, as a self-consciousness?' Each party has to show the other that it is not an object, simply immersed in life; that it is more than simply an organic, edible thing, but rather that it is made of some real substance that can survive negation. It has to show, prove, to itself and to the Other, its transcendent character, its worthiness of desire. To do this, self-consciousness must risk its life. It is only through risking life that one wins recognition of one's value as more than merely animal existence.

To struggle to the death is to struggle for recognition as independent self-consciousness. To risk one's life is to risk misrecognition, to risk estranging oneself, alienating oneself from one's membership of the community. One risks one's life and struggles to the death when one steps outside, when one reaches out towards the Other and confronts the difference. One risks death, puts one's life on the line, by risking estrangement from membership and risking not being recognized by Other. Canadians perform such outrageously foolhardy and heroic risking all the time, but as I will also show, we do not risk enough, for institutions like official multiculturalism and political correctness to a large extent seek to ensure that the encounter between differences is risk-free.

The emigrant to Canada risks estrangement from the shared life of the parent society, and the same immigrant risks misrecognition and estrangement in the new collective. The Ukrainian woman from Regina who brings her Pakistani boyfriend to meet her parents risks estrangement and alienation at home; she risks also the misrecognition by his community, and of his desire for her. And of course the same goes for him, he risks as much, perhaps more. How can they take such risks? Because they must; they must prove to themselves that they are not immersed in life; that they are more than simply elements suspended in the object categories of race and ethnicity that stand indifferently to one another. They risk misrecognition in order to gain greater recognition as subjects, as 'real people.' By risking estranging themselves from the communities of which they are secure members, by showing their desirability for Others outside of that community, they increase their desirability to and their recognition by both their familiar communities and one another. They play for the desire of multiple Others by playing them off against one another. This is what literally makes life worth living: to risk everything, by transgression, by stepping into the interzone, which is as close by and at hand as going to the party with your friend from Brazil.

The Restaurant at the End of the Trans-Canada Highway

'An all-Canadian pig-out': The banquet-sized premises of this squat roadside inn are divided into a couple of separated areas. I pass on the dark bar and I enter the cheerfully lit, floral surroundings of the main dining room. The chairs are softly padded, and the properly distanced tables are arranged in small sections that are screened from each other by beautiful plants.[114]

This is an approving review, not just of a restaurant, but of a Canadian restaurant, and implicitly it is an approving review of Canada, for the restaurant is a metaphor for Canada. Note the approval of size, of spaciousness, of the separation from the dining area of the bar – Quebec, always associated with excess enjoyment, drinking, romance in the sultry darkness, temptations which the (rest-of) Canadians can sample, or pass on. The restaurant is a squat roadside inn: like most of Canadians, it squats by the side of the Trans-Canada highway, surrounded by wonderfully floral natural scenery. The chairs are softly padded, we're comfortably well off, and we know it, and we're proud of it, that underneath our backsides is a generous welfare state and health-care system to lean back on when we're old and satisfied by our pig-out.

The reviewer approves of the unpretentiousness of the restaurant, the no-nonsense, hearty menu; self-deprecating ('nothing too fancy') but not understated ('well varied, well done, generous portions'). We can enjoy the unique flavour of what we choose from the ample multicultural menu: a great variety of ethnic enjoyment is represented albeit in a somewhat massified – less distinctive = more palatable – form, from T-bones to tandoori. The reviewer approves of the restaurant being bright and spacious. Canadian values of conversational openness, disclosure, frankness correspond here to the bright, open-plan design of the restaurant. Spaciousness, discretion, politeness, table distance, screening; the restaurant is a tolerant space that can accommodate all comers – families, lovers, business lunchers, there is enough room between tables that a multitude of enjoyments can happen simultaneously, without infringing upon one another.

The restaurant can tolerate a great range of enjoyments: we can all see one another's enjoyments, eat and squabble with our noisy families, swing a deal over lunch, take a break from the endless highway, or charm and seduce one another. And the presence and visibility of the diversity of enjoyments, the openness and brightness of the place, allow one the vicarious pleasure of access to other enjoyments if one so desires – and it is precisely this that makes this Canadian restaurant enjoyable.

But the tables are properly distanced – 'properly' distanced, mind you. It's not accidental, but planfully orchestrated that we keep a polite distance from one another. And it is that very distancing – our arrangement into small sections, screened from one another by beautiful plants (the colours and charms of multiculturalism), a discursive means of inscribing 'proper distancing' on the social, by which we are present for one another's enjoyment and simultaneously distanced from one another's enjoyment – that makes dining in this restaurant, in the opinion of this reviewer, a four-star experience.

But also, of course – and this is precisely the problem of both roadside restaurants and Canada – it can tend to be a somewhat soulless and isolating experience, where people are polite and well mannered, but cool and indifferent towards one another, where interaction is impoverished (suspicious eavesdropping on each other's conversations and ethnocentric evaluations of each other's table manners); where the poetry of the nation is a tasteless 'All-you-can-eat Italian/Chinese lunch buffet, plus thirty-item salad bar.' What is at stake in this particularly Canadian restaurant is the problem of a dialectic of distancing and integration which official multiculturalism tries to solve, to reconcile polarities of closeness and remoteness so that patrons have the privacy to enjoy their own particular enjoyment in such a way that their enjoyment of their enjoyment contributes to a collective spirit of enjoyment.

Hannah Arendt says that Socrates was the first to use *dialegesthai* (talking something through with somebody) systematically (Arendt 1990, 81). Socrates began with the *doxa*, that is the formulation in ordinary speech of the reality of the world, the truth 'as it appears to me,' the opinions of the 'ordinary man,' as it were. Socrates' assumption is that the world opens up differently to everyone, according to one's position in it, and that the 'sameness' of the world, its commonness, its 'objectivity,' resides in the fact that the same world opens up to everyone, and that despite all differences between people and their positions in the world, and consequently their *doxai* (opinions), 'both you and I are human.' There is an infinite number of ways of being in the restaurant, but what is common to us is our enjoyment of being there. In current parlance, Socrates is acknowledging the infinite possibility of perspectives on social reality, the multiplicity of standpoint epistemologies on which *doxa* is constituted and defended, the grounds on which we express our opinions honestly and publicly as 'this is truly how things appear to me.' But Socrates' position is very different from the formulations of standpoint epistemologies that are now in vogue in Canada.

Standpoint epistemologies[115] are characterized by the epistemological privileging of certain members over others. It is held that the oppressed and inferior position (standpoint) occupied within the social order grants some members unique insight and understanding of history and social dynamics that is unavailable to dominant groups and to those in positions of power. This epistemology is traditionally held by Marxists, for example, who accord epistemic privilege to the working-class subject. It has also been a position adopted by feminists such as Dorothy Smith (1987), who argue that women's standpoint as an oppressed group gives them the epistemic privilege of being able to perceive with particular clarity 'the everyday world as problematic.' Oppressed Others enjoy a privileged vantage point from which to critically view the prevailing social order because they have the least to lose in the event of its dissolution. Accordingly, the oppressed know, and only the oppressed can know, how they are oppressed. It follows that 'men and women of privilege,' to use the current idiom – academics, public representatives, or otherwise – cannot unproblematically speak 'about' the oppressed, and certainly not 'for' them, not 'in their interests,' since their own interests as 'people of privilege' are tied to the preservation of the status quo.

Flaws in standpoint epistemologies are revealed by the tendency for standpoints to proliferate in an infinite regress of categories of oppression and marginalization, and on top of this the tendency to hold a hierarchy of privileged epistemologies that compete for primacy. This becomes manifest in the paradoxical disjuncture between epistemological advantage and political consciousness; i.e., that while the oppressed are held to be the most privileged epistemologically, they often appear as the least politically conscious or enlightened; and, more commonly, in the assertion that there is a foundational, basic oppression, an oppression 'of last instance' (usually the oppression of the proletariat, though the oppressions of gender and race have also been accorded this primacy) to which a special, crucial, epistemological privilege is granted, and to which all the others, though 'significant' and 'important,' are secondary.

Standpoint epistemologies, upon which the politically correct categorization of the social is based, whether they are articulated from the grounds of class, race, gender, sexual orientation, or any Other sign of marginality or oppression, are profoundly problematic. In so far as standpoint epistemologies privilege certain members who are conceived essentially as 'Native,' 'Woman,' 'Worker,' etc., engaged in historically privileged struggles – the worker's revolution, the battle against patriarchy, the fight for self-determination – they are exclusive, divisive, and ultimately prone to forms of the very totalitarianisms that they oppose.

Socrates neither endorses the relativism arising from the infinite proliferation of identities/standpoints/epistemologies/*doxai* nor seeks the privileged standpoint, the *unum verum*, the one truth. Socrates' position is that there is a kernel of truth in every *doxa* that if brought to light would provide the basis of our mutual recognition of our common interest; we could pursue what's best for all of us, the 'common,' or 'public' good. Socrates hoped to further the common good by what he called *maieutics*, the art of midwifery; he wanted to help people give birth to the truth of their *doxai*.

Socrates' praxis of *dialegesthai* and *maieutics* helps us to address the central problem in contemporary Canadian political culture, the problem that underpins and always threatens to unravel the threads of this essay: namely, those who constitute the sometimes explicit, always implicit 'we' of this essay, can seem themselves to be not 'othered' by Otherness, but rather the agents and beneficiaries of reflexive self-realization. It seems that the 'we' seeks the Other's desire, seeks enrichment, excitement, eroticism, existential exposure through the Other, but 'we' does not experience the potential of extinction, elimination of the standpoint from which the 'we' is asserted. In short, there are structural asymmetries between subject positions that constitute 'we' and 'Others,' such that 'we' is never structurally endangered while 'Other' is.

In Socrates' model of helping to give birth to the truth in *doxa* we see that it is an unavoidable condition of discourse that one speaks from a particular position, which then becomes institutionalized as the point of authorship, of a (potentially) problematic authority. It unavoidably constitutes a 'we-ness' and an 'Other-ness' in an asymmetrical form. We also know that this 'we' cannot speak for the Other, that any hermeneutic gesture, any *verstehen* of the Other, will be inadequate, and that all such gestures will differ only in the degree of conceit with which the 'we' fails to recognize the persistence of the asymmetry. Foucault argues that the best 'we' can do is to speak like another Other; that the 'we' become aware of its own lack, incompleteness, contingency on the Other. To show the reflexive self-realization of the 'we' through the agency of the Other is the beginning of this process, and this is what I have sought to do here.

This epistemological question of exposing the conceit of the 'we' anticipates a question that arises after, or more precisely at the same time as, the exposure of the conceit of the 'we.' This is the issue of the emergence of practices that seek to redress the asymmetry of the discursive field. That is to say, that *the* question at the centre of the postmodern political landscape is how the many and proliferating Others, constituted and endangered in their otherness by their asymmetrical relation to the 'we' and their mutual isolation from one another, can be constituted as a new hegemonic 'we' of others. This 'we Others' is what would constitute the common sense of a new left hegemony in the project of radical and plural democracy envisaged by Laclau and Mouffe. This 'we Others' of a new left hegemony never fully succeeds in reaching closure on the question of the dynamics of inclusion/ exclusion, i.e., in being fully inclusionary. There is always a 'they' that falls outside of the 'we.' Thus the 'we' is a vanishing point, an allusive/elusive ideal that expresses the desire for a radical and plural democratic community. The task of discursively constructing institutions that aspire to that ideal begins with *maieutics*.

Socrates' metaphor of midwifery carries both the connotations of the delight, wonder, and goodness of bringing new life into the world and the very heavy connotations of labour, pain, time, effort, and difficulty attendant to birth. Bringing the truths of *doxa* to light would be painful; poiesis is agonal, but unless we work through the process nothing new comes into the world but repetitions of the old *doxai*. Socrates wanted to make the city more truthful by delivering all of the citizens of their truths, by getting them to talk things through with one another. 'The dialectic brings forth truth *not* by destroying doxa or opinion, but on the contrary reveals doxa in its own truthfulness' (Arendt 1990, 81).

Arendt says that this kind of dialogue, which doesn't need a conclusion in order to be meaningful, is most appropriate for, and most frequently shared by, friends.

Friendship to a large extent, indeed, consists of this kind of talking about something that the friends have in common. By talking about what is between them, it becomes ever more common to them. It gains not only its specific articulateness, but develops and expands and finally, in the course of time and life, begins to constitute a little world of its own which is shared in friendship ... Politically speaking, Socrates tried to make friends out of Athens' citizenry.   Arendt 1990, 82

Aristotle, says Arendt, 'explains that a community is not made out of equals, but on the contrary of people who are different and unequal. The community comes into being through equalizing. This equalization takes place in all exchanges, as between the physician and the farmer ... the political, non-economic equalization is friendship.' In other words, what Arendt is saying here is that the synthetic moment of the dialectical encounter of antagonistic different identities is friendship. Friendship is that moment in relationality, achieved by the dialectical process of talking it through, which cancels the opposition and preserves the difference. 'The equalization in friendship does not of course mean that the friends become the same or equal to each other, but rather that they become equal partners in a common world – that they together constitute a community.' Community is what friendship achieves, and this equalization in friendship, and the community arising from friendship, provides both the ground of ethics and social solidarity in the context of 'the ever-increasing differentiation of citizens that is inherent in agonal life' (Arendt 1990, 83).

The political element in friendship is that in the truthful dialogue each of the friends can understand the truth inherent in the other's opinion. Friendship is the commitment to the ideal of working out the truths inherent in difference, fostering and enjoying the emergence of a community through the poiesis of innumerable dialectics. By this, one friend understands how and in what specific articulateness the common world appears to the other, who as a person remains forever unequal or different. 'This kind of understanding – seeing the world from the other fellow's point of view – is the political kind of insight par excellence,' Arendt says. How does this relate to the problem of hegemony and radical democracy?

The outstanding virtue of the statesman ... consists in understanding the greatest possible number and varieties of realities ... as those realities open themselves to the various opinions of the citizens, and at the same time in being able to communicate between the citizens and their opinions so that the commonness of this world becomes apparent. If such an understanding – and action inspired by it – were to take place without the help of the statesman, then the prerequisite would be for each citizen to be articulate enough to show his opinion in its truthfulness and therefore to understand his fellow citizens. Socrates seems to have believed that the political function of the philosopher was to help establish this kind of common world, built on the understanding of friendship in which no rulership is needed.

Arendt 1990, 84

Socrates would have had his work cut out in contemporary Canada! Canada is friendly to the multiplicity of *doxai*, but there is a lack of *maieutics*. The discourses of official multiculturalism and political correctness institutionalize friendliness toward the fact of the existence of difference; they purport to value cultural diversity – i.e., the fact of *diversity* itself is valued.

Multiculturalism purports to value *tolerance* of the fact of diversity – i.e., diversity remains diverse, we value tolerating *doxa as doxa*. Multiculturalism institutionalizes the fact that 'everyone has an opinion,' but then leaves it at that. It preserves the different *doxai*, but it also preserves the opposition between them.

The discourses of official multiculturalism and political correctness do not seek to work out the truths inherent in difference and thus cancel the opposition by bringing the common world into view. Instead they promote the infinite proliferation of points of view, standpoints, different identities on which antagonistic *doxai* are grounded. In so far as multiculturalism refuses to take up the responsibilities of *maieutics* and work through the difficulties of labour, the truths inherent in difference cannot be born, and all manner of morbid symptoms appear – xenophobias, ethnocentrisms, closed conversations of sect, sex, creed, and colour. The banquet-sized restaurant expands spatially, more tables are added, new goodies appear in the salad bar, but it remains as coldly and properly distanced as ever. Friendliness towards the multiplicity of *doxai* is at best only the very minimum condition for the cultivation of friendship, community, and the pursuit of the common good. Official multiculturalism is a form of the colonization of the lifeworld in which the discreet distancing which members negotiate between one another and which assures the degree of privacy necessary for enjoyment becomes a juridico-bureaucratic valuation of *doxa* coupled with a refusal, perhaps a fear, to take on the responsibilities of *maieutics*.

To begin the *maieutics* we must first begin to think about 'breaching' strategies. What is the equivalent here of shitting with the bear in the forest? We need to go to the restaurant and systematically set about doing some violence to the conventions that keep our tables 'properly distanced.' In the spirit of Garfinkle's ethnomethodology[116] we might come up with ways to show the forces that keep the tables separated and the conversations private, that maintain a favour for distance over integration. We'll have to violate the conventions of political correctness and multiculturalism and learn again how to sin gladly, for the discourses of political correctness and multiculturalism inscribe and reinscribe boundaries, not the poetry that is being composed at the frontiers of the nation.

What sort of practices would do violence to the imaginary of discontinuity, and bring continuity to light in Canada today? What would work now to violate the discontinuity of multiculturalism and show continuity? What sacrifice is needed to show us this, to remind us of our love of our symptom? We don't want to lose the enjoyment of the endurance of the lack of

Canada through the pursuit of the fulfilment of our desire for Canadian continuity, or for just as much continuity as a symbolic order constituted by discontinuity can sustain. At this point I can only suggest a few general domains as topics for future research.

Is the social charter, or medicare, or the Charlottetown accord the sacrificial object? No. Unless they can be elevated to the status of sublime objects, their erosion, dismantling, or failure may have no great effect in uniting Canadians in their defence or promotion. An urgent task for parties concerned with human rights, social justice, and health care in Canada, I would argue, is to set about elevating these institutions to the status of sublime objects in the public imaginary. But that is not my immediate concern here.

The particularity of Canada is the enjoyment of the endurance of the lack of particularity, the values of tolerance and unpretentiousness. It is this articulation that would have to be violated to bring the continuity of Canadians to light: tolerance by ritualized intolerance, unpretentiousness by arrogant pretence. Such sacrifices would violate the enjoyment of endurance of lack of particularity, either by claiming particularity (Heritage Front, separatism, political correctness) or, in the other direction, by some action that would show that enjoyment of endurance of lack of particularity wasn't a particularity, wasn't worth defending against the Heritage Front and special interests. When we violate the symptom – the particularity of the enjoyment of the endurance of the lack of particularity – then we see the real: the hollowness and arbitrariness of tolerance and unpretentiousness, the nothingness/everythingness that the symptom shields us from. We come to see the symptom as all that there is, and accordingly, we reaffirm our love of it, our responsibility for it and the need to defend it.

But there is another level at which breaching is needed. What Canada wants is a comedic response to the discourses of political correctness and official multiculturalism. As we have seen, the joke is the symptom that points us not just to the law to which we are subject, but to the lack in the law, and comedy's double action gives us a break from the law and simultaneously reaffirms it. Jokes about politeness show us that in Canada this is the authority we are under, the humour we are in thrall to. One last joke to illustrate the point:

How would you know that a Canadian had broken into your house?
There would be an extra quart of milk in your fridge.

Even when we try to enjoy ourselves by some transgressive act (burglary is the example here), we are denied our enjoyment by our enslavement to the conventions of being polite towards the Other. Even when the Other is the victim of our transgression, it's only good manners to bring a little something if you pay someone a visit. If you are going to steal the Other's enjoyment, at least be polite about it and leave a small token of reciprocal equalization. Thus the typical idiom of Canadian racism is polite and well mannered: a university professor and a management consultant, presentable, articulate, and very civilized. One of my students told me of an exchange that she overheard between two little girls, in which one child (black) asked the other (white) for something. The little girl replied: 'I'm sorry. I don't play with or speak to black children.'

The strange thing is that not just racism but political correctness and official multiculturalism are anchored in the lifeworld in norms of etiquette, politeness, good manners, and discretion, justified in terms of values of tolerance and unpretentiousness, and ultimately grounded in enjoyment of endurance of lack of particularity. Multiculturalism and racism are both legitimated in terms of the obviousness of the coincidence of their principles with the rules of etiquette of being-with-Others in the everyday lifeworld: 'But of course people are entitled to celebrate and enjoy themselves in whatever way they see fit. I wouldn't come into your house and tell you what to have for dinner, would I?' Or, 'That kind of thing might be acceptable back where you come from, but you're in Canada now. If I went to live at your house you would expect me to conduct myself appropriately; you're living in our house, you're welcome, but we expect you to speak our language and to do as we do.'

It is patently obvious that we need the law of political correctness and official multiculturalism to protect us from the real, the underlying foundational antagonism of the social. In the absence of these laws, racial hatred, misogyny, homophobia, and all forms of xenophobia would know no check. In fact, we see plenty of evidence that despite the law the repressed returns. But the rules that protect us are somehow too restrictive; they permit us all to be in the restaurant together, but they prohibit our enjoying our meal, or enjoying it with one another. In Foucaultian terms, one could say that, in much the same way as the proliferation of expert discourse about sexuality serves to delimit and define 'good sex,' and thereby paradoxically infringes upon the enjoyment of sexuality, the discourses of political correctness and official multiculturalism disallow enjoyment in the political body by inscribing codes of 'good behaviour' that govern our interactions with one another.[117]

Of course there is resistance to this practice of power, the emergence of reverse discourses of 'political incorrectness' (which are quite distinct from the counter-discourses of 'the backlash' and anti–political correctness represented by the Reform party and REAL Women). Political incorrectness is a response articulated from *within* the categories: Camille Paglia (1992), the anti-feminist feminist, Callaghan's cartoons in Toronto's *Eye* magazine about disability (Callaghan himself is paraplegic). And notice how politically correct Canadians respond to Paglia or Callaghan. They see them as brash, arrogant, rude Americans, who offend the rules of good manners that govern our interactions with women and the disabled.

We can see in Callaghan the beginnings of a response to the disciplinary power of political correctness as it relates to disability. One of the rules of etiquette, for example, is the injunction: 'Don't focus on the wheelchair, focus on the person in the wheelchair.' A very ordinary and everyday rule of behaviour that shows in a small way the positive contribution of political correctness to the collective moral heritage. Callaghan subverts this law by a series of cartoons that, for example, exaggerate not focusing on the wheelchair so that the fact of the wheelchair is absurdly missed; or that present the person in the wheelchair as such an asshole that focusing on the wheelchair is a welcome relief; or that highlight the extreme discomfort of the able-bodied person who makes the *faux pas*; or that show the extreme discomfort of the person in the wheelchair at the obviousness and contrived conversation of the person who is being too self-consciously politically correct.

Callaghan's cartoons (a) expose the lack in the able-bodied subject – our discomfort with difference (differently abled bodies cause us anxieties about our own inabilities), or our inability to live up to the standard of the law (try as we might, we still make the occasional *faux pas*). (b) They expose the lack in the law itself, that when enforced too literally it is absurd and irrational, and/or tyrannical. (c) Callaghan attunes our perception of both these lacks (which were previously hidden) to the tranquillized obviousness of the fact of the lack in the disabled person, which we had previously taken to be the only lack. This is the achievement of the subversive art of comedy: Callaghan collects all our laughter by attuning the lacks to one another. He unites the able-bodied and the differently abled, and the Law of the Father in a new synthesis. A richer collective enjoyment is made possible by the artful comedic violation of the rule of polite, correct behaviour that had previously been sacrosanct.

For the moment it seems obvious that this kind of direct subversive response to the laws of political correctness and official multiculturalism can only be launched from securely within the categories. A white man cannot tell a joke about an ethnic woman, neither can a black person tell a joke about a Korean (it's not quite as much a mortal sin as the first case, but it's a definite no-no all the same, according to the Race Relations Commission). But my argument has been that it is politeness and good manners, rules of etiquette *in general*, that ground political correctness and official multiculturalism. Therefore, if we wish to loosen up the law of official multiculturalism while simultaneously endorsing it, an appropriate mandate for Canadian comedy would be to violate and subvert politeness and etiquette in all its forms. The outrageous 'Much Music' cartoon 'Ren and Stimpy' may provide us with a good model for subversive comedic art for contemporary Canada.

Along with 'breaching' the conventions of distancing, we need to think about collecting, or, if you will, of hegemonically articulating. Breaching leaves us with chaos, and anger and fear are as likely to emerge from confusion and disruption as are friendly interaction and shared enjoyment. Poiesis needs the moment of violation to get started, but then it needs artful improvisation in order to constitute the solidarity of the emerging form. The stand-up comedian then might provide us with a model for the hegemonic articulator, the one who brings to light the continuity between the tables in the restaurant, signified by their shared laughter at what they have in common. The best examples of the improviser, the stand-up comic as hegemonic articulator, are such Americans as Robin Williams and Jerry Seinfeld; while Canadian comics again seem to institutionalize the *doxa*, characterize the type – the hoser (Bob and Doug), the European (Dieter, the Scotsman), the Conehead, the chicken lady, the innocent klutz (Leslie Nielsen's Frank Drebbin in *Naked Gun*). But this may not be as problematic as it appears. As the individual American comedian mirrors the form of the singular presidency, the Canadian form is the comedy troupe – Kids in the Hall, Codco, SCTV, etc. – and further study might tell us much of how the troupe establishes a reflexive equilibrium between the *doxai* that their diverse characters represent to build up a picture of the common life of Canadians.

The hegemonic articulator as comedian, either charismatic leader or troupe, has to bring to light a cyborg multicultural continuity that political correctness and official multiculturalism denies. I have already shown the grounds on which a shared, enjoyable, radical, and plural democratic project could be articulated: shared values of tolerance and unpretentiousness grounded in the enjoyment of the endurance of lack of particularity, a shared ironic conceit allowing enjoyment, an enjoyment in commitment to partiality and incompleteness (evident in vernacular idiom), and a vulnerability/openness that invites attunement with Others in our sense of humour (already practised in our comedy). Now we need to produce the register in order for the stand-up to address the restaurant of cyborgs, who have no idea that they are cyborgs, and bring their shared continuity to light for them enjoyably.

(un)FIN. Eh!

Enfin, the Symptom: A Monumental Returning of the Repressed

In the centre of Ottawa stands a monumental representation of a crack in Canadian culture; simultaneously a sublime object, a *point de capiton* that attempts to suture a Canadian identity, and, ironically, a point at which Canada's embarrassing pudendum is spectacularly exposed to the light of day. This is a monument, a memorial, built to remind Canadians, and other visitors to Canada's capital, of the role Canada has played in international peace-keeping with the United Nations. Its purpose is to remind people that Canadians value keeping the peace between antagonists in faraway places – Africa, the Middle East, the former Yugoslavia. It implicitly raises the claim that we Canadians know a thing or two about managing antagonism and maintaining peace, order and good government. It is a phallic representation (as phallic as phallic representations of Canada go!) of Canada's desire and of Canada's firm resolve to boldly go into global trouble spots and do the business of peace-keeping. The peace-keeping monument seeks to attract the gaze to our own purported heroism. It is a monument to our desperate desire to be anointed by the Other who is traumatized by antagonism, our desire to be acclaimed in the gaze of the international community as having integrity, maturity, identity; to be recognizable, self-conscious, self-certain, to be free of our own antagonism.

The monument consists of three large lifelike statues of Canadian military personnel, positioned at the apex of two broken jagged concrete walls which approach each other at an angle of about fifteen degrees, but which do not meet. The monument attempts to represent how official multiculturalism and political correctness have solved Canadian antagonism, but it shows instead how deeply ingrained hierarchies of privilege and stereotyped role confinement are in contemporary Canada, and the persistence of solitudes of gender, race, and ethnicity, despite the rhetoric of the official ideology. A white male officer gazes blankly through binoculars through the rear of the Parliament buildings, to the empty allure of the north, oblivious to what is immediate. A woman with a field radio, crouching, kneeling, faces across the river to Quebec; she desires to communicate with them, it seems, she's sensitive, and she's got the technology. A black man, strong, armed, silent, will protect us, but from whom? He stands facing downtown! All three have their backs to the rift behind them, and their backs to one another. They are clustered at the apex of the rift, but at different points on it. They are facing away from the trouble, which is amongst them and behind them. They want to avoid it rather than deal with it. The real conflict yawns open at their backs and under their feet. It is not the antagonism amongst the

Others in Rwanda or in Bosnia but their own history that gapes open behind them in a jagged broken swathe.

The real trauma is buried deeply in the history of the childhood of the nation. It is a trauma that is repressed, but is constantly emerging in the pathological symptoms of our dealings with one another. Our terrible anxiety is that our heroic humanitarian interventions in Bosnia, in Somalia, might appear instead as ignorant, fumbling, naïve, and dangerous; that our (un)pretentious posturing on the world stage as a paragon of humanitarian, multicultural, and democratic virtue might be revealed as a hollow sham; that Canada might appear instead as the original architect of apartheid, the practitioner of an almost perfect genocide; that the crawl-spaces and cupboards of Canadian culture might be shown to be crammed with severed limbs and petrified skeletons. Our anxiety is that the gaze of the international community might discern our guilty secret behind the pretentious imposture of quietly confident unpretentiousness; the 'perfectly normal, just-blending-in' cover of the pervert. Here is Stephen Lewis, a former Canadian ambassador to the United Nations:

The treatment of Native people [is] without question the Achilles heel for Canada in the human rights arena. It undermined our influence, our prestige, our reputation. It made less compelling the human rights arguments we were making. It was very humiliating, very embarrassing.[118]

The childhood trauma for Canada, which all the antagonism around identity is symptomatic of and reenacts, is the historical and ongoing annihilation of Native peoples. The constitution of Canada resulted in the denigration of Natives to the status of pure objects, to be systematically consumed (assimilated) or annihilated. Hegel shows that in the struggle to the death for self-consciousness between the master and the slave, as the master objectifies the slave the master loses his subjectivity himself and becomes infused with the slave's thing-like quality (1977, 114–15). The master's identity (in this case Canada's) is contingent upon being recognized by an equal self-consciousness, and in so far as Canada systematically objectifies and annihilates Natives it destroys the very possibility of assuring the integrity and and self-certainty of its own identity. Canada cannot solve its identity crisis, it cannot even begin to attain subject status free of guilt and anxiety, without working through this trauma, and this is the jagged and broken abyss that yawns open and creeps up behind the blind, dumb, and solitary figures on the monument, threatening to engulf them.

It is only as the slave regains subjectivity through his endurance of facing

death and through the work of resistance that the master too regains subjectivity and identity. The clearest expression of this process in recent history is
that of South Africa. It is only as Mandela and black South Africans recover
their subject status through resistance that de Klerk and white South Africans begin also to reemerge to the gaze of the international community less
as brutes, more as fellow human beings. Is there a comparable process in
Canada, a returning of the repressed that Canada could avail itself of to go
back to the future, as it were, to work through history to alter the present
and give us some respite for the future from the endless repetition of our
annihilation of the Other?

Perhaps. We can see that this is what is at stake in the current discourse
surrounding Native self-government, the most striking aspect of which is
the extent to which Native self-government is a desire not only amongst
Natives but also amongst what Natives call the 'settler' community. That is,
non-Native Canadians desire that Natives be autonomous, self-governing
subjects, capable of giving Canada the recognition that it needs. But this
desire is a thoroughly ambivalent desire on the part of the settler community, for there is tremendous reluctance to confront the real of the ongoing
annihilation of Natives in Canadian history. The more typical practice is a
continuing repression and sublimation, endless inquiries, volumes of reports
of commissions, on Native justice and on conditions on reserves, reshuffling
meagre funding, band-aid crisis responses to the chronic deep wounds of
a campaign of obliteration, while Canada neurotically prances about on
the world stage, covering up, rather than stripping naked. Oka constituted a returning of the repressed, but has Canada availed itself of the
opportunity ...?

Notes

1 Hegel 1977. This is Hegel's concern throughout the *Phenomenology*, but is most explicitly formulated in the section on the lordship and bondage of consciousness. See in particular 110–11.

2 These three commentators are generally representative of the critical discourse on Canadian multiculturalism in recent years, a discourse not only emerging from reactionary conservative and mainstream liberal sources but also increasingly articulated by commentators 'from within,' as it were; i.e., commentators strongly supportive of the idea of multiculturalism but critical of its current formulation and modus operandi.

3 Jameson 1991, 16–17. The first chapter of Jameson's *Postmodernism, or the Cultural Logic of Late Capitalism* is a revised and expanded version of a famous analysis originally published by Jameson in the early 1980s. The analysis has appeared in different stages of development; e.g., in *New Left Review*, and in Hal Foster's edited collection of essays on the postmodern, *The Anti-Aesthetic* (1982). In its most recent appearance, Jameson adds this commentary on political correctness and political fragmentation as further symptoms of the condition of postmodernity.

4 Hebdige 1988, 185–98. The key features that Hebdige outlines here (the chapter is entitled 'Staking Out the Posts') collect and represent the diverse tendencies and currents of the postmodern condition.

5 This is a general theme in Edward Said's recent work. In a public lecture to the graduate program in Social and Political Thought at York University in April 1993 on politics in the new world order, he spoke of the possibilities offered by what he referred to as the 'nomadic imaginary's' ability to cope with 'transcendental homelessness.'

5 Laclau and Mouffe 1985, 137. Laclau and Mouffe have individually and collectively been developing this theme over the past ten years, and there is

now a substantial body of primary literature and secondary commentary. For an example of the backlash from an old 'New Left' orthodoxy, see Wood 1986. Some of the most interesting developments of Laclau and Mouffe's themes have appeared in the *Phronesis* series, also from Verso.

7 Cited in Ferguson 1976.

8 Bordo 1990. Bordo develops this as a critique of the political difficulties confronting contemporary feminist projects that attempt to recognize and represent the diversity of subject positions contained by the category 'women,' but it is equally applicable to an analysis of the difficulties facing multiculturalism.

9 See Marshall Berman's (1988) excellent interpretation of the *Manifesto*, particularly the chapter 'Marx, Modernism and Modernization.'

10 See the preface to Wollstonecraft [1792] 1992.

11 The definition and etymology of 'monster' is taken from the *Oxford English Dictionary*.

12 For critical interpretations of Frankenstein's monster as a metaphor for modernity see, for example, Law 1991; also Hindle 1994.

13 Marx, cited by Berman 1988, 20.

14 Donna Haraway's 'A Manifesto for Cyborgs' (1991) draws from a convergence in the contemporary literature. Though divergent in other respects, Habermas's critique of the colonization of the lifeworld by system media (*Theory of Communicative Action, vol. II*) and Foucault's analyses of the development of the institutions of disciplinarity (*Discipline and Punish, The Order of Things*) are an elaboration of Max Weber's critique of rationalization. The image of the cyborg in this negative guise as dehumanized subject first appears in the closing lines of Weber's *Protestant Ethic and the Spirit of Capitalism*, where in a chilling prognosis he predicts a race of 'specialists without spirit, hedonists without heart' whose only goal would be 'rationalized acquisitiveness,' populating a society resembling an 'iron cage' (1986, 181–2). This vision of dehumanization in postmodern technoculture has appeared recently as the 'Borg' species in 'Star Trek: The Next Generation.' Haraway develops this critical metaphor by showing that this is only one aspect of the cyborg, that rather than simply dehumanization we may see also at the present conjuncture the possibility of emancipatory reconfigurations of human subjectivity.

15 Haraway 1991, 150–2. I am paraphrasing/quoting Haraway here, as it is not her objective to 'define' the cyborg, but rather to suggest a poiesis of cyborg solidarity.

16 My reading of Heidegger is based on primary sources (listed in the bibliography) and from commentaries on Heidegger, especially Steiner 1978, Kaufmann 1975, and Macquarrie 1978.

17 This interpretation of Heidegger's method and its relationship to ethnomethodology comes via Foucault. See Dreyfus and Rabinow 1982, xxi.

18 This is developed throughout Lacan's corpus. See, for example, Lacan 1978, 49–54. For interpretive discussions see, for example, Anthony Wilden's 'Lacan and the Discourse of the Other,' in Lacan 1994, 194–7, and of course Žižek's development of the concept (1989; 1991, 21–34; 1993, 35–7 and 166–9).

19 Ethnomethodology is most famously associated with the work of Harold Garfinkle, e.g. 1967.

20 Lacan 1978. The concept of *object petit a* is developed throughout the text; e.g., 103–5 and 145–8. See also the discussion, clarification, and elaboration of the concept in Žižek 1989, 1991, and 1993.

21 My concept of ironic conceit is derived from reading explorations of irony by Meucke, Blum, and Hutcheon. However, the ironic sensibility, as developed by Meucke and Hutcheon at least (Blum's formulation is superior), doesn't do justice to the self-deception involved in the motivated masking of the real, outlined above. The thoroughly paradoxical character of the attitude which I'm describing combines a conceit of security of closure with an ironic openness.

22 My discussion here owes much to a graduate student seminar on 'The Method of Analysis' by Alan Blum at York University, Toronto, during the academic year 1993/4.

23 Cited in Leupiu 1991, 15.

24 See Žižek's discussion of the ethics of 'going through the fantasy' (1989, 124–9).

25 See, for example, Laclau's discussion of this in his essay 'God Only Knows' (1991).

26 Žižek 1991a. See in particular 11–12.

27 See Bataille's discussion of the relationship between sacrifice and continuity (1986, 81–8).

28 A method recommended by Alan Blum and Peter McHugh (1984, 144).

29 The persistence of a kernel of enjoyment is discussed by Žižek (1990).

30 See the discussion of the nation-thing as kernel of enjoyment in Žižek 1990.

31 W. Gardiner, speech to the Reform party convention, Markham, Ontario, 16 April 1991.

32 Hegel 1977, in particular the sections 'Self-Consciousness, the Truth of Self-Certainty,' and 'Lordship and Bondage,' 104–19.

33 Žižek develops this Lacanian theme in Žižek 1990.

34 This story was carried by the *Toronto Sun* as a running feature over several months of 1990 and is typical of the moral panic frequently instigated by some sections of the media around issues of ethno-racial difference in Canada.

35 W. Gardiner, speech to the Reform party convention, Markham, Ontario, 16 April 1991.

36 Reform party promotional literature, 'What Is Reform?' distributed by the Reform Party Information Office during 1991–2.

37 Spicer 1991. See also the *Group Discussion Kit*, which provided some of the terms of the coast-to-coast public discussion on which Spicer's report was based.

38 The CN Tower and the retractable roof on the SkyDome.

39 This formulation of the Jew as symptom of the non-existence of society and thus as a historical scapegoat of social antagonism appears in several places throughout the text, and indeed throughout Žižek's work.

40 See the discussion 'Beyond the Positivity of the Social: Antagonisms and Hegemony' in Laclau and Mouffe 1985, especially 111–12, 137.

41 For a thorough discussion of this controversy, see Coombe 1993. Incidentally, the Sikh Mountie has since won his case and wears his turban as part of the recognized uniform of the RCMP.

42 The Franklin voyage was an ill-fated expedition by the British Admiralty in the late nineteenth century to find a north-west passage to the Far East across the North Atlantic through the polar ice field. Franklin's ships were trapped by the ice floes and were lost without a trace. Only recently have some of the frozen bodies of members of Franklin's crew been finally recovered.

43 I found this pamphlet in the Toronto Public Reference Library under the general heading 'Domestic Architecture.' The pamphlet was printed in Winnipeg in 1973.

44 I examined a random sample of thirty-five cookery books from general and specialized Toronto bookstores.

45 Based on a random sample of issues of *Canadian Living* over the past ten years. Source: Metro Toronto Reference Library.

46 A Canadian Air Force Hercules crashed in darkness near Alert in the high Arctic in the dead of winter 1990. Several of the crew members were recovered alive during the course of a rescue mission conducted under appalling weather conditions. This report of Mulroney's remarks was carried by the *Globe and Mail* approximately two weeks after the rescue.

47 From the 'Tilley Endurables' Mail Order Catalogue, Don Mills, Ontario, 1990. See also weekly advertisements in the *Globe and Mail*.

48 See Lefort 1988. See in particular the introduction, and the essay entitled 'The Question of Democracy,' 10–20.

49 See the chapter 'How Did Marx Invent the Symptom?' in Žižek 1989.

50 My understanding of irony is informed by a variety of sources, the most important of which is Alan Blum's usage (1978) and Blum and McHugh (1984). David Meucke's discussion in his seminal book *Irony* (1970) and recent work on Canadian irony by Linda Hutcheon, notably 1990 and 1991.

51 Hutcheon 1990, 14–15. *'Aporia,'* meaning doubt, is most famously associated with Socratic dialogues, which seek the truth but conclude in uncertainty.

52 See Butler 1990, and also her essay on psychoanalysis and feminist theory in Nicholson 1990.

53 My interpretation here is based on several days of field work in the Royal Ontario Museum, and inspired by my reading of Donna Haraway's brilliant essay 'Teddy Bear Patriarchy: Taxidermy in the Garden of Eden,' in Haraway 1990b. See also Torgovnik 1990.

54 Ben Wicks's cartoon strip 'Bill' appears daily in the *Toronto Star.*

55 Bacon 1825, 254. For a discussion of the centrality of this theme in the discourse of science from Bacon and the founding fathers to the present, see Adorno and Horkeimer 1982, 3–42, and also Harding 1986.

56 See the concluding passages of Weber 1986, 181–3 – his famous depiction of life in the iron cage. See also 'Some Consequences of Bureaucratization,' where he speaks of 'little men clinging to little jobs'; 'cogs in a machine, who aware of that, their one concern is with becoming bigger cogs,' in Coser and Rosenberg 1964, 472–3.

57 For an elaborate account of subjectivization, see the chapter 'Panopticism' in Foucault 1979, 195–228.

58 'Wilding' refers to the practice of group robbery, whereby a group of youths rush someone and steal 'big ticket' items such as leather jackets, designer sports shoes, and personal stereos. Occasionally the group targets a shop. A small number of such incidents occurred in Scarborough, Mississauga, and downtown Toronto during 1992–3, and occasioned a moral panic, led by the tabloid press.

59 'The Stranger,' in Simmel 1971. See also Wolf 1964.

60 *Company of Strangers*, Montreal, National Film Board, 1990.

61 That language is the house of Being is a Heideggerian formulation, developed throughout his work. For a discussion of this theme in existentialist philosophy see Macquarrie 1978, 140–53. This formulation is in harmony with the centrality of the symbolic order in the Lacanian architectonics.

62 This discussion is owed to Matthew Trachman of the Graduate Program in Sociology, York University, Toronto, who argued this convincingly in a paper presented to the annual conference of the Canadian Learned Societies Association, Queen's University, Kingston, Ontario, June 1990.

63 See for example Simmel's essay, 'Conflict as a Form of Sociation,' in Simmel 1971, 70–93.

64 Barbara Owl and Russel Means, cited by Churchill 1991/2.

65 Simmel, 'Sociability,' in Simmel 1971, 127–40. See, in particular, 129 and the footnote.

66 See in particular Foucault 1988a, and the essay 'The Ethic of the Care of the Self as a Practice of Freedom' in Foucault 1988b, 1–20.

67 See especially Heidegger's discussion of the ethics of *Dasein* in Heidegger 1962, 225–35.

68 For an elaboration of the idea of the 'bricoleur' see Laclau and Mouffe 1991, particularly 100–2. The essay also appears in *New Left Review,* no. 166 (November–December 1987).

69 See Kaufmann 1975, especially the introductory discussion by Kaufmann.

70 From an essay entitled 'In Search of Canada' by V.S. Pritchett, in *Reader's Digest* July 1965.

71 Foucault's general thesis is developed most forcefully in Foucault 1991. See particularly the chapter 'Panopticism.'

72 Baudrillard articulates this argument in his essay 'The Masses: The Implosion of the Social in the Media,' Baudrillard 1985.

73 Baudrillard, 'The Ecstasy of Communication,' Baudrillard 1982, 128. (This is a slightly different version of Baudrillard 1988b.)

74 See Jameson's discussion of schizophrenia in 1991, 26–31. For his discussion of pastiche as an emancipatory practice with which to counter cultural schizophrenia see Jameson 1988.

75 See Steiner's discussion in Steiner 1978, 36.

76 From Greenpeace literature 'Greenpeace' supplied by the London (UK) office, 1993.

77 For an elaboration of the reflexive modernization thesis see Beck, Giddens, and Lasch 1994.

78 See Žižek's discussion of the question 'Chez voi?' in Žižek 1989.

79 *Aporia* is associated particularly with Socrates, for his dialogues, after searching very thoroughly for the answer, conclude inconclusively. The question remains unanswered, but unanswerability is regarded as occasioning further dialogue. For Socrates the puzzlement of *aporia* shows us that the truth coincides with the path towards Truth.

80 Foucault coins this phrase to describe Deleuze and Guattari's *Anti Oedipus.* He says that the book is best approached as 'erotic art,' that is 'less concerned with "why" this or that, than with "how" to proceed. How does one introduce desire into thought, into discourse, into action? How can and must desire deploy its forces within the political domain and grow more intense in the process of overturning the established order? Ars erotica, ars thoretica, ars politica.' Foucault, Preface to Deleuze and Guattari 1977, xi–xiv.

81 Coupland 1991. Coupland has since published a number of other explorations of contemporary suburban generation subcultures, including *Shampoo Planet, Life after God,* and most recently a look at computer geeks and cyber-culture.

82 'Loss of historicity,' Jameson argues, is one of the defining characteristics of the postmodern condition. See Jameson 1991, 21–5.

83 See Mouffe's discussion of politics as the pursuit of the intimations of tradition in her essay 'Radical Democracy: Modern or Postmodern?' (Mouffe 1989, 39).

84 This is a composite hypothesis, derived from Baudrillard's essay 'The Masses: The Implosion of the Social in the Media' (1985) and his *The Ecstasy of Communication* (1988).

85 We can get a sense of Baudrillard's America from the following lines: 'I went in search of astral America, not social and cultural America, but the America of the empty absolute freedom of the freeways, not the deep America of mores and mentalities, but the America of desert speed, of motels and mineral surfaces. I looked for it in the speed of the screenplay, in the indifferent reflex of television, in the film of days and nights projected across an empty space, in the marvelously affectless succession of signs, images and faces, and ritual acts on the road' (Baudrillard 1988a, 25).

86 This quotation and the one that follows are from the cover flap of Coupland's *Generation X*.

87 See the endorsement and development of Spivak's argument in Butler's essay 'Gender Trouble: Feminist Theory and Psychoanalytic Discourse,' in Nicholson 1990, 325.

88 For an interesting discussion of this theme see Hutter 1978.

89 From a popular poem by Robert Service called 'The Cremation of Sam McGee,' which tells the gothic horror/comic story of a Arctic traveller who froze to death (apparently) but when his colleagues tried to cremate the 'corpse' he thawed out and came back to life!

90 Luckily Carmen introduced me to this excellent tradition during my first winter in Toronto. Lacan is also familiar with the practice, though not, I hope, with Carmen! See Lacan 1994, 72 n11.

91 Review in *Cinema Canada* no. 138 (1987), 28.

92 I owe this to Ron Cadeaux of the Department of Anthropology, York University, Toronto, a folklorist and a native of the Ottawa Valley.

93 It is interesting to note the similarity between Frye's work and Fanon's account of the symbolic order in colonial Algeria. In the process of objectification of the Other, note the chain of equivalences: veiled women = palm trees = sand dunes = indocile nature, etc. 'In Algeria there is not simply the domination, but the decision to the letter not to occupy anything less than the sum total of the land. The Algerians, the veiled women, the palm trees and the camels make up the landscape, the *natural* background to the *human* presence of the French. Hostile Nature, obstinate and fundamentally rebellious, is in

fact represented in the colonies by the bush, mosquitoes, Natives, and fever; and the colonization is a success when all this indocile Nature has finally been tamed. Railways across the bush, the draining of swamps, and a native population which is non-existent politically and economically are in fact one and the same thing.' Fanon 1969, 250.

94 The screenplay has also been published (Egoyan 1993).

95 Gibson's most famous piece is probably *Neuromancer* (1984). For a discussion of the significance of the cyberpunk novel as an aid to the cognitive mapping of the condition of postmodernity, see Jameson 1991, 38.

96 Isabella Valancy Crawford, *Malcolm's Katie: A Love Story* (1884), cited by Frye 1977, 35.

97 Standard Canadian art books concur on this. See for example, Boulet, R. *The Canadian Earth: Landscape Paintings by the Group of Seven* (Thornhill: Cerebrus, 1982).

98 From a critical review by Hector Charlesworth, in *Saturday Night*, 1916, information incorporated in an exhibition of work by the Group of Seven at the Art Gallery of Ontario, Toronto.

99 See Torgovnik 1990. The primitive, Torgovnik shows, is defined in terms of whatever the non-primitive Modern has wanted the primitive to mean, according to what suits our purposes (9).

100 A survey of standard reference books on Canadian art, or a visit to the pre–Group of Seven exhibition in the Art Gallery of Ontario and the National Gallery in Ottawa, will attest to this.

101 Henry Miller, *Sexus*, cited in Deleuze and Guattari 1977, xv.

102 Marshall Berman, author of *All that Is Solid Melts into Air* (1988). Speaking at the University of Toronto, 4 May 1993.

103 See Žižek's discussion of this Hegelian formulation in Žižek 1989, 207–9.

104 David Cronenberg's interpretation of Burroughs's *The Naked Lunch* in his 1992 film of the same name.

105 This observation appears in a footnote to Freud's *Civilization and Its Discontents*. See Freud 1961, n53 n3.

106 This is usually stated explicitly and unambiguously. See for example the lyrics of 'Fight the Power' on Public Enemy's album *Fear of a Black Planet*.

107 From a report on the CBC Television Evening News in February 1993.

108 Cited in Corrigan 1981, 5.

109 This critique of political correctness appears in Foucault's Preface to Deleuze and Guattari 1977, xii.

110 Cited in Corrigan 1981, 18.

111 The insightful fan is Professor Steven Katz, of the Department of Sociology,

Trent University, Peterborough, Ontario. (Thanks for the rides to Toronto, Steve.)

112 Hegel 1977, 104. This section owes much to Professor Rebecca Comay's brilliant seminar on Hegel's *Phenomenology of Spirit*, in the Department of Philosophy, University of Toronto, 1992–3.

113 This memorable phrase is Professor Comay's.

114 A review of a Scarborough restaurant, *Now* magazine, Toronto, 14 November 1991.

115 For an elaboration of this argument see Keohane 1993.

116 One of the principles of ethnomethodology was to disrupt the flow of ordinary social interaction in order to reveal the web of a taken-for-granted, or lifeworld, in which action takes place. See Garfinkle 1967.

117 This is a general theme of Foucault's work, that what may initially appear as a liberalizing reform turns out to be an elaboration of a discourse of power and control. See, for example, Foucault, 1988.

118 *Ottawa Citizen*, 3 January 1990.

Bibliography

Adorno, Theodore, and Max Horkheimer. 1982. *Dialectic of Enlightenment*. New York: Continuum

Anderson, Benedict. 1991. *Imagined Communities*. London: Verso

Althusser, Louis. 1984. 'Ideology and Ideological State Apparatuses.' In *Essays on Ideology*. London: Verso

Arendt, Hannah. 1990. 'Philosophy and Politics.' *Social Research* 57:1. 73–103

Atwood, Margaret. 1972. *Survival: A Thematic Guide to Canadian Literature*. Toronto: Anansi

Bacon, Sir Francis. 1825. 'In Praise of Human Knowledge' (Miscellaneous Tracts Upon Human Knowledge). In vol. 1 of *The Works of Francis Bacon*, ed. Basil Montagu: London

Bakhtin, Mikhail. 1984. *Rabelais and His World*. Bloomington: Indiana University Press

Bataille, Georges. 1986. *Erotism: Death and Sensuality*. San Francisco: City Lights Books

Baudrillard, Jean. 1982. 'The Ecstasy of Communication.' In *The Anti-Aesthetic*, ed. Hal Foster. San Francisco: Bay Press

– 1985. 'The Masses: The Implosion of the Social in the Media.' *New Literary History* 16. 577–89

– 1988a. *America*. San Francisco: Bay Press

– 1988b. *The Ecstasy of Communication*. New York: Autonomedia

Beck, Ulrich, Anthony Giddens, and Scott Lasch. 1994. *Reflexive Modernization*. Cambridge: Polity Press

Beckett, Samuel. 1991. *Trilogy: Molloy, Malone Dies, The Unnamable*. New York: Norton

Berman, Marshall. 1988. *All That Is Solid Melts into Air*. New York: Penguin

Bhabha, Homi. 1990. *Nation and Narration*. London: Verso

– 1994. 'Signs Taken for Wonders.' In *The Location of Culture*. London: Routledge

Bibby, Reginald. 1990. *Mosaic Madness*. Don Mills: Stoddart

Blum, Alan. 1978. *Socrates: The Original and Its Images*. London: Routledge

Blum, Alan, and Peter McHugh. 1984. *Self Reflection in the Arts and Sciences*. New Jersey. Humanities Press.

Bordo, Jack. 1993. 'Jack Pine, Wilderness Sublime, or the Erasure of the Native in the Group of Seven?' *Journal of Canadian Studies* 27:4

Bordo, Susan. 1990. 'Feminism, Postmodernism and Gender Scepticism.' In Nicholson 1990

Boulet, Robert. 1982. *The Canadian Earth: Landscape Paintings by the Group of Seven*. Thornhill: Cerebrus

Buitenhuis, Peter. 1977. 'E.J. Pratt.' In Staines 1977

Butler, Judith. 1990a. *Gender Trouble: Feminism and the Subversion of Identity*. New York: Routledge

– 1990b. 'Gender Trouble: Feminist Theory and Psychoanalytic Discourse.' In Nicholson 1990

Churchill, Ward. 1991/2. 'Colonialism, Genocide and the Expropriation of Indigenous Spiritual Tradition in Contemporary Academia.' *Border/Lines* 23 (Winter), 39–41. 'The Native Issue,' special issue compiled by a guest editorial collective of Native Canadian writers

Cooking Collections: Canadian Feasts from Land and Sea. 1988. Ottawa: Federation of Womens' Institutes of Canada

Coombe, Rosemary J. 1993. 'Tactics of Appropriation and the Politics of Recognition in Late Modern Democracies.' *Political Theory* 21:3 (August). 411–33

Corrigan, Robert, ed. 1981. *Comedy: Meaning and Form*. New York: Harper and Row

Coser, Lewis, and Bernard Rosenberg, eds. 1964. *Sociological Theory: A Book of Readings*. New York: Macmillan

Coupland, Douglas. 1991. *Generation X: Tales for an Accelerated Culture*. New York: St Martin's Press

Deleuze, Gilles, and Félix Guattari. 1983. *Anti-Oedipus: Capitalism and Schizophrenia*. New York: Viking

Derrida, Jacques. 1991. *A Derrida Reader: Between the Blinds*. Ed. Peggy Kamuf. New York: Columbia University Press

Dreyfus, Hubert L., and Paul Rabinow. 1982. *Michel Foucault: Beyond Structuralism and Hermeneutics*. Chicago: University of Chicago Press

Durkheim, Emile. 1975. *Sociology and Philosophy*. New York: Free Press

Egoyan, Atom. 1993. *Speaking Parts*. Toronto: Coach House Press

Engel, Marian. 1976. *Bear*. Toronto: McClelland and Stewart

Fanon, Frantz. 1968. *Black Skin, White Masks*. New York: Grove Press
- 1969. *The Wretched of the Earth*. New York: Grove Press
Ferguson, Ted. 1976. *A White Man's Country*. Toronto: Doubleday
Fleras, Augie. 1992. *Multiculturalism in Canada*. Toronto: Nelson
Foucault, Michel. 1980. *Power/Knowledge*. Brighton: Harvester
- 1988a. *The History of Sexuality* vol. 3: *The Care of the Self*. New York: Vintage
- 1988b. *The Final Foucault*. Ed. James Bernauer and David Rasmussen. Boston: MIT Press
- 1989. 'Friendship as a Way of Life.' In *Foucault Live. Semiotext(e)* Foreign Agents Series. New York: Semiotext(e). 203–9
- 1991. *Discipline and Punish*. Harmondsworth: Penguin
Freud, Sigmund. 1961. *Civilization and Its Discontents*. New York: Norton
- 1981. *Jokes and Their Relation to the Unconscious*. Harmondsworth: Penguin
Frye, Northrop. 1971. *The Bush Garden*. Toronto: Anansi
- 1977. 'Haunted by a Lack of Ghosts: Some Patterns in the Imagery of Canadian Poetry.' In Staines 1977. 22–46
Garfinkle, Harold. 1967. *Studies in Ethnomethodology*. Englewood Cliffs, NJ: Prentice-Hall
Gibson, William. 1984. *Neuromancer*. New York: Ace
- 1993. Interview. *Now* magazine, 9 Sept.
Habermas, Jurgen. 1976. *Communication and the Evolution of Society*. Boston: Beacon Press
- 1984. *Theory of Communicative Action II*. Boston: Beacon Press
Haraway, Donna. 1990. *Primate Visions*. New York: Routledge
- 1991. 'A Manifesto for Cyborgs.' In *Simians, Cyborgs, and Women*. New York: Routledge. 149–181
- 1992. 'The Promises of Monsters: A Regenerative Politics for Inappropriate/d Others.' In *Cultural Studies*, ed. Lawrence Grossberg et al. New York: Routledge. 295–337
Harding, Sandra. 1986. *The Science Question in Feminism*. Ithaca: Cornell University Press
Hebdige, Dick. 1988. *Hiding in the Light*. London: Routledge
Hegel, G.W.F. 1977. *The Phenomelogy of Spirit*. Oxford: Oxford University Press
Heidegger, Martin. 1962. *Being and Time*. New York: Harper and Row
- 1975. 'The Way Back into the Ground of Metaphysics.' In Kaufmann 1975
Hewison, Richard. 1981. *Monty Python: The Case Against*. New York: Grove Press
Hilderly, Bob, and Ken Norris. 1988. *Poets 88*. Kingston: Quarry Press
Hindle, M. 1994. *Mary Shelley's 'Frankenstein,' or the Modern Prometheus'*. Harmondsworth: Penguin

Hobsbawm, Eric, ed. 1983. *The Invention of Tradition*. New York: Cambridge University Press

hooks, bell. 1991. *Yearning: Race, Gender, and Cultural Politics*. Boston: South End Press

Hutcheon, Linda. 1990. *As Canadian as ... Possible ... under the Circumstances.* Toronto: ECW Press

– 1991. *Double Talking: Essays on Verbal and Visual Ironies in Canadian Art and Literature*. Toronto: ECW Press

Hutcheon, Linda, ed. 1992. *Splitting Images: Essays on Verbal and Visual Ironies in Contemporary Canadian Art and Literature*. Toronto: ECW Press

Hutter, Horst. 1978. *Politics as Friendship*. Waterloo: Wilfrid Laurier University Press

Jameson, Fredric. 1982. 'Postmodernism and Consumer Culture.' In *The Anti-Aesthetic*. ed. Hal Foster. San Francisco: Bay Press

– 1988. 'Regarding Postmodernism: A Conversation with Fredric Jameson.' In *Universal Abandon*, ed. Andrew Ross. Minneapolis: University of Minnesota Press. 3–30

– 1991. *Postmodernism, or the Cultural Logic of Late Capitalism*. Durham: Duke University Press

Joyce, James. 1961. *Ulysses*. New York: Vintage

Kaufmann, Walter. 1975. *Existentialism from Dostoevsky to Sartre*. Second edition. New York: New American Library

Keohane, Kieran. 1993. 'Central Problems in the Philosophy of the Social Sciences after Postmodernism: Reconciling Consensus and Hegemonic Theories of Epistemology and Political Ethics.' *Philosophy and Social Criticism* 19:2. 145–69

Kroker, Arthur. 1986. *Techology and the Canadian Mind*. Montreal: New World

Lacan, Jacques. 1978. *The Four Fundamental Concepts of Psychoanalysis*. New York: Norton

– 1994. *Speech and Language in Psychoanalysis*. Trans. Anthony Wilden. Baltimore: Johns Hopkins University Press

Laclau, Ernesto. 1985. 'New Social Movements and the Plurality of the Social.' In *New Social Movements and the State in Latin America*, ed. David Slater. The Hague: SEDLA. 27–42

– 1990. 'The Impossibility of Society.' In *New Reflections on the Revolution of Our Time*. London: Verso

– 1991. 'God Only Knows.' *Marxism Today*. December. 56–9

Laclau, Ernesto, and Chantal Mouffe. 1985. *Hegemony and Socialist Strategy*. London: Verso

– 1991. 'Post Marxism without Apologies.' In *New Reflections on the Revolution of Our Time*. London: Verso

Law, John, ed. 1991. *A Sociology of Monsters*. London: Routledge

Leacock, Stephen. 1968. *Laugh with Leacock*. Toronto: McClelland and Stewart.

Lee, Spike. 1989. *Do the Right Thing*. Universal City: MCA Home Video

Lefort, Claude. 1988. *Democracy and Political Theory*. Cambridge: Polity

Leupiu, A. 1991. *Lacan and the Human Sciences*. Nebraska City: University of Nebraska Press

Li, Peter. 1990. *Race and Ethnic Relations in Canada*. Toronto: Oxford University Press

Marx, Karl, and Friedrich Engels. 1964. *The Communist Manifesto*. New York: Monthly Review Press

Macquarrie, John. 1978. *Existentialism*. New York: Pelican

McGregor, Gaile. 1985. *The Wacousta Syndrome: Explorations in the Canadian Langscape*. Toronto: University of Toronto Press

Meucke, David. 1970. *Irony*. London: Methuen

– 1982. *Irony and the Ironic*. London: Methuen

Mouffe, Chantal. 1989. 'Radical Democracy: Modern or Postmodern?' In *Universal Abandon*, ed. Andrew Ross. Minneapolis: University of Minnesota Press

Myers, Mike. 1993. 'Wise Guys: Why Are Canadians So Funny?' *Maclean's*. 26 July

Nader, Ralph. 1992. *Canada Firsts*. Toronto: McClelland and Stewart

Newman, Peter C. *Empire of the Bay: An Illustrated History of the Hudson's Bay Company*. Markham: Viking

Nicholson, Linda, ed. 1990. *Feminism/Postmodernism*. New York: Routledge

Nietzsche, Friedrich. 1967a. *Thus Spoke Zarathustra*. Baltimore: Penguin

– 1967b. *Will to Power*. New York: Random House

Paglia, Camille. 1992. *Sexual Personae*. Harmondsworth: Penguin

Pritchett, V.S. 1965. 'In Search of Canada.' *Reader's Digest*. July. 163–74

Rorty, Richard. 1989. *Contingency, Irony and Solidarity*. New York: Cambridge University Press

de Sade, Marquis. 1948. *Les cent-vingt Journées de Sodome*. Paris: Oeuvres Completes

Scarry, Elaine. 1992. *The Body in Pain: The Making and Unmaking of the World*. New York: Oxford University Press

Scott, Joan. 1992. 'Multiculturalism and the Politics of Identity.' *October* (Fall). 12–19

Simmel, Georg. 1964. *The Sociology of Georg Simmel*. Ed. Kurt Wolff. New York: Free Press

– 1971. *On Individuality and Social Forms: Selected Writings*. Ed. Donald Levine. Chicago: University of Chicago Press

Smith, Dorothy. 1987. *The Everyday World as Problematic: A Feminist Sociology*. Boston: Northeastern University Press

Spicer, Keith. 1991. *Citizens' Forum on Canada's Future: Report to the People and Government of Canada*. Ottawa: Government Publications Office

Staines, David, ed. 1977. *The Canadian Imagination: Dimensions of a Literary Culture*. Cambridge, Mass.: Harvard University Press

Steiner, George. 1978. *Heidegger*. London: Fontana

Torgovnik, Marianna. 1990. *Gone Primitive*. Chicago: University of Chicago Press

Weber, Max. 1986. *The Protestant Ethic and the Spirit of Capitalism*. New York: Macmillan

Wilden, Anthony. 1972. *The Imaginary Canadian*. Vancouver: Small Press

Wollstonecraft, Mary. [1792]1992. *A Vindication of the Rights of Woman*. Harmondsworth: Penguin

Wood, Ellen. 1986. *The Retreat from Class*. London: Verso

Woodsworth, J.S. [1909]1972. *Strangers within Our Gates; or Coming Canadians*. Toronto: University of Toronto Press

Žižek, Slavoj. 1989. *The Sublime Object of Ideology*. London: Verso

– 1990a. 'Eastern Europe's Republics of Gilead.' *New Left Review* 183 (October). 50–63

– 1990b. 'The King Is a Thing.' *New Formations* 1. 19–37

– 1991a. *Looking Awry: An Introduction to Jacques Lacan through Popular Culture* Cambridge, Mass.: MIT Press

– 1991b. *For They Know Not What They Do*. London: Verso

– 1993. *Tarrying with the Negative*. Durham: Duke University Press

Index

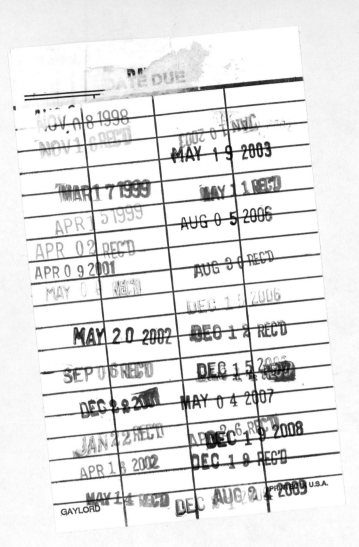